It is rare for a church leader to bring both clarity of thought and passionate emotion to the needs of the future church. Dan Kimball does both, and he speaks as somebody who actually lives in the trenches. I'm grateful for his wisdom.

John Ortberg, AUTHOR OF *IF YOU WANT TO WALK ON WATER, YOU'VE GOT TO GET OUT OF THE BOAT*

In his research and ministry to post-seeker-sensitive emerging generations, Dan Kimball is emulating the apostle Paul: "I have become all things to all men so that by all possible means I might save some. I do all this for the sake of the gospel."

Luis Palau, LUIS PALAU EVANGELISTIC ASSOCIATION

The future of the church in North America hinges on innovators like Dan Kimball and the ideas presented in this book. Vintage Christianity can be applied to new and existing congregations to help reach the next generation.

Bob Buford, FOUNDER OF LEADERSHIP NETWORK AND AUTHOR OF *HALFTIME*

Cool hair, bright mind, passionate heart—Dan Kimball belongs to the tribe of men and women who creatively advance the cause of Christ. His commitment to mission and context lays an important foundation for any conversation about style and innovation.

Erwin Raphael McManus, CULTURAL ARCHITECT, MOSAIC, LOS ANGELES, CALIF.

I am inspired and thrilled whenever I see a church leader wrestle with how the church can more effectively reach a generation in a shifting culture. Dan Kimball's ministry and learning will stretch and challenge all of us who long to lead the bride of Christ to its greatest potential.

Nancy Beach, DIRECTOR OF PROGRAMMING, WILLOW CREEK COMMUNITY CHURCH

This book will challenge you to do some hard thinking and rethinking about how your church can engage with the emerging culture in your unique setting, with you and your team as unique individuals, in the unique moment in which you are living . . . whether you're ministering in an established church rich in tradition, or in a new church-plant wide-open with freedom. No book can make your ministry easy, but a good book like this can help you rise to the challenge.

Brian McLaren, AUTHOR OF *MORE READY THAN YOU REALIZE*

Dan Kimball shines a spotlight (or more precisely, lights a bank of candles), illuminating the mystery-laden "postseeker" world. Churches dare not ignore the perspectives and preferences of the emerging generation as they take the gospel into the future.

Marshall Shelley, EDITOR, *LEADERSHIP* JOURNAL

We constantly come into contact with youth workers, pastors, and church leaders who want to understand the postmodern shift and its implications for their churches but are intimidated by most of what's written on the subject. Dan's book distills complex ideas into bite-sized chunks that are understandable without being simplistic. And he doesn't stop there: he offers practical discussion of real-life implications for their ministries.

Tic Long, PRESIDENT, YOUTH SPECIALTIES EVENTS

Dan Kimball has advice for the church that all of us need to hear. It is time to return to vintage Christianity.

Chris Seay, AUTHOR OF THE GOSPEL ACCORDING TO TONY SOPRANO
AND PASTOR OF ECCLESIA IN HOUSTON

I'll never forget the first time I heard Dan Kimball communicate at his church in Santa Cruz. His words just hovered in the room, they were so present and timely. And in this book his words fall off the pages into your life to inspire and hang in your mind and heart, provoking thought and feeling long after your first encounter.

David Crowder, SPARROW RECORDS RECORDING ARTIST
AND MUSIC AND ARTS PASTOR,
UNIVERSITY BAPTIST CHURCH, WACO, TEX.

Once in a while, a book comes along that oh so simply and effortlessly describes reality. In the world of ministry, this is one of those books.

Sally Morgenthaler, FOUNDER, SACRAMENTIS.COM
AND AUTHOR OF WORSHIP EVANGELISM

This book is a wonderful, detailed example of what a purpose-driven church can look like in a postmodern world. My friend Dan Kimball writes passionately from his heart, with a deep desire to reach emerging generations and culture. While my book The Purpose-Driven Church explained what the church is called to do, Dan's book explains how to do it with the cultural-creatives who think and feel in postmodern terms. You need to pay attention to him because times are changing.

Rick Warren, SADDLEBACK CHURCH,
AUTHOR OF THE PURPOSE-DRIVEN LIFE

Being tested in the laboratory of his own effective ministry, Dan continues to learn and to model a passion for the unreached souls of emerging generations. He deserves honest and thorough evaluation. Read this book at your own risk. To many it may look threatening, but it may open your eyes to reality and to a refreshing hope for our children and grandchildren.

Howard G. Hendricks, DALLAS THEOLOGICAL SEMINARY

Dan has the courage to model revolutionary thinking and the wisdom to encourage reconciling action. This book is both a blueprint and a blog of transformation.

Spencer Burke, CREATOR OF THEOOZE.COM

Dan is a practitioner, not merely a theorist. He is no armchair strategist. He is on the front line of reaching this generation. This is a practical book. However, it moves beyond merely presenting methodology to addressing fundamental issues. The book offers a biblically based approach to ministry but clearly states there is not one way to do ministry. Some of what is presented is new and innovative. Then, Dan breathes new life into a centuries-old method of communing with God.

Les Christie, CHAIR, YOUTH MINISTRY DEPARTMENT,
SAN JOSE CHRISTIAN COLLEGE

I have served with Dan for ten years in high-school ministry, in Graceland, and now in starting Vintage Faith Church, and I am privileged to call him a close friend. This book will open your eyes to the incredible opportunities for kingdom influence that the emerging church has in post-Christian America. The coolest part of this book to me is that it all has really been lived out in the context of our local community, vintage-faith style.

Josh Fox, PASTOR OF WORSHIP ARTS, GRACELAND/
SANTA CRUZ BIBLE CHURCH AND VINTAGE FAITH CHURCH

What I appreciate about this book is that what you are reading is coming from a practitioner. I have had the privilege of working with Dan for many years, and I have seen him live out and learn and put into practice what he writes about in this book. He isn't just a theorist.

Chip Ingram, PRESIDENT, WALK THRU THE BIBLE

the EMERGING church

Dan Kimball

the EMERGING church

Vintage Christianity for NEW GENERATIONS

WITH COMMENTARY BY: Rick Warren Howard Hendricks Brian McLaren
Sally Morgenthaler Chip Ingram Mark Oestreicher

ZONDERVAN™

GRAND RAPIDS, MICHIGAN 49530 USA

ZONDERVAN™

The Emerging Church
Copyright © 2003 by Dan Kimball

Requests for information should be addressed to:

Zondervan
Grand Rapids, Michigan 49530

Library of Congress Cataloging-in-Publication Data

Kimball, Dan.
    The emerging church : vintage Christianity for new generations / Dan Kimball.
      p.   cm.
  Includes bibliographical references.
    ISBN 0-310-24564-8
    1. Public worship.   2. Evangelistic work.   3. Non-church-affiliated people.
  4. Church work with young adults.   I. Title.
    BV15 .K48   2003
    250–dc21

                                                  2002152349

Interior design by Tracey Moran

Printed in the United States of America

04 05 06 07 08 /❖ DC/ 10 9 8

Contents

Deconstructing Postmodern Ministry, Candles, and Coffee

Part 1

Reconstructing Vintage Christianity in the Emerging Church

Part 2

by
Rick Warren

In ministry, some things must never change, while other things must be constantly changing. God's five purposes for his church are nonnegotiable. If a church fails at worship, fellowship, discipleship, ministry, and evangelism, it is no longer a church. It's just a social club. On the other hand, the way or style in which we fulfill these eternal purposes must continually be adjusted and modified, because human culture is always changing.

The word contemporary literally means "with temporariness." By nature, nothing contemporary is meant to last forever. It is only effective for a while, and it is only relevant in that particular moment. That's what makes it contemporary. What is considered contemporary and relevant in the next ten years will inevitably appear dated and tired in twenty.

As a pastor, I've watched churches adopt many contemporary styles in worship, programming, architecture, music, and other elements. That's okay, as long as the biblical message is unchanged. But whatever is in style now will inevitably be out of style soon, and the cycles of change are getting shorter and shorter, aided by technology and the media. New styles and preferences, like fashions, are always emerging.

Let me give you a word of advice. Never attach your church to a single style; you'll soon be passé and outdated. At Saddleback Church, we've changed styles of worship, programming, and outreach many times during our first twenty years, and we'll continue to do so because the world keeps changing. The only way to stay relevant is to anchor your ministry to unchanging truths and eternal purposes while being willing to continually adapt how you communicate those truths and purposes.

This book is a wonderful, detailed example of what a purpose-driven church can look like in a postmodern world. My friend Dan Kimball writes passionately, with a deep desire to reach the emerging generation and culture. While my book *The Purpose-Driven Church* explained what the church is called to do, Dan's book explains how to do it with the cultural-creatives who think and feel in postmodern terms. You need to pay attention to him because times are changing.

In the past twenty years, spiritual seekers have changed a lot. In the first place, there are a whole lot more of them. There are seekers everywhere. I've never seen more people so hungry to discover and develop the spiritual dimension of their lives. That's why there is such a big interest in Eastern thought, New Age practices, mysticism, and the transcendent. Today seekers are hungry for symbols and metaphors and experiences and stories that reveal the greatness of God. Because seekers are constantly changing, we must be sensitive to them like Jesus was; we must be willing to meet them on their own turf and speak to them in ways they understand.

You probably won't agree with everything you read in this book. Dan freely (and humbly) admits that he has sometimes painted with a broad brush in some of his comparative charts and has exaggerated the differences between old and new, modern and postmodern, yesterday's ministry and tomorrow's. Generalizations are *generally* wrong. But please don't let this view, or any other view you may disagree with, cause you to dismiss this important book. Dan has something vital to say, and the church needs to hear it.

Remember: the world changes, but the Word doesn't. To be effective in ministry, we must learn to live with the tension between those two. My prayer is that God will use this book to raise up a new crop of churches which, like David in Acts 13:36, "served God's purpose in his own generation." We need churches that are both purpose driven and postmodern, timeless and timely at the same time. May God use you for that purpose.

Too often in recent years, church leaders have acted as if being sensitive to seekers means sliding into a one-size-fits-all, franchise, clone, mimic-*the*-model mentality. Too often, we exchanged one set of rigid traditional styles and methods and ways of thinking for equally rigid "contemporary" ones. Too often, we have acted without sufficient reflection, without thinking deeply about the profound relationships between church and culture, between past and present and future, between our methods and our message. And we have been gimmick-prone and thoughtlessly (sometimes desperately) pragmatic, without being as innocent as doves and as wise as serpents (Matt. 10:16).

Since I first met Dan, he has impressed me as refreshingly different from all these trends. A true learner and innovator, he asks great questions. He reads widely and deeply. He thinks and rethinks, painful as that can be! Through this book, you'll be stimulated to do the same.

You'll be challenged to do some hard thinking and rethinking about how your church can engage with the emerging culture in your unique setting, with you and your team as unique individuals, in the unique moment in which you are living, whether you're ministering in an established church rich in tradition or in a new church plant wide open with freedom. Wherever you are, you have limitations and resources, disadvantages and advantages that are your own; they are your unique challenges and your unique opportunities. No book can make your ministry easy, but a book like this can help you rise to the challenge.

This book will offer you stimulating new ideas and practical suggestions to engage our emerging culture with the gospel. Our understandings of the gospel constantly change as we engage in mission in our complex, dynamic world, as we discover that the gospel has a rich kaleidoscope of meaning to offer, yielding unexplored layers of depth, revealing uncounted facets of insight and relevance. No doubt, as we move into the postmodern world, we will look back and see ways in which our modern understandings of the gospel were limited or flawed, and no doubt, we must be humble and careful, because we can (and will) make the same mistakes in our new context.

But that's our challenge, and when you turn the last page of this book, you will feel more motivated and equipped to face that challenge . . . and to see it as a thrilling opportunity and privilege.

The Graceland staff and community: On my living room floor in extended prayer is where the idea of the Graceland worship gatherings and approach to ministry was formed with Josh Fox and Rollyn Zoubek. Over the next several years, Josh Fox, Heather Margo, Christine Beitsch, Jessica Ivan, Ursula Haas-Macmillon, Erik Hopper, and Joe Schimmels were at some point part of the Graceland staff. Gracelanders themselves are also a very, very big part of this book, since it is their lives which helped shape the ministry and ideas which are written within.

So many leaders who faithfully served Jesus were part of the Graceland team and in many ways helped write this book without even realizing it. Rod and Connie Clendenen, Steve and Caren Ruppert, Tom and Debi Rahe, Fred and Bebe Barnes, Robert Namba, Bonnie Wolf, and others through the years were beautiful examples of generations imparting their faith down to those younger.

Santa Cruz Bible Church: I need to thank Chip Ingram and the elders and staff of Santa Cruz Bible Church. They gave me the holy privilege of serving Jesus in youth ministry for many years. Here I was allowed to think of different ways of approaching ministry and to experiment by starting the Graceland worship gatherings. Through Santa Cruz Bible Church, Josh Fox and I are once again exploring new ground and extending the vision to reach the emerging culture, launching the first ever Santa Cruz Bible sister church: Vintage Faith Church (www.vintage church.org).

Emergent, Leadership Network, and other emerging church leaders: I have been stretched and influenced in my rethinking of church and ministry through many dialogues and friendships with explorers and thinkers such as Brian McLaren, Doug Pagitt, Brad Cecil, Sally Morgenthaler, Tony Jones, Brad Smith, Spencer Burke, Dieter Zander, Denny Henderson, Mark Oestreicher and Tic Long from Youth Specialties, Paul Allen, Daniel Hill, along with the many other emerging leaders and churches with whom I have had the privilege of engaging in conversation.

Without these people, I truly don't know if I would have survived the journey so far. Through them I learned I was not alone and that there are

11

others out there feeling the same thing in the air and asking the same questions, so I realized I wasn't just going totally crazy. I seriously can't thank them enough for how God has used each of them in my life, ministry, and philosophical sanity. In particular, Leadership Network (www.leadnet.org) and Emergent (www.emergentvillage.com) have really been used by God to help rebirth my viewpoint of church and ministry as we look to where God is moving and shaping the emerging church. It is a joy to be part of the Emergent-YS board and a thrill to wonder where God will take this new movement next.

Becky and Skip and Jan: Becky, my wife, helped with virtually everything in this book, since we are a team as we serve Jesus in ministry together. My parents, Skip and Jan, also have shaped my thinking of what a family and church community could be through the beautiful example they set for me as parents. This helped me understand the love of God for his children.

Paul Engle and John Raymond: Paul and John from Zondervan have been so incredibly encouraging to me in this process, making my first writing experience a joyful one. I so appreciate that they both have been pastors and thus understand ministry and the challenges we face in the emerging church.

The commentators in this book (see bios at the end of the book): I thank Chip, Rick, Brian, Mark, Sally, and Dr. Hendricks for taking the time to read and contribute to this book. Their comments and various insights make this book more of a diverse voice than a single one.

Introduction

> **See to it that no one takes you captive through hollow and deceptive philosophy, which depends on human tradition and the basic principles of this world rather than on Christ.**
>
> —Colossians 2:8

Have you ever tried typing the words *emerging church* and *postmodern* into your favorite search engine on the internet? I did. I could easily have spent hours viewing the results from church sites, webzines, discussion groups, and blogs that show how God is moving among emerging leaders around the world. Turning from my computer, I scanned a catalog on my desk from a major book distributor and counted a dozen or more new books on this topic. Clearly interest is growing in how the church can reach out to emerging generations in what some call a postmodern or post-Christian context.

I am absolutely thrilled! Church leaders are realizing that changes in our culture can no longer be ignored. Perhaps we've been awakened by the diminishing number of people from younger generations in our churches. Perhaps the Spirit of God is stirring among us, giving us an unsettling feeling that church the way we know it must change.

✝ We *must* think about the emerging culture because too much is at stake

I believe with all my heart that this discussion about the fast-changing culture and the emerging church *must* take place. While many of us have been preparing sermons and keeping busy with the internal affairs of our churches, something alarming has been happening on the outside. What

e·merg·ing

adj. newly formed or just coming into prominence *v.* to come to light, being discovered[1]

once was a Christian nation with a Judeo-Christian worldview is quickly becoming a post-Christian, unchurched, unreached nation. Tom Clegg and Warren Bird in their book *Lost in America* claim that the unchurched population of the United States is now the largest mission field in the English-speaking world, and the fifth largest globally.[2]

New generations are arising all around us without any Christian influence. So we must rethink virtually everything we are doing in our ministries.

✛ A clear and present danger when reading this book

I frequently engage in conversations in which individuals eventually ask questions like, "What type of music will bring young people to our church?" or, "What is the model for starting a new worship service to reach emerging generations?" Lots of these questions focus on ministry methodology.

But this focus poses a danger we need to address up front in this book: the danger of focusing on ministry methodology without understanding and addressing foundational issues that are far more important. So let me mention three assumptions from which I write.

✛ 1. There is no single model for the emerging church

Instead of one emerging-church model, there are hundreds and thousands of models of emerging churches. Modernity may have taught us to look for a clean model to imitate. But in today's postmodern context, it's not that simple.

However, you can see striking patterns developing among churches that are connecting with post-Christian hearts and minds all across America, as well as in England. I'll refer to several examples in this book. But please remember, there's no one-size-fits-all way of doing things, because you can't box-in the emerging church. It will be made up of large churches, small churches, and home churches, multiracial and intercultural churches, inner-city, rural, and suburban churches. I hope you will see this book not as a how-to manual for a church model but as a stimulant to get you thinking about what God might have you do uniquely in your context.

✛ 2. The emerging church is more of a mindset than a model

I have learned that emerging leaders have the same heartbeat. They realize something needs to change in our evangelical churches if we are to reach and engage the emerging culture. They realize we need to change how we think of the church, rather than merely change our forms of ministry. Emerging leaders are not afraid to remove the modern-ministry lenses we have been viewing "church" through and put on a new set to reexamine all we are doing. The emerging church must not try to simply replace the outer wrappings of our ministries. We must look at the inner core with a new mindset.

✝ 3. The emerging church measures success missionally

The modern church has been criticized for bragging (or being ashamed) when we count the three B's (buildings, budgets, and bodies), for directly or indirectly measuring our success using these criteria alone. The emerging church needs to beware of the same trap. We can't produce success merely by starting to use candles, artwork, the practice of *lectio divina,* and prayer labyrinths. Success is more than having an alternative worship gathering that has become the hottest thing in town, attracting hundreds of younger people.

> The emerging church must redefine how we measure success: by the characteristics of a kingdom-minded disciple of Jesus produced by the Spirit, rather than by our methodologies, numbers, strategies, or the cool and innovative things we are doing.

How should we measure success in the emerging church? By looking at what our practices *produce* in the called people of God as they are sent out on a mission to live as light and salt in their communities (Matt. 5:13–16). By seeing if people in our church take social justice and caring for the needy seriously as part of the mission Jesus did. We must measure success by looking for the same characteristics that the Spirit of God commended in the emerging missional Thessalonian church of the first century: "And so you became a model to all believers in Macedonia and Achaia. The Lord's message rang out from you not only in Macedonia and Achaia—your faith in God has become known everywhere. . . . They tell how you turned to God from idols to serve the living and true God, and to wait for his Son from heaven, whom he raised from the dead" (1 Thess. 1:7–10).

The emerging Thessalonian church was praised because their mission and message "rang out" as their faith had "become known everywhere" (1:8). Paul taught them to have their daily life "win the respect of outsiders" (4:12). Because of this reputation and outward missional focus, many came to know Jesus and "turned to God from idols" (1:9). The Thessalonians experienced an intensity of mission and love in their church (4:9–10). They took holy and pure living seriously (4:1–7). These are the types of measurements by which we should judge success.

I write these words with great personal concern. I've often engaged in conversations with other ministry leaders, each of us zealous and excited by all the new things we are trying in our emerging churches and ministries. We talk about philosophers and new theological insights, share about rave worship-events in England, dialogue on experiential worship, and sometimes criticize what modernity has done to the church. But what is too often sadly missing from our discussion is talk about the characteristics so esteemed in the Thessalonian church. So as you read this book, ask how the Spirit of God can use it to produce characteristics like we see in the Thessalonians.

I have divided this book into two parts. I hope you'll resist the temptation to jump to part 2, where we will walk through some practical ministry issues, because part 1 is critically important. If we don't understand the causes of the symptoms, our treatment is likely to be merely cosmetic, lacking in effectiveness.

In part 2 we will focus on rethinking leadership, spiritual formation, the church's mission, and evangelism. We will also look at how various churches across the nation are changing their worship services to meet the needs of the emerging culture.

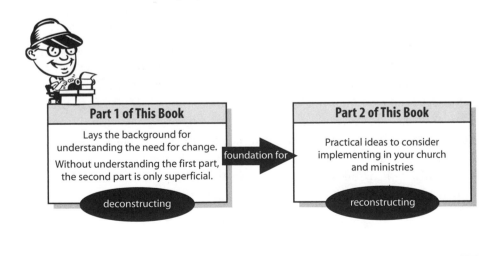

Part 1 of This Book	Part 2 of This Book
Lays the background for understanding the need for change. Without understanding the first part, the second part is only superficial.	Practical ideas to consider implementing in your church and ministries
deconstructing	reconstructing

foundation for

May our hearts beat fast when we think of how our churches can be known for their love, for the way they pray, for how they share Jesus, instead of being known merely for a style of preaching, music, artwork, or candles. The emerging church is about the Spirit of God producing missional kingdom-minded disciples of Jesus no matter what methodology we use. The emerging church is about love and faith in a post-Christian world. The emerging church is about Jesus.

Let me introduce you to a friend of mine named Sky, who is typical of the emerging generations. When you turn to the opening chapter, you'll hear his story.

What I appreciate about Dan's book is that what you are reading is coming from a practitioner. I have had the privilege of working with him for many years, and I have seen him learn and put into practice what he writes about in this book. He isn't just a theorist.

—CHIP INGRAM

DECONSTRUCTING
Postmodern Ministry, Candles, and Coffee

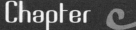
The Anti-Christian, Antichurch, Post-Christian Seeker

> " **Not all who wander are lost.**
>
> —J. R. R. Tolkien

✛ "Hello. My name is Sky, and I'm not a Christian."

Twenty-four-year-old Sky walked up on the stage during our Sunday night worship service and stood next to me. Sky was creative and artistic, an intelligent thinker who majored in photography at the University of California Santa Cruz. He had an introverted personality and was a little nervous, but he courageously stood beside me, dressed in his polyester Santa Cruz retro-artist fashion attire and displaying great, extended sideburns (which I personally admired). I handed him a microphone, and he began to tell his story with a plain and direct statement. "Hello. My name is Sky, and I'm not a Christian."

I could feel the ripple of surprise coming from the people as his words sank in. I suspect that many were expecting to hear Sky share a testimony of how Jesus had changed his life. But on this night, we had been talking about the importance of having true friendships with those who are not church attenders. I had been explaining how Jesus spent time with nonreligious sinners (Matt. 9:10). What better way to teach on this subject, I decided, than to hear the perspective of someone who doesn't believe in the Christian faith? Someone who would actually be considered a nonreligious sinner.

Sky stood there in front of several hundred of his peers and told them why he was not a Christian. His reasons, sadly, echoed those I had heard, and continue to hear, over and over from people in emerging generations whenever Christianity is brought up.

✢ "Christianity is a man-made organized religion."

Sky shared how he was raised in a nonreligious home. His parents, who had divorced when he was young, never encouraged him to attend church. In fact, they were rather distrustful of Christians and had rejected the church. As Sky grew up, he was taught by his parents to intelligently think for himself, and his own observations led him to believe that Christianity was a man-made organized religion filled with man-made rules based on opinions and politics.

✢ "Christians are close-minded, judgmental people."

From all he had experienced, Sky felt that most Christians are closed-minded and judgmental. Whether the issue was sexual, ethical, or moral preferences, Christians were always ready to point out how others were wrong and how they were always right. He shared how he strongly felt it was silly for the church in this age to cling to its dogmatic opinions. He felt that Christians were very shallow thinkers to believe that they had the only true answers.

✢ "Christians are arrogant to think they alone have the only true religion."

Sky shared that in his viewpoint, all religions and worldviews should be considered of equal value and beauty. He felt that the criticism and condemnation he had heard Christians inflict on nonbelievers was harmful and inexcusable. He shared that it really is arrogant to think that Christians alone have the one true religion and the only way to God. For all of these reasons, he testified, he not only rejected Christianity but was actually repelled by it. Although he described himself as a very spiritual person, he made it clear that Christianity was one of the last religions he would ever consider following. He offered his perspective on Christians as a word of caution to those there that night, lest they make these mistakes in their interactions with others like him.

But Sky's story wasn't over yet.

✢ Some "very different and unusual" people

Recently, about two years after the night he had shared his "anti-testimony," Sky joined me in front of his peers once again on another

Sunday night. Like the first time, Sky spoke into a microphone, but now we were standing waist deep in water in the baptistry. This time, instead of explaining why he wasn't a Christian and the reasons he didn't believe, Sky boldly and passionately declared, "I love Jesus and want to serve him with all my life."

Although he still looked the same with his very cool extended sideburns (although he wasn't wearing his usual polyester in the baptistry), this was quite a different Sky than the one who had stood on the stage two years ago. I could sense his passion as he shared what had occurred in his life. He even had to stop talking for a brief moment as his voice choked with emotion. Sky's story didn't include any type of major trauma, nor had he hit bottom in some area of his life. He simply told the story of how he met someone where he worked who introduced him to a few Christians who were what he called "very different and unusual" people.

Sky shared that as he got to know these particular Christians and became friends with them, for the first time he had actually seen Jesus in people who claimed to be his followers. He said he hadn't expected that there could ever be a group of Christians whom he felt he could relate to. He said that the way they befriended him and lived their lives for Jesus in front of him, despite their even knowing what he believed, caused him to think. He said that this is what eventually led him to regularly go to the place where they gathered to worship on Sunday nights.

✛ Compelled to be in the presence of believers worshiping

Standing in the baptistry, Sky thanked everyone present that night for the part they had each played in his decision. He explained that they were the first Christians he had ever seen actually worshiping God in a seriously spiritual way. He told them how much it impacted him when he would come on Sunday nights and see people his age singing songs of joy to God, praying on their knees, and taking Jesus very seriously. He never realized that Christians seek and encounter God in this way. It was a very unusual thing to him, seeing this, and it was so unlike anything he had ever experienced that he felt compelled to keep coming back. He said he was haunted by the images of people worshiping like they were, so he kept returning.

Sky told everyone how eventually one Sunday night, during a time when we allowed people to sit quietly and reflect and pray, he made a decision. Sky particularly liked the times of silence and heart-searching in the worship service. On this evening, while sitting at a table, he realized that he wanted to know the Jesus that he was experiencing through his friends and on Sunday nights at the worship service. He told everyone how he bowed his head into his hands and prayed (I quote Sky word for word here), "Lord, I don't understand everything that it is to follow you, but I have seen your power at work in other people and felt your presence. I want you to be my savior and to be the center of my life." Sky shared how he later found out that at the very moment he was praying, his friends were sitting nearby, all intensely praying for him.

☩ Sky's story didn't end with a salvation prayer to get him to heaven

Sitting in one of the first rows that night as he spoke from the baptistry were Sky's mom and dad. Although neither are Christians, they came to watch their son's baptism, knowing how much it meant to him. Sitting near his parents were Rod and Connie Clendenen, Sky's midweek Bible study leaders and spiritual mentors. Rod is eighty years old, and he and his wife, Connie, open their home every Wednesday night to lead a group of primarily twenty-somethings in in-depth studies of various books of the Bible. Rod and Connie have become a big part of Sky's life, even though he and they are generations apart in age. Sky felt that as he explored Christianity, he needed to seriously study the Bible. In fact, he had made a commitment to read through the entire Bible before his baptism. It took him nearly two years, but he did it. Sky now helps lead his Bible study from time to time and is passionate about aligning his life with the teachings of Jesus. Sky constantly is allowing other nonbelievers to see how God transformed his life and makes it a point never to get too consumed with "church" at the expense of those who need to see Jesus in him now.

+ Evangelism to an anti-Christian, antichurch, post-Christian seeker

After I baptized Sky that night, people applauded and praised God with great enthusiasm. A young nonbeliever with strong antichurch and anti-Christian views had been transformed into a devoted follower and disciple of Jesus. And it had happened quite outside the lines of the modern "seeker-sensitive" prescription for church growth.

There are two ways of understanding the term seeker-sensitive. My use of the term in this book could be confusing if you don't grasp this. In one sense, we all should be seeker-sensitive in terms of being sensitive to seekers as a lifestyle. Jesus was very sensitive to seekers, and we should be too. But the fact is that the term seeker-sensitive has also become known as a methodology of ministry, in particular a certain type of worship service. This second sense is primarily what I mean when I use the term in this book. Confused? Let's look at some definitions.

Seeker-Sensitive As a *Lifestyle*

Being seeker-sensitive as a lifestyle means that we are sensitive to spiritual seekers in all that we do. This can apply to our conversations with those seeking; it can apply to how we design any style of worship service. In this sense, it is not a style or methodology of worship; it is a lifestyle approach to how we live as Christians in relation to being sensitive to seekers of faith.

Seeker-Sensitive As a *Style*

Currently in our culture, when someone refers to a seeker-sensitive worship service or approach, they many times are referring to a methodology or style of ministry—a strategy of designing ministry to attract those who feel the church is irrelevant or dull. This often involves removing what could be considered religious stumbling blocks and displays of the spiritual (such as extended worship, religious symbols, extensive prayer times, liturgy, etc.) so that seekers[1] can relate to the environment and be transformed by the message of Jesus. Generally, seeker-sensitive services function as entry points into the church, and the church offers deeper teaching and worship in another meeting or setting. This is primarily what I mean when I use the term seeker-sensitive in this book.

Sky did not come to know Jesus and become part of a church because of a well-rehearsed drama sketch, polished four-point preaching, flawless programming, or new padded theater seats. It wasn't because we met in a well-lit, contemporary, bright and cheery church facility where we removed the religious symbols, stained glass, and churchy atmosphere to make "seekers" more comfortable. It wasn't because we used secular songs in the church meeting so he could relate to them, or cut musical worship to a minimum in the fear that it would cause someone like Sky to be turned off. In fact, Sky experienced almost the opposite.

Being sensitive to seekers is not a style of worship! I could show you hundreds of different styles being used by seeker-sensitive churches, including surfer seeker-services, cowboy seeker-services, artistic seeker-services, ethnic seeker-services, liturgical seeker-services, and postmodern seeker-services. That's because not all seekers are alike.

Being sensitive to the mindset of unbelievers is a biblical attitude (1 Cor. 14:23) modeled by both Jesus and Paul. It is loving lost people enough to try to relate to them on their level (whatever that is) so Jesus can save them. In a postmodern world, building that bridge will be hard work, but this book can show you how to do it. It begins with not expecting nonbelievers to act, think, or feel like believers until they are.

—RICK WARREN

25

When he attended his new friends' worship gathering, he experienced more of a "post-seeker-sensitive" approach to ministry and worship services. This approach is really nothing new at all; in fact, it is simply going back to more of a raw and basic form of "vintage Christianity."

Post-Seeker-Sensitive

Going back to a raw form of vintage Christianity, which unapologetically focuses on kingdom living by disciples of Jesus. A post-seeker-sensitive worship gathering promotes, rather than hides, full displays of spirituality (extended worship, religious symbols, liturgy, extensive prayer times, extensive use of Scripture and readings, etc.) so that people can experience and be transformed by the message of Jesus. This approach is done, however, with renewed life and is still "sensitive" as clear instruction and regular explanation are given to help seekers understand theological terms and spiritual exercises.

In fact, I later learned from Sky that if we had offered the type of things typically associated with a "seeker-sensitive service," he wouldn't have been interested. If he was going to take the time to go to a church service, he told me, he wanted to experience an authentic spiritual event in which he could see if God was truly alive and being worshiped. If he attended the service his Christian friends went to, and discovered that we took away the crosses and anything that looked religious and didn't open the Bible and had fewer times of prayer and singing, he would have felt Christians were either embarrassed by or were trying to hide what they believed. To him, this would have been hypocritical and even a turn-off to church.

Many of the very things that we removed from our churches because they were stumbling blocks to seekers in previous generations are now the very things that are attractive to emerging generations.

How ironic! So many of the things I had once worked so hard to eliminate in order to be seeker-sensitive, to avoid offending or confusing a seeker like Sky, were exactly the things he found the most influential in his decision to become a Christian. For Sky, a seeker-sensitive (style, not

lifestyle) approach would have been a complete failure and possibly even detrimental. Sky comes from a generation that grew up in a changing post-Christian culture, a culture different from that of the generations that grew up when the seeker-sensitive movement started. We need to recognize that we are moving into a post-seeker-sensitive era.

By no means do I discount the value of seeker-sensitive-style ministry. I know for a fact that God has used it in phenomenal ways and will continue to use it. But our culture is changing. Previous generations grew up experiencing church as dull or meaningless, and so the seeker-sensitive model strove to reintroduce church as relevant, contemporary, and personal. But emerging generations are being raised without any experience of church, good or bad. As in Sky's case, when he first went to church, his desire was for a spiritual, transcendent experience. To have removed the overtly spiritual would have seemed very strange to him.

✠ The emerging church exists in a post-seeker-sensitive world

In the following chapters, we will learn more about what led to Sky's conversion and what he was drawn to in his Christian friends and in the worship services they attended. We will look at what people in emerging generations are finding attractive (and not so attractive) about the Christian faith and today's church. Sky's story is not isolated; all across America I am hearing similar accounts repeated over and over. I believe Sky's former opinions about Christianity are quickly becoming the norm. If you aren't yet hearing opinions like Sky shared, it is only a matter of time before you do. I believe there are many Skys in your local community, perhaps many more than you realize. But the good news is that they are spiritually open.

I believe we are at a point in church history where we need to rethink some of our assumptions and reexamine some of our presuppositions about church and ministry. As we will discuss in the next several chapters, the emerging church is emerging in a very quickly changing world. So we need to change how we go about our ministry.

✠ A new wave of change

In recent times, the wave of change came to the church with the seeker-sensitive movement. Another wave of change is now breaking on our shores. This shouldn't surprise us. Time passes, new generations are born, cultures change, so the church must change. We see this in ancient church history, in European church history, as well as in American church history. Many call the change we are now experiencing as moving from a modern to a postmodern era. Some call it moving from a Christian to a post-Christian culture. Sky and others like him probably wouldn't call it anything at all or want to be labeled as post-anything. However, emerging generations are definitely being shaped by the culture, probably much more than they or we realize.

The type of change I am talking about is not just about what happens in the church service, with the music, or with the small group strategy. These are only surface issues. It is really a revolutionary change that affects almost everything we do—even what comes to our minds when we say the word church.

✛ No matter how the culture or church ministry changes, Jesus never changes

You may be thinking, "I'd like to see emerging generations reached, but how the heck can I ever keep up with all the waves of cultural changes?" Amid our anxiety, remember that although ministry methodology, church, and culture change, Jesus never does.

"Jesus Christ is the same yesterday and today and forever" (Heb. 13:8). He is the same Jesus now as he was in the Upper Room and as he appeared to Paul on the road to Damascus. He is the same Jesus as when Martin Luther nailed his ninety-five theses to the door of Castle Church in Wittenberg. He is the same Jesus as when the Enlightenment was in full force. Modern world, postmodern world, post-postmodern world ... Jesus never changes. He is the reason for and the focus of all that we do. He is our anchor, no matter which direction the tide may be taking us.

We must not forget that cultural change doesn't surprise Jesus. I don't think Jesus is looking down, saying, "Oh no! I wasn't expecting this postmodern shift. What do we do?" We can take great comfort in the fact that we are merely experiencing a period in history, and that in the perspective of eternity, this is but a blip on the screen. However, it is a reality, and emerging church leaders must be students of world and church history so we can gain perspective on all of this.

✛ A return to vintage Christianity

In today's world, emerging generations have no anchor or truth to hold onto. So as they hear and experience Jesus as the truth and the anchor for the very first time, the hope for the future is incredibly optimistic. As the emerging church returns to a rawer and more vintage form of Christianity, we may see explosive growth much like the early church did. These new cultural waves of change may bring the greatest opportunity we have had in a long time to see many antichurch, anti-Christian, post-Christian seekers like Sky meet the eternal Jesus.

EMERGING THOUGHTS

1. Do you know anyone like Sky? Would you say his or her criticisms of the church and Christians are the same, or are there other critcisms you are hearing from those in emerging generations?

2. If you don't know of anyone like Sky, do you feel that people like him don't exist in your community, or that you are just not in the right circles to have met them? What might be some ways you could meet people like him in your area?

3. What would you say someone like Sky would like about your church right now if he visited? What would you think he might find that would confirm his preconceptions about Christianity?

4. Are you worried or excited about the changes in the culture? Why? If you feel more anxious than excited, how could you go about finding comfort in the fact that although culture may change, Jesus always remains the same?

How I Moved from Being Seeker-Sensitive to Post-Seeker-Sensitive

2

> **To the Jews I became like a Jew, to win the Jews. To those under the law I became like one under the law (though I myself am not under the law), so as to win those under the law. . . . To the weak I became weak, to win the weak. I have become all things to all men so that by all possible means I might save some.**

— 1 Corinthians 9:20, 22

I was brand-spanking new to ministry in the late 1980s. My first responsibility at Santa Cruz Bible Church was to lead a high school group of eleven teens. I vividly remember the first night, looking into the faces of those students and having no idea what to do.

So, like most eager new pastors, I made my pilgrimages to Willow Creek Community Church near Chicago and to Saddleback Church in Orange County, California. At Willow Creek my heart was broken for those who don't know Jesus. I learned to appreciate the value of excellent ministry programming and how to see the church through a seeker's eyes. From Saddleback I learned the importance of approaching all ministry with purpose and strategy. I learned the importance of removing "religious" barriers so that we could communicate the message about Jesus all the more clearly. I also studied popular books on ministry methodology and attended seminars and conferences to sharpen my pastoring skills.

+ Disco balls, smoke machines, and Jesus

Over the next several years, I took these modern principles, values, and models to heart and strove to implement them in the high school ministry. We wrote a mission statement, designed a strategy, and defined our ten core values, and soon we were off on a mission to impact the five public high schools in Santa Cruz County. At our midweek outreach, we desired to be seeker-sensitive to teenagers, so we used dramas, a rock band, a fog machine, videos, special lights, even a disco ball hanging from the ceiling. Each week, we taught strong biblical messages on sex, self-esteem, and all the typical issues that teenagers face. By the mid-1990s, our midweek seeker-sensitive-style outreach service had grown from eleven high school students to 250 to 300, an exciting thing in a relatively small beach community such as Santa Cruz. This large group was broken down by schools into smaller gatherings so that leadership could meet and befriend students personally. Over half the teens were also part of small group Bible studies and Sunday morning high school classes, where they received deeper teaching and worshiped. A high percentage of those students participated in leadership roles. We were privileged to see many teens come to know Jesus using the very principles I had been taught. Several of these teens have now gone into full-time vocational ministry. It was an extremely thrilling time! We experienced a great deal of genuine success in changed lives, clear evidence that God's hand was on the ministry.

✠ Feeling the first waves of change from emerging post-Christian generations

But the story doesn't just happily end there. I had assumed that we had locked into a strategy that worked and that we would go on like this forever (or until Jesus returned). However, after several years of fruitful ministry, I began to notice a subtle, disturbing trend. Something was changing. I could sense it in the conversations I had with teenagers. I could feel it in the response to the outreach program we were leading. I could hear it in the questions that students were asking. I didn't know it yet, but we were feeling the effects of emerging generations being born into a post-Christian (and what I will define here as a post-seeker-sensitive) world.

Little by little, I began to recognize that non-Christian students, who had once been impressed by all of our programming, dramas, media clips, and topical messages, were showing less and less interest. With technology now so accessible to teenagers that they could easily create their own flashy video clips, seeing it in church was no big deal. Fancy PowerPoint presentations lost their uniqueness as students were creating their own presentations for school. The special effects in the video games they were used to went far beyond what we could ever offer. Their lives were fast-paced as it was; coming to church for yet another fast-paced experience was losing its impact.

+ By the way, which God are you talking about?

But the change I was sensing had to do with more than programing. No longer was it so simple to tell students, "God loves you." Now they were asking, "By the way, which God are you talking about?" They all seemed for the most part to believe in a god, but they were exposed to a wide variety of world faiths and other ways of viewing him . . . or her.

To make matters even more complex, these changes weren't limited to our high schoolers. Many of our graduating seniors were also having a hard time connecting with the church's existing college ministry and integrating with the main adult services of the church. The churched teenagers who were raised in Christian homes that taught them Judeo-Christian values and had a history with contemporary Christian culture, values, and language seemed more likely to make the transition. But those who had come to the faith out of non-Christian backgrounds did not connect as easily. We knew the problem was not that our college ministry or adult church services were dull or irrelevant. Our church was vibrant, alive, with great contemporary worship and phenomenal preaching.

But somehow it wasn't connecting with the hearts of these young adults. These patterns haunted me. What should be done? We were doing all the things that had once been so effective. We had great sound equipment and lighting, we had our strategy, we had our mission statement, we had a great track record of producing disciples of Jesus. Where were these new questions coming from? You can imagine how frustrated and puzzled I felt.

So I began making phone calls. I telephoned a select group of healthy and growing churches all across America and asked questions such as, "Are you seeing any changes in your youth and college ministries?" "Are younger generations attending your adult worship services?" "In your community, what percentage of people in younger generations attends local churches?"

I was not alone; the same thing was surfacing all across America.

Good warning: any program or paradigm or model or system that purports to be timeless—or, for that matter, "guaranteed to work"—is to be avoided at all costs!

—MARK OESTREICHER

Contrary to much of our current thinking about the importance of powerful youth ministries to the lifelong spiritual development of future adults, research proves otherwise: a teenager who attends a church's worship service on a regular basis and does not attend youth group is more likely to continue to attend church worship services as an adult than a teen who is active in youth group but doesn't attend worship services with other age groups.

—MARK OESTREICHER

The answers I heard fascinated me. From coast to coast, many of the nation's largest and most successful churches were experiencing the trend we'd been observing in Santa Cruz. Some patterns emerged:

- ➡ Non-Christian youth and younger adults were not responding to outreach methods that had been very successful in the past.
- ➡ Youth and young adults generally were not connecting with the contemporary, modern church service and seeker-sensitive approach that was very successful with earlier generations.
- ➡ Youth, college, and young-adult ministries were overall confused about what to do and were definitely in a state of transition.

✠ From a sense of relief to a sense of panic

At first, as I understood I was not alone, I felt a huge sense of relief. But then a sense of panic arose. If this truly was a national trend, the longer-term implications could be devastating. How will we reach future generations if the methods of ministry that had always worked with previous generations were not as effective with the emerging generations? What happens if this generation grows up rejecting church, and then their children grow up with no concept of the Christian faith taught to them? And then their children? What would our future churches look like if emerging generations are not reached? How would we make Jesus known to this new, emerging culture?

✠ Unplugging the smoke machine and raiding the church attic

I was pretty much at a loss as to what to do. Then late one night I happened upon the band the Cranberries playing an *Unplugged* concert on MTV. It was an all-acoustic performance. The stage was draped with a dark, rich fabric and lit by candelabras. It looked more like a grandmother's attic than a rock-concert venue, and I was struck by the simplicity of it. No fancy light shows or drum-set risers. I also noticed how close the audience was seated to the musicians. There wasn't a giant separation between the two groups. Rather, they were sort of all together in a "community." I immediately felt that there was something very interesting to this "unplugged" approach.

MTV obviously studies culture and knows their audience, so maybe they were on to something here. Besides, going unplugged would be a heck of a lot easier than gearing up for our usual Wednesday night full production. So a few weeks later, as summer began, we tried an unplugged experiment for our midweek meetings.

Instead of all the flash and lights, we set up only candles. I felt that this would add a sort of catacombish feeling to our meetings, reminiscent of the early Roman church in hiding. I played up this catacombs angle to the high schoolers as we launched this new approach. (I actually thought I was the first one ever to bring candles into a non-Catholic church. I had no idea that other leaders across the country were doing exactly the same thing.) Instead of the well-rehearsed dramas and flashy videos, we simply had a few high schoolers reading sections of Scripture while sitting on stools. Instead of speaking from a high stage and having the band playing loud electric music, we set up a lower stage and the band went acoustic. We raided our church attic and set up old props and funky furniture we found to give it an eclectic bohemian sort of look. I wasn't sure what to expect, but what happened next only puzzled and surprised me all the more.

✛ "I like this. This is really spiritual."

The loud rock-pop music of our typical Wednesday night events was usually met with high-pitched screams and yells. But as our unplugged evening unfolded, I could hear the voices of the high schoolers rising in worship. When I got up to speak, instead of the rustling of squirming teenagers in the back, there was stillness. One particular group of more hard-core skater kids who normally caused a lot of disruption sat quietly to listen. Please remember, this was not our Sunday morning believers high school services; this was our outreach night. We typically hired security officers to patrol the grounds at these events.

When one of the unplugged nights ended, one teenager waited to speak with me. He was one of our more disinterested and unresponsive teens, and I was dreading what he would say. I was expecting him to tell me how dull and boring the evening had been and that he wouldn't be coming back. Instead, he smiled and gave a nod of approval. "I like this," he said. "This was really spiritual."

What an incredible thing to hear! Here we had been trying so hard to remove all aspects of the spiritual in order to communicate God's love to this teenager, seemingly to no avail. Now that we had almost completely reversed our tactics, we finally seemed to be getting through. This was fairly mind-tweaking. Non-Christian teenagers now desire spiritual experiences? I knew Christian teenagers desired the spiritual, but the non-Christian?

Dan's use of the word panic brings back a powerful moment when the force of this shift hit me. It was the late '70s, and I was in graduate school studying literature. I was in a literary criticism class (literary criticism was the portal through which postmodern thinking entered the American academy), and we were discussing Stanley Fish's *Self-Consuming Artifacts*. I remember thinking, "If this way of thinking catches on, the whole world changes." And then I remember a shiver running up my spine: "And I'm not sure the Christian faith can handle the change." It took almost twenty years for me to muster the courage to grapple more directly with the issues that sneaked into my brain in that class that day.

—BRIAN MCLAREN

Wait! Some of you, while reading this, went to Illumina-tions.com and ordered a few dozen candles! If you simply copy Dan's methods like he tried the smoke machines and disco ball (really, Dan, a disco ball?), you're setting yourself up to run into the same wall he ran into ten years ago. Just adding candles and unplugged music to what you are doing is not the answer to your problems.

—MARK OESTREICHER

Instead of turning them off, this was causing them to desire to know God more? Of course teenagers still need plenty of fun events and Jell-O Olympics and all-night shut-ins. But now we need to recognize that perhaps this culture is forcing their spiritual hunger to surface all the more. Their desire is to *experience* God and not just be told about him or told about the things he doesn't like, which also happen to be the things they want to do.

This is what began my personal journey out of a seeker-sensitive-style approach to church and outreach. I was beginning to grasp that culturally we are now truly in a post-seeker age. Realizing this, I could identify with what the apostle Paul said in 1 Corinthians 9:22: "I have become all things to all men so that by all possible means I might save some." I then began to be post-seeker-sensitive in how I approached all aspects of ministry, moving to a rawer and more vintage approach.

Then I began wondering if adults were also feeling the same desire for a spiritual experience rather than a seeker-sensitive-style one. Was the feeling of change transcending youth to impact adults as well?

✢ Post-seeker-sensitive adults too?

We began our research by gathering several young adults, both believers and nonbelievers, for a series of brainstorming sessions. We took them to some contemporary, modern church services and met afterward to ask questions about their impressions of the services. What they said was absolutely fascinating and mind-tweaking. As we had found with teenagers, many of the things we had brought into our church to make the services contemporary and relevant were the very things the young adults didn't like. (I will tell you more about their comments in chapter 13.) Some of the things I had never even noticed before were very noticeable to them. Many of the things they thought a church should be like were never mentioned in any of the seminars or conferences I had ever attended.

The changes in our culture are influencing emerging generations to crave a raw and vintage approach to Christianity and church. Therefore, contemporary seeker-sensitive methodology goes against what connects with them most deeply.

And so we took their ideas and impressions about church and began to think and pray. We experimented by starting a Sunday-night worship gathering called Graceland. We chose the name because it took something familiar in pop culture (Elvis' mansion) and fused it with spiritual meaning. (Plus, I was a big pre-1960 Elvis fan!) We wanted a name that was not commonplace in Christian circles, wouldn't sound corny to the unchurched, and would reflect our heart as a community where you experience God's grace. We began by taking the same approach we had with the unplugged high-school ministry events and tailoring it to an older age group. Our intention was to create a gathering specifically for young adults (18–30 years old) but soon found that teenagers, as well as those over thirty, wanted to attend. So we eventually turned it into a worship service for all ages. In a few short years, it grew beyond anything we could have imagined with hundreds attending, many of whom were there for their first ever church experience. Many Christians who had become disillusioned with their evangelical church experience became part of the church. If we had continued with our modern methods of ministry and our seeker-sensitive-style approach, I don't believe we ever would have seen this happen. Although a vintage and post-seeker approach attracted primarily younger generations, it was fascinating to see the number of people outside of the 18–30 year old age range who related to and hungered for this ministry approach. I believe we must recognize that even though the seeker-sensitive approach has reached many in older generations, a significant percentage of people in those generations were not drawn to the contemporary seeker approach to church and ministry.

+ Please, please, please ... this is not just about the worship service

So far, I've talked a lot about the "meeting" or church service in my stories. But I believe what is happening goes far beyond that. In the case of some emerging churches, there may not even be a meeting like we think of one now. In fact, the worship service itself is by no means where we should focus all of our attention. Rethinking the emerging church involves rethinking almost *everything* we do. The worship service is but one part of it.

✢ The journey may be unknown, but that can make it all the more exciting

You and I live in a fascinating time in church history. This book was written to take us on a journey during this fascinating era of sweeping change, a journey to an unknown destination. There are no easy routes, no maps or trail markers. Culture is changing quickly and there are many unknowns. But even so, we can take brave steps of faith and move forward. God called Abram to go on a journey without telling him his destination (Heb. 11:8–10). Those of us who are called to ministry to emerging generations find ourselves in a similar situation. Like Abram, if we call upon God to guide us, he will. Just as we are facing new cultural issues, so did Abram as he left his home in Ur and went into a different culture in Canaan. But if we rely not on our own tactics and human wisdom but on God's leading, we can trust that the "architect and builder" of our faith will guide us. We can step out on the journey and look forward to whatever it is he has in store for the emerging church.

EMERGING THOUGHTS

1. **Is there anything or anyone in the story of what happened in our youth ministry that you can relate to in your own church experience?**

2. **How would you say the emerging generations in your community and church would initially respond to the idea of a rawer and more vintage, spiritually up-front experience?**

3. **Where would you say your current church barometer is on a scale from being seeker-sensitive to being post-seeker-sensitive? Or is your church somewhere else?**

Understanding the Past to Understand the Future

3

> **" . . . men of Issachar, who understood the times and knew what Israel should do.**
>
> —1 Chronicles 12:32

✚ "Why aren't younger people coming to my church anymore?"

At a recent conference I found myself engaged in a conversation with the senior pastor of a very large, well-known church primarily of baby boomers. This was the first we had met. Although I immediately found him to be confident, intelligent, and articulate, after a few minutes of cordial exchange I sensed an urgency rise in his voice and saw puzzlement in his eyes. It wasn't long before he spoke straight to the core of the issue. "What is going on with younger people?" he asked. "Why aren't they coming to my church anymore?"

This was no backward dying church. It had great facilities with state-of-the-art media equipment. Since a lot of money had been invested in their young adult and college ministry over the past couple of years, it seemed to be poised for success. But they failed to experience growth from younger generations. The pastor said that despite all his successful years of ministry as a self-described student of church growth, he was stumped and very concerned for the future of his church. He shook his head in bewilderment and said, "I just don't understand this postmodern thing."

No one can deny that great attention has been paid in recent years to the development of various church models designed primarily to reach baby boomers and those of a modern mindset. Seeker-sensitive and seeker-driven churches have changed the church culture of America and have accomplished absolutely wonderful things for Jesus. Many people have had bad church experiences and returned to the church, while multitudes of others have been introduced for the first time to a contemporary life-changing faith and church experience. God is still using these churches in great ways and will continue to do so.

✣ A megachurch in almost every town, yet an unsettling trend is occurring

Today, you can find a megachurch in just about every major populated area. Worship centers have been transformed into contemporary auditoriums. You can now walk into a number of churches and find sound systems that cost thousands of dollars and PowerPoint presentations of Bible verses projected onto cineplex-sized screens. Worship teams that once consisted of an organist and a piano player now include a drummer and electric guitarists. We have replaced straight-backed pews with cushioned theater seating. Preachers have adapted to speaking to large audiences using motivational and powerful communication techniques. The church has become acclimatized to many aspects of our culture.

Yet most churches seem to be grappling with a growing problem today. In spite of all these contemporary additions and amendments, we're losing ground. Younger people for the most part are staying away from churches and are even more interested in exploring other world faiths or spiritual beliefs.

For those who need statistical data, researcher George Barna provides some critical observations:

- ➡ Out of all the age groups, those ages 18 to 32 are the least likely to describe themselves as religious, as Christian, or as committed Christians.[1]
- ➡ Young adults today in the US seem the most open to exploring faiths other than Christianity.[2]
- ➡ Young adults are avoiding church: Church attendance is declining by generation.[3]
- ➡ Compared with teens throughout the past twenty years, today's teenagers have the lowest likelihood of attending church when they are living independent of their parents.[4]
- ➡ The data regarding young adults also pose the possibility that churches are losing ground in terms of influence and may need to consider new approaches.[5]

Here in the Northeast, megachurches (among white Protestants) aren't nearly as popular as they are many other places. Nor are they popular in Europe. This may be simply because the culture here is more pervasively postmodern (yes, even more so than in southern California, though probably not more so than San Francisco, Seattle, or Minneapolis), and postmodernity tends to shy away from the big and powerful, the organized and slick. Where megachurches are found, they tend to draw nominal Christians into a more vibrant Christian life, rather than reach more hard-core unchurched folks. By the way, some of the most hard-core unchurched here are the sons and grandsons of hard-core evangelicals.

—BRIAN MCLAREN

TOO MUCH COFFEE MAN   BY SHANNON WHEELER

HERE'S THE CHURCH,

HERE'S THE STEEPLE,

OPEN THE DOORS, WHERE ARE THE PEOPLE?

ACROSS THE STREET,

IN THE BAR...

OPEN THE DOORS... AND THERE THEY ARE!

© 2002 Shannon Wheeler. www.toomuchcoffeeman.com / Used with permission.

Church leaders are noticing this trend and are discussing ways to address it. We saw evidence of this at a forum held by Leadership Network (www.leadnet.org), hosted at Santa Cruz Bible Church. The purpose was to explore the concept of starting new services within existing churches as a way to reach out to the emerging culture. We were initially expecting fifty to seventy-five people but quickly discovered how hot this issue is. Approximately 250 pastors and leaders attended the conference, from many different denominations and churches of different sizes, many with memberships of several thousand. Time and again that week, and multiple times since, the same questions were being asked: "Why aren't younger people coming to our churches anymore?" And, "I don't understand this postmodern thing."

+ Oh no, not yet another discussion on the "postmodern" word

I know that for some, the word postmodern has become overused and overanalyzed, so you may be tired of hearing about it. You may be thinking, "Oh no, not yet another discussion on postmodernism." If that's your reaction and you can honestly say that you grasp the broad concept of postmodernism, then you may want to skip the next two chapters. It may be redundant for you, but in order for others to be able to grapple with the methodology and ministry issues covered in the later chapters, I couldn't just ignore providing an introductory overview, since it lays the groundwork for the second part of the book.

Others may have heard about postmodernism, but it remains a fuzzy concept for them. All you know is that "postmoderns don't believe in absolute truth." If that's you, then I think you will find this brief introduction valuable; hopefully it will clear up some of the confusion. By no means do you need to be an expert or know who all the postmodern philosophers are, but at least a general understanding will be beneficial to your church and ministry.

For others, if you bristle and brush off postmodernism as a fad or buzzword that has no impact on the church, then the question I need to ask you is, Where are all the younger people in your church? You may have Christian young people who have been raised in your church, but what about the population of emerging generations in your community? Is your church homogenous? New generations are now becoming the mainstream of the emerging culture and probably cannot relate to what many churches are doing now.

✥ The key to understanding the future is to understand the past

When we hear that cultural changes are occurring, our initial reaction may be to try to pinpoint the new problems and then tweak our ministries to fix them. If we don't see younger people coming into our churches today, perhaps we should just add some hip songs to the worship set. Or maybe if we turn the lights down and add some candles, we'll be addressing this "postmodern thing" and emerging generations will return to our churches. However, it's futile to try to fix a surface issue without knowing the cause. We need to be like the men of Issachar, who *understood the times* and were able to discern what they should then do.

Throughout our history, major periods of cultural transition have drastically affected our view of the world. Francis Schaeffer traced these time periods in his book and video series *How Should We Then Live?* Philosophers and sociologists call this our epistemology, or you could say our worldview. Our worldview consists of the presuppositions and the foundation upon which our life's meaning and purpose are based.

It impacts our values, the way we process information, and how we draw our conclusions. It determines how we think about God, humanity, and religion. Our worldview affects the way we see not just "the church" but also individual church organizations. Our worldview is the lens through which we see everything.

Most of us would agree that worldview cultural shifts have taken place throughout human history and that they are not simply the fabrications of philosophers and professors. One cannot deny, for instance, how the printing press, the Reformation, and the Enlightenment each tremendously changed culture and even the church as we entered the modern era. Now in the early years of the twenty-first century, many believe that we are now experiencing the next great cultural shift, even if it isn't happening overnight. Entire books have been written which explore these shifts and

epis·te·mol·o·gy

n. (Greek *episteme*, "knowledge"; *logos*, "theory") the philosophical theory of the method or basis we use to obtain our knowledge

pre·sup·po·si·tion

n. what we believe or assume in advance

their effects in depth. If you desire a deeper understanding, please do read the great books out there written by experts on this subject (see appendix C).

> We need to look into our past in order to understand how we got where we are today. Then we can begin to discern where the emerging church may be heading in the future.

By no means can I do justice to three thousand years of world history with a few paragraphs and charts. But for the purpose of this book, we need to at least understand and see that throughout history, significant changes do take place. When we realize that, perhaps we won't fear the changes needed for the emerging church.

✝ Understanding the past

I recently engaged in a conversation with someone who was born in a primitive area of western Africa and is now serving as a pastor there. As we talked about postmodernism, I realized how foreign this issue is to the situations he faces. In many ways, he is dealing with a premodern worldview among the tribal groups to whom he ministers. My attempt to map out all this history really did not have much to do with his situation. So I recognize how Eurocentric and basic is the brief look at history which follows. However, I hope it conveys the necessary points in a way that's quickly understood and remembered to equip us for cultural change in the American church.

The dates on the following table are mere approximations, reflecting the time when change was occurring, not when it exactly began or ended. Because we are beginning another shift, many may disagree or fail to see that it is happening. But just because you cannot see the ramifications doesn't mean it isn't reality. Changes like this take decades to see fully in day-to-day life.

The year 2000 in the chart was chosen as a transitional point for postmodernism merely because we began to see such a large degree of postmodern philosophy evident in our culture. Some say postmodernism started at the fall of the Berlin Wall; others argue for 1969, the year of Woodstock; some trace it back even further. Since there is no exact year, I am using an approximate date for the sake of showing we are living at

> Many otherwise intelligent church leaders make the mistake of seeing postmodernism as a narrow, generational issue. Yet the record indicates otherwise, as even an honest, fifteen-minute perusal of the subject would reveal. Postmodernism has all the well-developed philosophical, aesthetic, and cultural underpinnings that characterize broad periods of time.
>
> —SALLY MORGENTHALER

43

the beginning of it. In the next chapter let's take a look more specifically at our time period and how we may see some of these changes in our day-to-day lives and what they mean to our ministry.

A Look at Major Worldview Shifts

	Ancient World 2500 B.C.–500 A.D.	Medieval World 500–1500	Modern World 1500–2000+	Postmodern World 2000+
Epistemology	Regional worldview. Time period of first historic civilizations. Deities were considered regional and territorial.	Judeo-Christian, God-centered worldview.	During the Enlightenment epistemology shifts to a man-centered trust in reason to discover truth.	Self-determined pluralistic view of culture and religion. Conflicting truths and beliefs are accepted.
Understanding	Power and faith were in the kings, empires, and local deities.	Power and faith were in the church.	Power and faith were in human reasoning, science, and logic, which also helped explain and interpret God.	Power and faith is in personal experience.
Communication	Oral communication and limited local historical records.	Manuscript and oral communication.	Printing press transforms communication.	Internet and media accelerate an instant global communication revolution.
Authority	Authority was in the revelation given through the oracles, poets, kings, and prophets.	Authority was in the Bible but only to be understood as taught through the church. The Bible was not in the hands of the people.	Authority was in reason, science, and logic and for Christians was in the reasonable interpretation of the Bible.	Suspicion of authority. The Bible is open to many interpretations and is but one of many religious writings.
Theme	"What is man that You are mindful of him?" —Psalm 8:4	"I believe in order that I may understand." —Anselm (1033–1099)	"Knowledge is power." —Francis Bacon "I think, therefore I am." —Descartes (1596–1650)	"If it makes you happy, it can't be that bad." —Sheryl Crow "Every viewpoint is a view from a viewpoint."

This chart has been adapted from the Leadership Network (www.leadnet.com) with input from Brian McLaren, who also discusses this topic in his book *A New Kind of Christian*.

44

EMERGING THOUGHTS

1. Think through the chart on worldview shifts. Have you ever looked at the church through an epistemological lens to see how it changed through time during each of these eras? Can you name any specific ways you know from church history that the church has had to adapt during these time periods?

2. Look again at the chart "A Look at Major Worldview Shifts." Does anything jump out at you in terms of recognizing the shift from modern to postmodern in your context?

3. Do you agree with or resist the idea that we are going through a postmodern change in our worldview? Give reasons for agreeing or disagreeing.

Beyond Postmodernism, Candles, and Cool

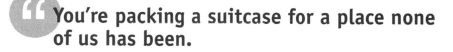

> ❝ **You're packing a suitcase for a place none of us has been.**
>
> —U2, "Walk On"

Christian leaders can be an interesting bunch. In this whole emerging church discussion, I hear all types of ideas on what is occurring culturally. I just had lunch with a rather conservative Bible college student who brushed off postmodernism and said it doesn't impact ministry. "All you have to do is preach God's Word," he said, "and ministry will then go on just fine." On the other hand, I get emails all the time from pastors telling me they know they need to do something and are planning on starting a radically different "postmodern service," but all they talk about is changing the style of what they're doing, which misses the point and meaning of postmodernism. Some people are just hearing about this term, and yet others are tired of hearing it.

The discussion in Christian circles does need to go beyond just using the word postmodern. It needs to go beyond candles and cool worship music. It is not about surface things that we generally describe as postmodern. Since postmodernism is still in the process of developing, we can't fully define the word postmodernism yet. We don't know when exactly postmodernism began or how long it will be around. We don't know where it will be taking us, or how much further it will shape the culture. Some people are even suggesting that we are moving into a post-postmodernism phase in which, now that postmodernism has deconstructed all that it needs to, we are actually building on postmodernism's foundation.

> A brilliant professor I know and respect said in a public forum that postmodernism is just a fad. I challenged him on this and offered him an out by saying, "You must have meant that the way the church is responding to the undeniable postmodern shift is faddish, right?" He paused for a long time, then conceded, "Okay, I suppose that's what I meant."
>
> —MARK OESTREICHER

✛ The word we can feel in the air, sense all around us, but cannot define

Whether or not we want to call this change postmodernism, something is happening that can be felt, heard, and observed in art, music, fashion trends, and in the lives of people in emerging generations. I appreciate the analogy of Plato's cave used by Tony Jones in the book *Postmodern Youth Ministry*. A man lives in a completely cave-bound society in which everyone inside believes that the cave is the only reality and is content with that. When the man finally steps out and sees the sun, the seasons, and the wonder of the world outside of the cave, he returns and tries to explain it to the people still inside. But they just call him crazy and refuse to listen. For several years I have had hanging on the wall beside my desk in the church office a cartoon based on Plato's allegory of the cave.

EVERYONE IS CHAINED IN A CAVE. THE PRISONERS SEE ONLY SHADOWS AND TAKE THEM FOR REALITY

ONE MAN ESCAPES. HE LEAVES THE CAVE AND SEES THE REAL WORLD

BUT... AH SHADDUP!

HE RETURNS, BUT DAZZLED BY THE LIGHT, SEEMS MORE STUPID THAN BEFORE.

From *Philosophy for Beginners* by Richard Osborne (New York: Writers and Readers Publishing Inc., 1992). Used with permission.

The reason I related to that man in the cave—enough to hang the cartoon up on my wall—is because many times I felt just like that when I tried to explain what I was feeling about making changes and doing things differently in ministry. I'd stumble with my words, have a hard time explaining why I felt like I did, but I knew without a doubt that something was happening. Maybe you feel a lot like the man in Plato's cave. Or maybe you've been one of the ones who refused to accept that change is occurring.

✛ The origin of postmodernity: a reaction against modernity

In his book *A Primer on Postmodernism,* Stanley Grenz tells how the term postmodern was used in the 1930s by writers and architects desiring

Not every church in the world bought into modernism, at least not as much as evangelicals, who swallowed modernism so completely many find it impossible to separate modernism from Christianity. But the African-American church never really bought into modernism. Neither did many streams of Christianity outside North America. There's no modernism to deconstruct for these folk, none of that baggage to be post of. Sure, they have other issues. But they have leapfrogged this issue that we'll be mired in for a while longer and are able to move directly on to new and fresh praxis.

—MARK OESTREICHER

to break out of modern molds and patterns of thought and creativity. The word postmodern was also used by historian Sir Arnold Toynbee in the 1940s to describe his observation of the beginning of a new phase of Western history. So the word postmodern represents a change in world-view moving from the values and beliefs of the modern era to the new postmodern era, which rejects many modern values and beliefs.

+ Not all of modernism is bad! Not all of postmodernism is bad!

Sometimes I hear modernism get bashed pretty badly in certain circles. But modernism actually produced wonderful things, great advances in the sciences, in medicine, and in technology. Modernism did line up well with many aspects of our faith. However, we need to understand how modernism also shaped some of our concepts of church and faith, concepts that aren't necessarily biblical. The Enlightenment assumed that human thinking can solve everything. So when modernism then assumed we could figure out God and systematize our faith, we went astray. What we need to do in the emerging church is to rethink what aspects or values of modernism became more or less accepted standards, rather than Scripture, for how we go about ministry.

In the same respect, not all of postmodernism is bad. In certain circles I hear postmodernism getting bashed frequently. Of course, we need to be discerning and wise as we think through any cultural change, whether it's small or major, like postmodernism is. But at the same time, there actually are many refreshing aspects of going back to a more transcendent view of God, allowing for mystery, and bringing back the supernatural view of life. We need to be thinkers and theologians more than ever in this day so we can discern the good from the bad and what is scriptural from what is man's methodology or philosophy, whether it's modern or postmodern. The post part of postmodernism doesn't mean we reject everything from modernism. It just means "after." So we are now moving into the "after modernism" time period, which of course will have lots of aspects of modernism in it.

Pure modernism held to a single, universal worldview and moral standard, a belief that all knowledge is good and certain, truth is absolute, individualism is valued, and thinking, learning, and beliefs should be determined systematically and logically. Postmodernism, then, holds there is no single universal worldview. All truth is not absolute, community is valued over individualism, and thinking, learning, and beliefs can be determined nonlinearly. Stanley Grenz explains that postmodernism "is an intellectual mood and an array of cultural expressions that call into question the ideals, principles and values that lay at the heart of the modern mind-set."[1] On the Emergent website (www.emergentvillage.com), postmodernism is defined as "an emerging culture that is characterized by having passed through modernity and pursuing something beyond modernity. Postmodernism should be distinguished from anti-modern, pre-modern, and hyper-modern. We do not believe it yet exists in its fully developed forms, but it is in its early formative stages, and for this reason can not be tightly defined beyond saying that it is beyond modernity."[2]

✛ Postmodernism in academia and architecture

As architects, writers, and philosophers began rejecting the confining modern values of systematic thinking, they began shaping a new postmodern philosophy. No longer did architecture have to be designed purely for function, nor music or art have to be placed in previously known categories. Postmodern philosophers began teaching that even language cannot have fixed or certain meaning but should be deconstructed, that is, pulled apart and rearranged. Since language is constantly shifting, according to postmodern thought, there can be many interpretations of a word or text, not just one meaning. As artists, philosophers, and architects rejected modern values and embraced postmodern ideas, this change was reflected in university classes, which in turn began influencing new literature, art, architecture, and even educational methods. Little by little as students studied this new form of creativity and philosophy, we began seeing actual changes slowly surfacing in experimental forms of music, movies, and the arts. We saw some of this rejection of modern values begin surfacing on university campuses in the 1960s.

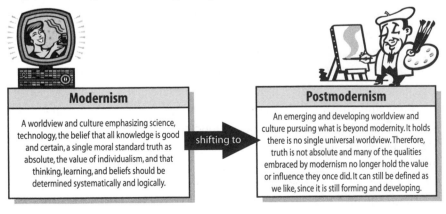

Modernism

A worldview and culture emphasizing science, technology, the belief that all knowledge is good and certain, a single moral standard truth as absolute, the value of individualism, and that thinking, learning, and beliefs should be determined systematically and logically.

shifting to

Postmodernism

An emerging and developing worldview and culture pursuing what is beyond modernity. It holds there is no single universal worldview. Therefore, truth is not absolute and many of the qualities embraced by modernism no longer hold the value or influence they once did. It can still be defined as we like, since it is still forming and developing.

⊹ From architecture and academia to pop culture

By the 1980s and 1990s, postmodernism no longer impacted only the academic realm or just the most politically active college campuses, nor was it embraced only by the most innovative artists and philosophers. Postmodernism was now fully making its way into pop culture, showing itself in fashion, music, television, movies, theater, arts, graphics, and literature. We began seeing its influence in our culture on a regular basis. The modern categories that we once knew and used began to shift and disappear as new postmodern ones formed.

Let's look at some examples from current pop culture. Country music, as viewed through a modern lens, sounds a certain way and its singers look "country" and talk "country." Country songs are played on country radio stations. Things fit into an expected order and package. It is comfortable and makes sense. We can wrap our arms around it and understand it.

But postmodernism is bringing interesting changes. For example, Garth Brooks is a contemporary country-western singer. As one would expect, he looks very country. He wears country-western ten-gallon hats and his shirts are country-western. The edge of his guitar shows mother of pearl western-style detailing. His smile is country-western. This makes reasonable and logical sense. We can put this in a neat package and understand it. His music matches his image with no contradictions.

But then a strange thing happened a few years ago. Brooks, in a post-modern twist, chose to "deconstruct" himself and his country image and to "reconstruct" himself as a grunge–punk rock star named Chris Gaines. Instead of a happy and smiling country-western Garth, we now have a brooding Garth (Chris Gaines) dressed in black. In his new persona, he released an album of a sort of grunge-pop music that fits no modern categories. Garth, in essence, is bringing together two opposing musical systems and two opposing fashion statements. This is postmodernism. Once, country-western stars were country-western stars, not deconstructed and reconstructed country and grunge-pop dual personalities. In fact, many country-western stars such as Shania Twain and Faith Hill are presenting images that are more and more like rock stars, even wearing late 1970s punk-rock leather jackets. Imagine what Hank Williams Sr. would think of this! It would probably be inconceivable to him.

Another example: The album cover of Madonna's self-titled record in 1984 reflects the look of the New York City dance club scene of the time. Her haircut, her jewelry and bracelets, and what she is wearing reflect the music on the album. Her music matched her image. This would be modern. It fits into a nice category.

But then there's the cover of a Madonna album *Music,* released in the year 2000. She has the image of a country-western sort of Texas oil woman whose clothes are country-western. She wears a country-western ten-gallon hat. The album title box has a very western-rodeo look. The fonts and graphics all scream country-western. Hank Williams Sr. would be very happy. But what kind of music comes from this image? It is far from country. It's techno pop. The music is almost the opposite of the image. Twenty years ago, if you saw this album cover in a store, there would be no question what type of music was within. But today, contradiction is accepted. You can't place this in a neat category anymore. This is postmodern.

(To view photos of Brooks' and Madonna's album covers, go to www.vintagefaith.com/albums. Links on this site will direct you to the relevant photos.)

These may be pedestrian examples of contradictions between image and music that may leave you wondering, "What does this have to do with church?" But keep reading; it has drastic ramifications for the church and the people we hope to reach.

+ From pop culture to everyday life and normal thinking

We are now experiencing postmodernism in everyday life. Postmodern values rapidly made their way into our schools, television shows, movies, advertising, magazines, and fashion. They have effected changes in the way we view the world, human sexuality, religion, and spirituality. The communications and media explosion brought by technology and the internet only speeded up the process. Image no longer needs to align with its original meaning (i.e., country music stars can look like rock stars, and rock stars can look like country stars). The lines are fuzzy, if they exist at all. Rock star Jon Bon Jovi currently wears a trademark straw cowboy hat, even though he is from New Jersey and plays nothing like country. Contradiction is accepted. Even the famous Smiley Face has been given a postmodern twist in a T-shirt design. The familiar image is given a contradictory meaning.

The spread of postmodern culture is accelerated as parents who have embraced postmodernism now teach others and raise their children.

It becomes more and more the normal way of life. But it affects more than just movies and music. It impacts values, ethics, sexuality, and virtually everything, including our view of religion and spirituality, which is where those of us in church ministry start coming face to face with the fruit of postmodernism.

✠ From everyday thinking to spirituality and into our churches

As emerging generations grow up, of course, we now see postmodernism impacting spiritual beliefs. A person can claim spiritual belief without living out that faith in any genuine way. Contradiction in spirituality is acceptable. And that is exactly what we are seeing.

Of course, there have always been people who didn't live out their claim to faith; in a modern world, this would be called hypocrisy. But in a postmodern world where the lines are blurred, it is simply a way of life. In a modern world, if a country singer like Garth Brooks were to dress up in grunge-punk clothing and enter a country bar, he would probably be beaten up. But in a postmodern world, the dichotomy is celebrated and the fashion lines are all blurred. The spiritual lines are blurred, too, as spiritual relativism is the norm, and the consequences are far more serious.

+ Sexual, pluralistic, pop Christianity is in vogue

When famous musicians receive awards on television, we hear them over and over publicly giving enthusiastic thanks to God or Jesus for their success, even though their music, image, and lyrics may be in contradiction to the Bible. There is no hypocrisy here. It is simply their personal viewpoint of God and Jesus. They feel there is no problem with the contradiction because to them, there isn't one.

An article in the *San Jose Mercury News* bore the headline, "Mixed Messages: Spears' Naughty Image Belies Her Christian Values."[3] The article reported Britney Spears' public claim to be a "born again Bible-belt Baptist." She even sang "Jesus Loves Me" at the audition that landed her a recording contract. Yet "she is a confusing postmodern mix of spirituality and teasing schoolgirl sexuality." We also see this troubling combination displayed in artists like Destiny's Child or Jessica Simpson, young women who are vocal about their Christian beliefs but send hypersexual messages through their appearance and lyrics. Beliefs blatantly contradict actions, and from a postmodern viewpoint, no harm is done.

I would have had such a huge problem with this a few years back! But now . . . A friend of mine who plays a key role in a large, evangelical youth gathering designed to teach teenagers how to share their faith recently asked me, "What's the least someone can 'do' and become a Christian?" I wasn't sure how to respond. (Sure, I know the "believe in the Lord Jesus Christ" answers.) We've focused on "doing" for so long that we've truly distorted Scripture through out tweaked modern grids. My friend followed up with, "Okay, then what's the least someone can believe to be a Christian?" Once again, I hesitated. Yup, I still believe salvation comes only through Jesus Christ. But does a little dose of Buddhism thrown into a belief system somehow kill off the Christian part, the Jesus-basics? My Buddhist cousin, except for her unfortunate inability to embrace Jesus, is a better "Christian" (based on Jesus' descriptions of what a Christian does) than almost every Christian I know. If we were using Matthew 26 as a guide, she'd be a sheep; and almost every Christian I know personally would be a goat.

—MARK OESTREICHER

It follows naturally, then, that we can select our religious beliefs much in the way we would choose what to eat for lunch at a salad bar. A popular sticker displayed in a youth-oriented clothing-store chain proclaims, "10% Angel—15% Princess—25% Diva—50% Goddess." I'm sure most junior high school girls don't actually believe themselves to be such an interesting amalgam of feminine mystique, but even so, this sticker offers a not-so-subtle example of postmodern spirituality.

According to this line of thought, we can fully embrace the contradictory mixing of the major world faiths. It isn't uncommon to see someone hold to a bit of Buddhist teaching and a little bit of Christianity, with even a trace of nature worship added to the mix. The difficult part for many of us to grasp is realizing that there is nothing wrong or contradictory with this approach to spirituality to individuals in the emerging culture.

A feature article in *Newsweek* recently pointed out that "young people are openly passionate about religion—but insist on defining it in their own ways."[4] This is only a normal and natural response being raised in a postmodern culture. We shouldn't be surprised.

⸙ Whether you believe in postmodernism or not, something is happening

A realistic snapshot of our developing postmodern world is provided by Dave Tomlinson in his book *The Post-Evangelical*. Although I do not agree with some of the theological conclusions Tomlinson makes, I do think he defines our world with great insight:

> The postmodern world is a world which understands itself through biological rather than mechanistic models; a world where people see themselves as belonging to the environment rather than over it or apart from it. A world distrustful of institutions, hierarchies, centralized bureaucracies and male dominated organizations. It is a world which networks and local grassroots activities take precedence over large scale structures and grand designs; a world in which the book age is giving way to the screen age; a world hungry for spirituality yet dismissive of systematized religion. It is a world in which image and reality are so deeply intertwined that it is difficult to draw the line between the two.[5]

He follows with a sharply challenging statement:

Those who think that postmodernism is a figment of the academic imagination, a passing fad, could not be more wrong. Postmodernism has flowed right out of the musty corridors of academia into the world of popular culture; it is on the pages of youth magazines, on CD boxes and the fashion pages of *Vogue*.[6]

Postmodernity and the spiritual relativism it brings completely pull the rug out from under most of our current, modern ministry strategy and methodology.

When we open our eyes and alert our senses, we begin to recognize the influence of postmodernism all around us. Look at magazine covers and advertising graphics; see how TV commercials are written and visually produced; listen to the dialogue of TV sitcoms and movies and to the lyrics of today's music. Observe fashion; learn what popular authors are writing. Consider the changes occurring in our methods of education. As we look in all of these directions, the implications for the emerging church are mind-boggling. More about that to come. As we move into the next chapter, we'll tackle something else that I often hear generally from older pastors and leaders. Perhaps it's been on your mind, too.

EMERGING THOUGHTS

1. When did you first hear of postmodernism, and how would you define it?

2. In what ways have you seen postmodernism impact culture in day-to-day life?

3. What ways do you see postmodernism impacting people's spirituality?

More Than a Generation Gap

5

> **After that whole generation had been gathered to their fathers, another generation grew up, who knew neither the LORD nor what he had done for Israel.**
>
> —Judges 2:10

✛ "One day they're all gonna grow up and be back in church."

"I'm telling you, these generations are no different than when I was a teenager or when I was in college." The pastor's face was flush with emotion. "When I was in high school, I rebelled and rejected church." He leveled a heated gaze right into my eyes. "When I got to college, I even explored some Eastern religions and experimented with some drugs. But then I got older. I got married, and when we had kids, I returned to my roots and came back to church."

Then he smiled, as if his case had been clearly made. "It is the same thing with young people today. They are just like I was. One day they're all gonna grow up and be back in church. All of this is simply a generation gap issue."

I quietly listened, and when he finished, I said, "You said you had kids and returned to your roots."

"Yep," he answered, "just like they will when they get older and come back to the church."

"What if their roots involved no church or Christian faith to begin with? What if the roots they put down while they were growing up were a pluralistic mix of world faiths, leaning toward more of a Buddhist philosophy? How can they return to their roots of church and Christianity if they don't have any roots there to return to?"

He sat for a minute looking a little puzzled and then responded, "I don't know what they will do then."

Earlier in American history, this pastor would have been right. But in recent years, teens and young adults have grown up in a world of postmodern, post-Christian values and perspectives. They simply have no Judeo-Christian roots to return to.

In Judges 2:10 we read of a time when "another generation grew up, who knew neither the LORD nor what he had done for Israel." If this could happen in ancient Israel, where God was such a central and visible part of the culture, couldn't it happen here today?

Let's take the "returning to your roots" concept and turn it into an imperfect but hopefully useful analogy. Plants have roots, so let's look at the two environmental factors necessary for their development:

1. The atmosphere: the light conditions, the temperature, the rain and humidity which the plant will intake as it grows.
2. The soil: the nutrients and water on which the roots feed as they grow.

Just as a plant depends on its environment to grow, a person develops according to his or her environment.

What would it be like for a person to grow up in a modern world in America?

In the modern era (A.D. 1500–2000), someone raised in America (after its birth as a colonized nation) would receive a primarily Judeo-Christian upbringing. For the most part, everyone grew up in an atmosphere that taught the values of the Judeo-Christian faith. Even if one was not a Christian, he probably agreed with most biblical values and ethics, tried to live by the Ten Commandments, understood many of the basic Bible stories, and knew what it meant that Jesus died for sins. When someone in the modern era thought of "God," generally the Judeo-Christian God came to mind.

In the modern era, a person would grow by taking in the nutrients of modern soil, including monotheism (belief in one God) and a rational, logical system of learning. Religion was a good thing in modern soil. A

Modern Era: Local Judeo-Christian "Atmosphere"

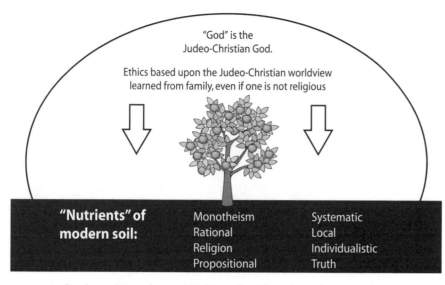

"God" is the
Judeo-Christian God.

Ethics based upon the Judeo-Christian worldview
learned from family, even if one is not religious

"Nutrients" of modern soil:	Monotheism	Systematic
	Rational	Local
	Religion	Individualistic
	Propositional	Truth

Growing up in a modern world, taking in the air from the modern atmosphere
and nutrients from the modern soil

Dan's analysis of the
post-Christian era is excellent.

—HOWARD HENDRICKS

modern person learned propositionally and was able to understand and master concepts by breaking them down into systems. Most people didn't travel a lot and viewed life through a hometown lens. Truth was knowable and absolute. The Bible, for most people, provided a reference point for all experience. It told the story of where life came from, its purpose, and its meaning.

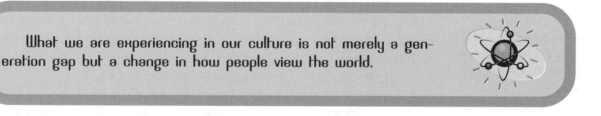

What we are experiencing in our culture is not merely a generation gap but a change in how people view the world.

What is it like growing up in a post-Christian era with a postmodern atmosphere and soil?

In the post-Christian era (beginning c. A.D. 2000), the values and beliefs of a person raised in America are shaped by a global, pluralistic atmosphere. This person has instant exposure to global news, global fashion, global music, and global religions. There are many gods, many faiths, many forms of spiritual expression from which to choose. In a postmodern

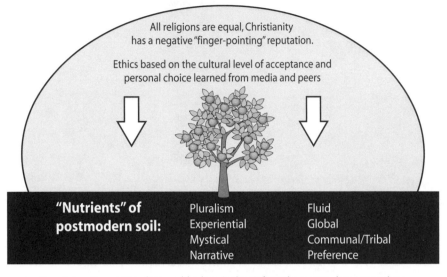

Post-Christian Era: Global Pluralistic "Atmosphere"

All religions are equal, Christianity has a negative "finger-pointing" reputation.

Ethics based on the cultural level of acceptance and personal choice learned from media and peers

"Nutrients" of postmodern soil:	Pluralism	Fluid
	Experiential	Global
	Mystical	Communal/Tribal
	Narrative	Preference

Growing up in a postmodern world, taking in the air from the postmodern atmosphere and nutrients from the postmodern soil

atmosphere, a person grows up learning that all faiths are equal but that Christianity is primarily a negative religion, known for finger-pointing and condemning the behavior of others. In this atmosphere, the Ten Commandments aren't taught and the Bible is simply one of many religious writings. Ethics and morals are based on personal choice, as families encourage their children to make their own decisions about religion and to be tolerant of all beliefs. A major influence on a postmodern person's ethics and morals is what they learn from the media and what is accepted by their peers. Although relativism is more of a norm in a postmodern world, most agree on some absolutes, such as the wrongness of excessive violence, murder, or evil like the September 11th tragedy.

In a post-Christian world, pluralism is the norm. Buddhism, Wicca, Christianity, Islam, Hinduism, or an eclectic blend—it's all part of the soil. The basis of learning has shifted from logic and rational, systematic thought to the realm of experience. People increasingly long for the mystical and the spiritual rather than the evidential and facts-based faith of the modern soil. The way people respond and think is more fluid than systematic, more global than local, more communal than individualistic. And in postmodern soil a high value is placed on personal preference and choice, as opposed to predetermined truth.

> In a post-Christian world, not only is preference personal but it is a constantly changing preference.
>
> —HOWARD HENDRICKS

✠ Why the tension and confusion?

We are now in transition as the modern era shifts to a postmodern era. Therefore, a mix of people with all types of worldviews live in America today. Generally, the older people are, the more modern they are. The younger they are, the more they will have known only a postmodern, post-Christian world and the more a postmodern atmosphere and soil will be normal to them. Those born into a postmodern, post-Christian world don't have the modern atmosphere and soil to remember. They don't have the modern roots to return to.

But it's still not quite as cut and dried as that.

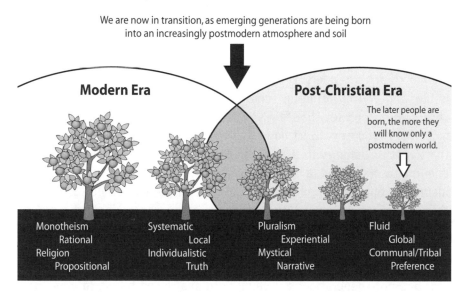

We are now in transition, as emerging generations are being born into an increasingly postmodern atmosphere and soil

Modern Era

Post-Christian Era

The later people are born, the more they will know only a postmodern world.

Monotheism	Systematic	Pluralism	Fluid
Rational	Local	Experiential	Global
Religion	Individualistic	Mystical	Communal/Tribal
Propositional	Truth	Narrative	Preference

✛ Some in younger generations are still modern

Because we are in transition, some people are born into a postmodern, post-Christian era who, in their local environment, grow up in modern atmosphere and soil. Many younger Christians growing up in Christian homes are very modern, as their parents enforced modern values. In some areas of the country, many people are still not feeling the full impact of postmodernism, and the younger people may still be very modern. Because we are in transition, we can't just say there is a postmodern generation born between certain years.

I recently talked with a father in our church who described his twenty-year-old son as being a postmodern. I hesitated to contradict him, but I believed he was missing the point. I know his son very well, and although to some degree he may be influenced by postmodernity, he is modern. He

> This is a good illustration to show how we can't define being postmodern by age alone.
>
> —HOWARD HENDRICKS

was raised in a Christian home where he was taught Judeo-Christian principles and ethics, and he views the world accordingly. He thinks and learns systematically and is drawn to using logic and reason to prove and understand his faith. It is how one views the world, what one values and thinks about life, that makes one postmodern, not because one falls into a certain age range.

✣ Modern churches are still attracting modern young people

Some contemporary modern churches today are drawing a large number of younger people. It may have to do with the demographics of the community and, of course, with the personality and philosophy of the church itself. Some communities are still very conservative, and people living in them would line up more with Judeo-Christian values even if they are not church attenders. If this is your situation, it's wonderful that God is blessing you by bringing some of the emerging generations to your church. But don't let that fool you into thinking you are reaching postmoderns. If you were to sit down and talk with them, would you find that the majority belongs to a more modern mindset? Were they fortunate enough to have had a Judeo-Christian upbringing? What about the increasing numbers of people in your community who do not come from this background? How will you reach emerging generations who do not resonate with your church? How will you reach those who grew up and "knew neither the LORD nor what he had done"?

Today there are definitely those in younger generations who are modern, but more generations are being born and raised taking in only postmodern soil and atmosphere and therefore are truly post-Christian, lacking any Judeo-Christian foundation to base ethics, morals, and life on. These generations will increasingly become the American norm and will make up the greater percentage of the population. For their sakes we *must* rethink our approach to ministry.

✣ Some in older generations are postmodern

On the other hand, we must not forget that although it's a small percentage, some people who were born in the modern atmosphere and soil thrive in and relate more to a postmodern environment. This was certainly the case for the first postmodern architects and writers of the 1930s and 1940s who found themselves uncomfortable with modern values and began freeing themselves from modernity. It was obviously more than an age thing for them, as they would be in their eighties and nineties now. We have some elderly postmoderns out there! Brian McLaren, in his book *A New Kind of Christian,* suggests that there may even be up to a third of baby boomers (born approximately from 1946–64) who are more postmodern than modern. And this third of the baby boomers are the ones who have not been drawn to churches who use a modern approach to ministry. All of this goes to say that a major worldview shift such as this is more than just a generational issue.

This is why when many churches started "Gen X" services to appeal to a certain age group (born 1964–83), they found that many people outside of this demographic resonated with the heart, methodology, and style of these services. For this reason, most of the so-called Gen X ministries I know of have now opened up to all ages.

✛ What all this means to our churches and ministries

After all that we have considered so far in this book, the big question is, What does this mean for our church and ministries? Here are several answers:

1. We cannot assume that everyone is going to learn, relate, and think the same way. The ministry methods we used for moderns are going to differ from what's used for postmoderns. While fundamental human needs, such as love and acceptance, will never change, we need to approach the emerging generations with new eyes and with different ways of going about ministry. We will deal with these differences in coming chapters.

2. We cannot blame emerging generations for believing what they believe. Remember, this is the only world they know.

➡ *Of course* they are going to view spirituality from a pluralistic viewpoint.
➡ *Of course* they are going to be drawn more to the mystical and experiential over the rational.
➡ *Of course* their view of sexuality is going to be much more open and tolerant.
➡ *Of course* they are going to view Christianity as the negative religion of finger-pointers. That is all they have seen and known, especially if they aren't born in Christian families. Instead of blaming them for what they believe, our hearts should be breaking for them.

Dan is right in emphasizing the importance of examining who attends your worship services if you are serious about reaching the emerging culture. While it is a laudable accomplishment that some churches are providing a place for young Christians to remain active in their faith, it is easy to propagate the myth that scores of non-Christian, postmodern younger people are being reached in the process. Not long ago, a very large high-profile church was courageous enough to find out who they were actually reaching every week. The result? Less than 3 percent of their young adult constituency came from an unchurched background.

—Sally Morgenthaler

3. We should not expect postmoderns to one day "grow up" and become modern. It's not an issue of age or musical tastes but of mindset. This means that someone influenced by postmodernism may be a Christian but drawn to worshiping God in a more postmodern way. He or she may learn differently or appreciate different church-building aesthetics and ministry values.

If we were to attend an evangelical Korean church in America, we would certainly expect the worship services and methodology to reflect the Korean culture, learning style, and approach to worship. We wouldn't expect them to one day "grow up" and feel comfortable in a modern, seeker-sensitive church service. So much beauty would be lost, and most likely they would not grow in their faith as they would in an environment more suitable to their culture.

Dan Allender, author of *The Wounded Heart,* speaking at the Willow Creek Leadership Summit in 2002, said, "We are principle-oriented, linear, simplistically driven people who want answers so much more than we want the person of Jesus Christ. The dilemma is we now live in a postmodern world that does not embrace, and will never reembrace, some of the core values of modernism."

Therefore, we cannot think that one day when postmodern generations hit a certain age they will convert to modernism and begin being, thinking, relating, and worshiping in a way foreign to who they are.

4. Modern leaders may have a difficult time understanding post-Christian ministry. This all may be difficult to grasp for those of us who have grown up with a modern mindset. We may have a difficult time understanding how postmoderns view life and what they value. If you are a modern-thinking pastor or a Christian leader, you might find it incredibly frustrating to think of doing ministry in a new way. It may feel "messy" and not fit into your accepted ministry systems. It might not resonate with your heart to worship in ways you're not used to, or to learn in ways that are not primarily cognitive, or to preach differently than you were taught in seminary.

This doesn't mean that you're not hip or contemporary, and by no means does it mean you are outdated. It simply means you have been born and raised with a modern viewpoint. God will continue to use you in great ways to reach those who think like you do. But there are other ways to think. As long as we are not conforming to the world (Rom. 12:1–2) and not failing to pay attention to sound doctrine (1 Tim. 4:16), and as long as we are producing disciples (Matt. 28:19), we should press ahead in seeking to reach others for Christ. But our modern categories and values just might need to be rearranged if we want to reach emerging generations.

✣ A two-centuries-old lesson from missionary Hudson Taylor

Many times friction and misunderstanding develops among church leaders because those who are engaging a postmodern, post-Christian culture want to think about and design ministry differently. Many times the older pastors or leaders, being modern in their viewpoint, don't understand why a different methodology is needed. So tension arises. Remember that Hudson Taylor, a missionary to China in the late 1800s, had problems explaining to his board in England why he wanted to do ministry differently than the "English way." He wanted to change everything, from his haircut and clothing to how he spent his time to his approach to missionary work. But his board did not understand or approve of the changes. Eventually, he had to start his own missionary board. Hudson Taylor understood that he was engaging in ministry to a different culture and mindset, and God used him in incredible ways. I believe we must view the emerging culture in much the same way, taking whatever costly steps are necessary to build the emerging church.

Postmodern thought may hit some dead ends as the emptiness of some of what it stands for is revealed. But we won't see a return to the way things were. Whatever comes after postmodernism will not be "Modernism: Part 2." Regardless of what you think of the evolution of our culture, it is clear that the changes we are seeing will not go away in a few years. Peter Drucker, a well respected management and business guru, writes in his book *Post-Capitalist Society:*

> Every few hundred years in Western history there occurs a sharp transformation. Within a few short decades, society rearranges itself—its world view; its basic values; its social and political structure; its arts; its key institutions.
>
> Fifty years later, there is a new world. And the people born then cannot even imagine the world in which their grandparents lived and into which their parents were born.
>
> We are currently living through just such a transition.[1]

Without mentioning postmodernism, Drucker describes a transition like the one we are seeing right now. We are witnessing with our own eyes a major cultural shift, as though we were living during the Reformation. This is no passing trend we can ignore, run away from, or shut out. Instead, we must engage the culture and passionately use this time in which emerging generations are very open to spiritual things to make disciples of Jesus.

We cannot afford to lose this opportunity. Jesus is the true living water (John 4:13–14) for all human beings, whether they are modern or postmodern. May our efforts direct people's roots toward the water that will bring them life. May we bring this living water to the generations who do not yet know the Lord or the things he has done.

In the next two chapters, we'll look at how other changes are taking form in our world.

EMERGING THOUGHTS

1. **Do you know anyone who has no knowledge of God or what he has done?**

2. **Where are you on the diagram showing the transition from the modern era to the post-Christian era (p. 61)? To what degree do you feel modernity has shaped you? How much influence do you think postmodernity has had on your life? How much influence has it had on your children?**

3. **Where would you say most of the people in your church are on the chart? How about the people in your community who aren't attending your church?**

4. **What do you think about the argument that the changes we are dealing with are mainly a generation-gap issue? Did reading this chapter alter any of your preconceptions?**

5. **Can you think of ways the story of Hudson Taylor may relate to differences of opinion among leadership in your church?**

Born (Buddhist-Christian-Wiccan-Muslim-Straight-Gay) in the USA

> " I go to synagogue, I study Hinduism . . . all paths lead to God.

—Madonna

On a beautiful Fourth of July afternoon, we gathered at my in-laws' house for a picnic. The American flag proudly waved in the breeze above picnic tables decked with red-checkered tablecloths. Even the paper plates, cups, and napkins bore American flags. We looked like a Norman Rockwell painting. As mealtime approached, my father-in-law led us in a wonderful prayer thanking God for our freedom. He then closed with a statement something like, "And thank you, Lord, for making us a Christian nation. Amen."

From my father in law's perspective, this was a true statement. After all, America has been considered a Christian nation for most of his adult life, and most of his friends are Christian. But I've thought back on the closing of that prayer many times, and I no longer believe it reflects our nation today.

+ God-Goddess-Buddha-Allah Bless America!

At the University of California at Santa Cruz, across town from my father in law's home, the non-Christian student religious groups on campus conspicuously outnumber the Christian groups. They have a Muslim group, a Buddhist group, a Bahai group, even a Wiccan group. Religious diversity such as once was found only in metropolitan areas now flourishes in suburbs and rural areas. You can't accurately say that we are a

Christian nation anymore, especially when examining the increasing spiritual diversity among younger people.

This change is impacting how we think through what the emerging church is going to look like and how we design and think of ministry. If we really desire to reach out to the emerging culture, then we need to become like the spies Joshua sent to look over the land across the Jordan. If we break out of our Christian circles, stop the busyness of church, and take a look at what is happening in our towns and communities, we may be surprised.

> *Then Joshua son of Nun secretly sent two spies from Shittim.*
> *"Go, look over the land," he said.* —Joshua 2:1

⊹ Thinking like a missionary in your local context

You may see average and not-so-average twenty-one-year-olds sipping cups of coffee at your local coffee shop, but do you really know them? Have you ever talked to them about what they believe? What do they think of Christians and the church? Perhaps you already know some Christian young people in your church, but they're not who I'm talking about. They likely already believe what you do. Can you say that you truly are listening to what is happening in the hearts and minds of emerging generations? Are you listening to what their musical poets and prophets are saying? If not, you may not understand their world and how they view it, and you probably won't be very effective in reaching them. Since we are no longer living in "Christian America," we once again need to see ourselves as missionaries.

+ America has become a new missionary frontier

Lesslie Newbigin was born and raised in England when it was a "Christian nation." In 1936 he went to India as a missionary, and for over thirty-five years he labored to share Jesus in a primarily Hindu country. In 1974, at the age of sixty-five, he returned to England and was quite surprised to discover that the Christian nation he had left behind had now become a mission field itself. But this was a mission field of a different sort.

Newbigin found that ministry in England was now "much harder than anything I met in India. The cold contempt for the Gospel is harder to face than opposition."[1] The difference was that people in India were hearing the gospel for the first time; but in his absence, England had become a post-Christian nation. The country was layered with preconceived notions about Christianity, which had developed into contempt for the faith.

This is a wild thing to think about! To say that it is easier to share the gospel in a pagan nation than in a country which has already heard it is a significant insight.

In only a few generations, the Christian nation of England changed to a post-Christian one. America is closely following the same pattern, particularly with emerging generations. What once was a "Christian America" has become a mission field itself.

Perhaps you recall that I mentioned in the introduction the observation of Tom Clegg and Warren Bird in their book *Lost in America:* "The unchurched population in the United States is so extensive that, if it were a nation, it would be the fifth most populated nation on the planet after China, the former Soviet Union, India and Brazil. Thus, our unchurched population is the largest mission field in the English-speaking world and the fifth largest globally."[2]

What an incredible statistic! What is the implication? As we approach ministry to the emerging culture—a post-Christian mission field—we need to use the same approach we would employ entering a foreign culture. We cannot go on seeing ourselves simply as pastors and teachers; we need to see ourselves as a new kind of missionary. And we must train people in our churches to do the same. We must dream missionary dreams. We must bleed missionary blood. We must pray missionary prayers.

Sad to say, the generations being born and raised in America today don't know who God is or what he has done, or what the Bible says about him, or who the true Jesus is. We have to start all over again in a nation once characterized by a Christian belief structure. Perhaps we aren't quite as secularized as England is, but we are quickly approaching it.

> *The harvest is plentiful but the workers are few. Ask*
> *the Lord of the harvest, therefore, to send out workers*
> *into his harvest field.* —MATTHEW 9:37–38

✟ The even harder challenge we face in a post-Christian world

As thrilling and exciting as it is to think about being a missionary right here in America, don't forget Lesslie Newbigin's observation that the contempt for the gospel he encountered in England was harder to face than the opposition he encountered in India. He went on to state that "England is a pagan society, and the development of a truly missionary encounter with this very tough form of paganism is the greatest intellectual and practical task facing the church."[3] And so we find ourselves facing the same challenge in America. People think they have already heard the gospel. And most have rejected it and are turning to other ways of approaching spiritual things.

✝ Growing up in a religiously diverse America

I experienced an odd moment recently after I agreed to join a panel discussion at the University of California in Santa Cruz. When the day arrived, I made my way to the cafeteria where the panel was to be held and was introduced to the other local religious leaders who had been invited. I was the Christian representative. To my right was a young man who practiced witchcraft and represented Wicca. To my left were a Hindu, a Muslim, and a Buddhist. As students asked questions and we casually answered, the oddness of the situation dawned on me. We live in a culture so religiously diverse that an evangelical Christian can sit beside a witch on a Q & A panel, both considered representatives of equally viable religious alternatives, and it can feel like "business as usual." In fact, I noted a surprising familiarity among the other representatives on the panel and sensed they understood each other's faiths better than they understood Christianity.

✝ We're truly not in Kansas anymore

One of the larger bookstores in downtown Santa Cruz carries only Eastern religious and New Age materials. On any given day, you would probably see a number of average moms and dads and younger people perusing the shelves for spiritual advice. A short walk away is a store where you can purchase all your Wiccan books and supplies. If you pause to see who is going in and out of this establishment, you might be surprised to find that it isn't just strange or gloomy people dressed in black velvet and gothic capes but mainly younger people who look like the kid next door, or like typical college students. The times are definitely changing as we see all types of religious faiths in mainstream America.

I recently was standing outside a store in an outdoor mall waiting for my wife, Becky, who was still inside. Sitting on the sidewalk reading a book was a girl in her young twenties who had the appearance of someone who might well be from Kansas. She was blond, had blue eyes, and was wearing a conservative floral dress. A friend joined her, and I watched her read from the book and begin praying. They even joined hands. They looked like two Christians praying. But as I was close enough to hear some of their words, I realized they were inviting spirits to indwell them to direct their Tarot readings. Here was a girl who looked like she was from Kansas, praying unashamedly out in the open prayers that the Scriptures would interpret as evil. Incredible! I wish Christians were that passionate about praying together in such a public place.

> *Paul then stood up in the meeting of the Areopagus and said: "Men of Athens! I see that in every way you are very religious."* —ACTS 17:22

☩ Choosing from a spiritual smorgasbord

Diana Eck, professor of comparative religion at Harvard University, has written a book called *A New Religious America: How a "Christian Country" Has Become the World's Most Religiously Diverse Nation*. If this title doesn't cause you to sit straight up and want to pay attention to all that is written within, then chances are you need a pretty strong wake-up call. Please read carefully these words from the cover of Eck's book:

> "The United States is the most religiously diverse nation in the world," leading religious scholar Diana Eck writes in this eye-opening guide to the religious realities of America today. The Immigration Act of 1965 eliminated the quotas linking immigration to national origins. Since then, Muslims, Buddhists, Hindus, Sikhs, Jams, Zoroastrians, and new varieties of Jews and Catholics have arrived from every part of the globe, radically altering the religious landscape of the United States. Members of the world's religions live not just on the other side of the world but in our neighborhoods; Hindu children go to school with Jewish children; Muslims, Buddhists, and Sikhs work side-by-side with Protestants and Catholics.[4]

+ The Buddhist is now your neighbor, the Muslim your child's schoolteacher

The copy on the cover of Eck's book goes on to comment that although this altering of the religious landscape is happening at a very fast rate, most Christian leaders are unaware of it.

This new religious diversity is now a Main Street phenomenon, yet many Americans *and most Christian leaders* [italics mine] remain unaware of the profound change taking place at every level of our society, from local school boards to Congress, and in small-town Nebraska as well as New York City. Islamic centers and mosques, Hindu and Buddhist temples, and meditation centers can be found in virtually every major American metropolitan area. There are Muslims, Hindus, and Buddhists in Salt Lake City, Utah; Toledo, Ohio; and Jackson, Mississippi. Buddhism has become an American religion, as communities widely separated in Asia are now neighbors in Los Angeles, Seattle, and Chicago. There are now Muslims worshiping in a U-Haul dealership in Pawtucket, Rhode Island; a gymnasium in Oklahoma City; and a former mattress showroom in Northridge, California. Hindu temples are housed in a warehouse in Queens, a former YMCA in New Jersey, and a former Methodist church in Minneapolis.[5]

✛ Why didn't you tell me there are lots of religions to choose from?

For those working with the emerging church, this diversity impacts not only how we evangelize but also how we teach and educate people to think about other faiths and beliefs. Even if people in emerging generations are not becoming part of these faiths, they are aware of the variety of them. Gary Lederman, a religion professor at Emory University in Atlanta, states that "the kind of pluralism we're seeing today is unheard of."[6] No longer is the Buddhist or the Hindu living on the other side of the world or only in cosmopolitan cities. This means our children are going to come home with questions about Buddha or asking their Christian parents, "Why do we think we are the right and true religion?"

> *I believe in God. I just don't know if that God is Jehovah, Buddha or Allah.* —ACTRESS HALLE BERRY

I personally love cultural diversity. I would want my children to appreciate the Native American culture and to listen to global music of all kinds. In our diverse culture, I would want my children to know about the origins and basic practices of Buddhism, Hinduism, Islam, and so on. But I know I must also teach them the origin and distinctives of Christianity. I must tell them why I choose to place my faith in Jesus and why I trust the Bible as being inspired. I need to teach them why I believe in one God and in Jesus as the way, the truth, and the life (John 14:6). How confusing it will be to our children if we ignore what is happening all around us.

✛ Choosing my religion

In order to think like missionaries, we need to recognize that America is a nation that offers an ever more accessible mix of spiritual choices, all perceived as equal. So we shouldn't be surprised to hear statements like the one Madonna said in a 1990 interview on *60 Minutes:* "I go to synagogue, I study Hinduism . . . all paths lead to God."

This is the religious anthem of those growing up in a post-Christian world: "All paths lead to God." We have lost the overarching story of God and man. So we piece together our own stories. What is interesting is that most people in the emerging culture have no problem believing in a "God." But this "God" is pieced together from a mix of world religions and various personal beliefs. Since having contradictory beliefs is not a problem in postmodern culture, this is acceptable. Though she embraces aspects of Hinduism and practices the Jewish mysticism of kabbalah, Madonna has no problem having her son baptized in an Anglican church.

> *Eastern thought, Western mysticism. I really dig the whole Hindu pantheon. And I just pull from all kinds of different things.* —ACTRESS MEG RYAN

On the cover of an issue of *Newsweek* featuring teenage spirituality ran the tagline "Searching for a Holy Spirit: Young people are openly passionate about religion—but insist on having it their own ways."[7] Religion can be assembled like a meal from a smorgasbord or salad bar. Bits and pieces from various faiths can be bundled together, even if they contradict one another. *Newsweek* stated that "teens might cobble together bits of several faiths: a little Buddhist meditation or Roman Catholic ritual, whatever mixture appeals at the time."[8]

+ Choosing my sexual orientation

Because emerging generations have such a limited knowledge of the God of the Bible, it's only natural that people are open to self-determined morality and diverse ideas about sexuality. Living together is almost the norm today. Straight, gay, bi—people consider sexuality simply a matter of preference. And because there is no universal reference point in a post-Christian mindset, how dare anyone say it isn't?

A non-Christian straight teenager attended a Christian camp with our youth group. One day toward the end of the week, she approached me with angry tears and handed me a scribbled note. In it she explained that she had heard comments about homosexuality made by one of the speakers, and she was horribly offended. How dare they tell people that being gay is wrong? She was not gay, but she had grown up with gay friends and felt that this was an absolutely sick and twisted thing to be communicating to all these "impressionable teenagers." She wanted to go home immediately and get as far away from Christians as she could. In a way, I couldn't blame her.

✣ We must realize that not everyone thinks like us

I truly understood her feelings because I heard that speaker too. For one thing, the speaker had not considered that not all of the teenagers at that camp (which interestingly was supposed to be evangelistic) grew up with the same standard of truth. His assumptions about the teenagers were invalid, so his approach was, in this teenager's case, not only ineffective but also offensive. He also showed no compassion in his message—no understanding. And unfortunately, his modern, linear approach to preaching was to use only evidences to prove homosexuality wrong, which only succeeded in making Christians and the church all the more repulsive to this girl. His approach backfired, only reaffirming this girl's skepticism about the open-mindedness of Christians. I ran into this girl recently. She had graduated from college, and she has no interest in the church and the faith. She'd had a taste of Christianity and doesn't want any more.

Now, I am not saying that we shouldn't preach about homosexuality or moral standards. Of course we need to. We need to speak about these things more than ever today. We need to be opening our Bibles and exploring what the Scriptures say about all types of ethical and moral standards. We need to know what it means to be holy. But we need to rethink how we preach about it. I am convinced that we can effectively preach and teach the same conclusions if we change our approach. (More on this in the chapter on preaching and communication.)

✣ We need to teach emerging generations because most parents aren't

A growing number of parents are reinforcing our culture's move toward religious pluralism and rejection of the exclusivity of the Christian faith.

An article in the *San Jose Mercury News* titled "Teaching Values without Religion: Parents Develop Methods to Raise Spiritual Kids Outside Organized Faiths"[9] showcased parents who are encouraging their children to choose their own faith outside of the established church. Many parents who abandoned Christianity over the past decade or two teach their children to choose for themselves their sexuality, morals, and ethics. Now, I am all for teaching children to "think" for themselves. In fact, I believe more than ever that we need to focus on encouraging children and teenagers how to discern good from evil (Heb. 5:14). This article simply illustrates how children growing up outside of Christian homes naturally are being taught personal religious pluralism, and this trend will only escalate in the years to come.

✛ The impact of the media and the internet

Something we cannot underestimate is the way that communications media affect our worldview. Just as the printing press transformed Europe in past centuries, we are in the midst of another communications revolution with the internet, which almost every household in America has access to. Unlike any other time in history, emerging generations have instant access to world news. What happens in China is news a few minutes later, complete with live visuals on our computer screens and TVs. We have global access to endless volumes of information, including about religion and world faiths of all kinds. This information changes how we see the world.

✢ *The X-Files* in El Salvador, Marilyn Manson in Jerusalem

Because we are in a global community, even trends in fashion, entertainment, and music are no longer merely regional. In rural Nebraska, white farm kids go to school dressed like New York City street rappers and talk using hip-hop slang. My wife and I recently visited the Old City of Jerusalem on vacation and found ourselves in the Arab quarter, an experience which truly felt like stepping back 2,000 years in history. Guess what we saw in the tiny, cluttered shops set into the ancient walls of the city? Marilyn Manson T-shirts for sale! When we were on a missions trip in the forests of El Salvador, the children were asking us questions about *The X-Files*.

We are not speaking to people who are generic, suburban, culturally naive, protected from the outside world. Emerging generations are

culturally sensitive and globally aware. No longer do they perceive things only according to their local context, or even only according to an American context. We need to communicate to them with a global awareness and a global conscience.

> Like missionaries respectfully entering a foreign culture, we need to approach our post-Christian culture with a gentle awareness of the prevailing worldview while boldly expressing the great news of Jesus and God's truth.

Despite the challenges of plurality and the diversity of people's views about spirituality, sexuality, morals, and ethics, I am greatly optimistic. I am finding that emerging generations really aren't opposed to truth and biblical morals. When people sense that you aren't just dogmatically opinionated due to blind faith and that you aren't just attacking other people's beliefs out of fear, they are remarkably open to intelligent and loving discussion about choice and truth.

+ An openness to hearing that Jesus is truth

In fact, I've seen that when Jesus and his teaching are offered as solid truth in the midst of a confusing and shifting world, people actually respond positively and with great relief. People are simply opposed to the self-righteous attitudes of those who unlovingly argue that they have the exclusive claim to truth.

But effectively conveying Jesus' teaching in a post-Christian world is no easy task.

EMERGING THOUGHTS

1. How would you describe the religious beliefs of the residents of your community? How many synagogues, mosques, and Buddhist temples are in your community? What percentage of people even attend local churches? You might find it revealing to call every religious organization, church, synagogue, and so on in your community to get a feel for their attendance and correlate that with your population.

2. Do you see yourself and your church as missionaries? Does the typical member of your church hold this view?

3. Could you have an intelligent discussion about world faiths with someone right now? Are you teaching the children and adults of your church about why you hold to Jesus in the midst of other faiths?

Chapter 7

I Like Jesus, but I Don't Like Christians

> **" I like your Christ, but I do not like your Christians. Your Christians are so unlike your Christ.**
>
> —Mahatma Gandhi

We filmed video interviews on the University of California Santa Cruz campus to show at our worship gathering. We asked each person we interviewed two questions:

1. What comes to mind when you hear the name Jesus?
2. What comes to mind when you hear the word Christian?

The answers to these questions brought me both joy and extreme sadness. Why? Because at the first question, students' faces light up in smiles. "Jesus was beautiful." "I want to be like Jesus." "Jesus was a liberator of women." "I'm all about Jesus." "I want to be a follower of Jesus." "Jesus was enlightened and had higher truth." What encouraging answers! Here we were on a post-Christian campus finding students eager to talk about Jesus. I realized they probably weren't familiar with the whole of Jesus' teachings, but they held a high opinion of Jesus as an extremely positive figure in history.

But at the second question, their expressions changed dramatically. Eyes looked downward, smiles turned to frowns and even pained expressions. "Christians have taken the teachings of Jesus and really messed them up." "I would want to be a Christian, but I have never met one." "Christians are dogmatic and closed-minded." "Christians are supposed to

be loving, but I've never met any who are." "Christians should be taken outside and shot."

Most discouraging of all was that only one person out of sixteen even claimed to actually know a Christian personally. Their conclusions were based on general observations and hearsay. What they knew of Jesus, they liked, but what they knew of Christians, they definitely didn't like.

> *When Pammy and I returned to school in the fall of my junior year, terrible news unfolded: our English teacher had become a born-again Christian.* —ANNE LAMOTT, *TRAVELING MERCIES*

✛ We probably wouldn't be attracted to Christianity if we weren't Christians

I can't blame those students for their opinions of Christians, since only one of the sixteen even knew one. If no one is living out their faith to them, how will they know anything different about Christians or who Jesus truly is?

> *How, then, can they call on the one they have not believed in? And how can they believe in the one of whom they have not heard?* —ROMANS 10:14

We are living in a wonderful time when younger generations are wide open to Jesus, but Christians are often the stumbling block. Let's take a look at some of the factors influencing people to think so negatively about Christians and Christianity.

✛ A sense of mistrust and caution toward Christians

A college student told me she was sitting at a bus stop on campus when another young woman asked what she was reading. When she told her that it was a book about Christianity, the woman recoiled with a grimace. "Oh, Christians," she said. "They are wicked people."

From a non-Christian perspective in post-Christian times, Christians are often considered the wicked ones, and perhaps understandably so. What is the common perception of Christians in the media? Recall the Christian televangelist scandals of the 1980s? Even those too young to have experienced them know about this part of Christian history. News reports show extremists protesting a whole spectrum of social and ethical issues, carrying signs bearing slogans such as "God hates fags." Prime time TV presents Christian characters such as Ned Flanders and his family on the cartoon show *The Simpsons*. Almost every time Christians are portrayed on television or in the movies, they appear somewhat unintelligent, mindless, even cultish, usually engaging in angry crusades to wipe out the evils of society and convert people to their point of view. Add to all this the public arrest of a pastor or priest for some sexual crime.

> *I became disillusioned by a lot of things that happened to me by Christian people.* —SCOTT STAPP, LEAD SINGER OF CREED

Christians are not the only people emerging generations have difficulty trusting. Picture growing up in today's culture, in which many come from families torn apart by divorce. Watch any sitcom and you may be surprised to see how much of the humor is based on lies between friends and family. And of course, many believe that politicians can't be trusted. Is it any wonder that we sense mistrust from those we are hoping to reach?

Because emerging generations live in this confusing and often disappointing world, we need a much more relational approach to ministry and evangelism. We need to rebuild trust and point to Jesus as the one who can always be trusted.

> *Do not let your hearts be troubled. Trust in God; trust also in me.* —JOHN 14:1

+ The strange world of Christian subculture

I had a rather shocking experience a few years ago in a Christian bookstore. I love Christian bookstores, and I frequent them often. But this time I was shopping for a book for a non-Christian friend to help him learn about Christianity in a way that he could understand. I walked into the store and immediately noticed the wide array of Christian T-shirts, many with cute and clever slogans. But as I tried to picture what my friend would think, I felt uneasy. The wording on the shirts was supposed to be evangelistic, but I felt that many of them would actually offend or just seem silly to my friend.

I turned to the music section, which featured CDs by a whole array of celebrity musicians, all of whom would be unknown to my friend. The

This is a convicting story!
—HOWARD HENDRICKS

music styles and the look of the musicians seemed to mimic certain secular bands, down to their hair, their dress, and even their facial expressions. Christian punk music, Christian heavy metal, Christian country and western—all were there. I saw numerous other products for sale—Christian sweatbands with Christian slogans, Christian tea bags with verses, Christian candy, even (I am not exaggerating here) Christian golf balls and tees. I found Christian dolls, Christian baseball hats, Christian jewelry, and (to me) some pretty ugly Christian art.

Then I looked at the Bible table and again pictured my friend becoming confused. I spotted Bibles for leaders, Bibles for women, the "Jesus Bible," the End Times Bible, the Athlete's Bible, the African-American Bible, Bibles endorsed by various celebrity preachers, and dozens of Bibles subcategorized in niches. I was almost surprised not to see a Bible for left-handed people or for people with red hair. I know these Bibles are produced to help people, but something about niche marketing the Bible to this degree made me feel uneasy. Especially as I imagined trying to explain to my friend why, even with all of these Bibles, most Christians are biblically illiterate.

In my flustered state, I actually bumped into a life-size cardboard promo cutout of a famous Christian radio preacher promoting his new book. At this point I was just too weirded out by the whole experience, so I left the store without purchasing anything at all. I sat in my car in silence for what must have been twenty minutes trying to comprehend what I had just experienced.

For those of us from a Protestant background, a great experiment to flesh out what Dan describes in the Christian bookstore is to spend some time in a Catholic bookstore. It seems mildly familiar yet culturally distinct. The norms and values "preached" in a Catholic bookstore are decidedly different from those in a Protestant bookstore.

—MARK OESTREICHER

Jesus and his teachings will not seem as strange or repellant to non-Christians as will the Christian subculture we have created. Emerging generations are actually very interested in Jesus, but many times Christians get in the way.

✢ Are you numb to the subculture we have created?

What happened in there? I'd been in that store dozens of times and had never noticed its strange subcultural atmosphere. I knew that Christianity itself requires some explanation, but what rattled me about what I'd seen in the store was that had my friend been with me, I would have had to explain more than just spiritual things to him. In fact, the store didn't look or feel very spiritual to me at all. That was the problem. Now,

I know that oftentimes beneath the surface is great content (usually), or at least positive intent. But picture this scene through the eyes of someone growing up in a post-Christian world.

✝ Christapalooza: 20,000 Christians convene ... God doesn't show

If you disagree that the Christian subculture often gets in the way, consider this quote from an article by a non-Christian young adult reporting for a secular music and entertainment paper. He called the article "Christapalooza: 20,000 Christians Convene at the Gorge: God Doesn't Show." He had attended a large Christian music festival, the kind which draws more than 20,000 people. I have attended this type of event and have even been a speaker at one. They have always seemed like great fun. From what I sense, mainly Christians attend these events to hear their favorite Christian bands. But listen to this reporter's non-Christian, post-Christian perspective:

> I have a difficult time locating any similarities between what Jesus says and does, and what the people—in particular the organizers—[at this festival] said and did.... Jesus is a beacon of righteousness who leads the way through a dark world to eternal peace, love, and eternal salvation; the Jesus of [the festival] is a blue-light special, pointing you to the quick fix of a righteous bargain in the shopping mall of endless consumption.
>
> These two versions of Christ, and the premises they entail, are antithetical. They negate one another, leading me to a very unsettling, unpleasant conclusion [about the festival]: It was, in the end, a very un-Christian affair.[1]

Note that he had come thinking that a Christian festival would represent the Jesus he had heard about. The Jesus who is a very spiritual being. The Jesus of the Bible, who, homeless, wandered across the land, living among the poor. The Jesus who was known for taking times of solitude and quiet as his normal way of life. The Jesus who overturned the tables of the money changers in the temple.

But what this young reporter saw was entertainment—screaming teens adoring their favorite bands, loud music, and tons of money being poured out by Christian consumers eager to buy Jesus products and other Christian paraphernalia. Now, you and I know that this is simply a fun way to spend a day or two. We are pretty sure that at least most of the bands and promoters love Jesus. But to someone who expected a spiritual event, it came across as foreign to him. Where was the Jesus he had expected? Where was the Jesus who was against making a profit in God's name and spent time with the poor and needy? Where was the Jesus who devoted quiet time to prayer in the garden or on a mountain? This reporter concluded that he wasn't there. So he subtitled the article "God Doesn't Show."

The Bible teaches us that we should "be careful, however, that the exercise of your freedom does not become a stumbling block to the weak" (1 Cor. 8:9). Perhaps we need to apply this scriptural principle to the subculture we have created. In many ways, our subculture may cause non-Christians to stumble. In fact, it may more than likely repel them. As we design ministry for the emerging church, we need to introduce people to Jesus, not to the Christian subculture of consumerism we have subtly created. We need to make sure we are not trying to see them "born again" into our Christian subculture and changed into one of us instead of being transformed by the Spirit into a disciple of Jesus.

+ A more personal look

Let's take this to a more personal level. What would someone who has grown up in a post-Christian world see when they enter your church building? What does your decor or paintings or posters on the walls communicate? What do you sell in your bookstore? What words do you use in your ministry statements or descriptions that may seem nice to you but horribly tacky to anyone outside of the Christian subculture? You may need to reexamine the messages you are sending through the eyes of those you hope to reach.

I recently saw the logo and mission statement of a church's college and youth ministry. It was a big shield and sharp sword with words underneath saying something about making Christ known to the lost. Now, I understand the biblical metaphor of a shield and sword, and I'm sure the church had good intentions. But what does this logo say to the post-Christian, college-aged student for whom this ministry was intended? What educated young adult wouldn't immediately associate these symbols with the evil Crusades of the Middle Ages and all the anti-Islamic bloodshed that took place in the name of Jesus? If we're serious about being missionaries, we need to be careful how we come across to those growing up in a post-Christian world.

✛ The new theology teachers and spiritual prophets

In the past, pastors and religious leaders of America generally defined spiritual terms for the average person. But this is no longer the case. A new group of prophets, philosophers, and theologians are teaching the emerging culture about spirituality and even Christian theology. I have been told that post-Christian generations have no interest in theology, but on the contrary, they are being taught theology all the time. They are even willing to pay for it.

Movie theaters all across America (and the world) show a steady stream of movies that deal with spiritual themes, sometimes humorously, sometimes seriously, sometimes subtly. Through movies, emerging generations are being taught theology. The angelology is being taught in movies such as *City of Angels,* in which an angel can fall in love and become human. Satan is defined as a lawyer (in *The Devil's Advocate*) or as a beautiful woman (portrayed by Elizabeth Hurley in *Bedazzled*). We learn that an angel in heaven can have sex with Satan and produce a child called Little Nicky (portrayed by Adam Sandler).

The doctrine of the afterlife is taught in *The Sixth Sense,* in which departed souls still wander around modern-day neighborhoods, and in *What Dreams May Come,* in which we learn that we can make our way out of hell into a pluralistic type of heaven. Eschatology (the study of the end times) is taught in movies such as *End of Days* (with Arnold Schwarzenegger) and *Lost Souls,* in which we hear about the meaning of 666 and the Antichrist.

Christology is taught in television specials such as Peter Jennings' "The Search for Jesus." Through this particular broadcast, over sixteen million viewers learned that most of what the Bible says about Jesus was made up by the early church and that the resurrection and other miracles didn't actually happen.

Homework assignment: If you've not spent time in the "religion" section of a large bookstore recently (Barnes and Noble, Borders), it's absolutely essential that you do. In fact, many of these stores have moved "Christianity" into a separate section, near the "religion" section, as to not contaminate the broader-minded stuff. Observe the people browsing. Notice the subcategories of books. Notice which books have multiple copies on the shelf, which often means that they sell more copies.

—Mark Oestreicher

We must understand that new definitions are being assigned to spiritual and theological terms by the new cultural prophets and philosophers of music, movies, and media. This affects what and how we teach.

Spirituality is taught quite often in popular music. Marilyn Manson's strong lyrics are derived from Christian themes twisted to opposite meanings.

The band Godsmack is public about their belief in Wicca. Bands today use religious symbols and imagery quite frequently. There are some subtle and truthful Christian themes in the music of bands like Creed and P.O.D., but overwhelmingly people are immersed in lyrics which send contradictory messages.

> *We are under siege from religious zealots and nuts . . . mostly*
> *Christians, so-called Christians. I'm talking about those hell-bent,*
> *holy rollers that sit around and try to control the country,*
> *the ones that are against abortion. . . . Those nuts. Those wackos.*
> —HOWARD STERN, NATIONAL RADIO AND TV HOST[2]

We may think that there is no harm to this. After all, in the past we've had movies such as *It's a Wonderful Life,* which featured an angel who wasn't quite biblical. But unlike past generations, which held to a Judeo-Christian worldview, emerging generations have no biblical grounding. We need to redefine for our listeners many theological terms and premises which are being incorrectly taught by popular culture.

Today celebrities serve as our culture's prophets and religious philosophers. What a famous actor does or believes carries much weight with those who look to them for fashion trends, hairstyles, and even religious influence. Celebrity lives and practices are scrutinized; movies are viewed and reviewed; the lyrics of songs are heard over and over.

> *We'll never tell [our fans] to do drugs, burn people's houses down, kill*
> *people, or worship Satan. I'm really into Jesus Christ, God, all that.*
> *I really am a big believer. I'm a Christian. I just happen to have a foul*
> *mouth, and I try to make kids laugh. But that's just me. I'm as*
> *God made me.* —TOM DELONGE, BLINK-182 GUITARIST-SINGER[3]

To add to the confusion, famous celebrities claim they are Christian and talk about God or Jesus yet promote a lifestyle contrary to Scripture. This "Christian" example, for many younger people, is the only one they know.

✛ An extreme openness to spiritual things

"First, I want to thank God!"
"Without Jesus, none of this would have been possible!"

God is now thanked from end zones and awards podiums so often that his name has almost become commonplace. While the credits rolled on a recent MTV Music Awards broadcast, a skit ran in the background featuring a white-haired deity directing a recording session in a studio. The producers jokingly surmised that God must be there with the musicians as they record, since they so often feel compelled to thank him. Spiritual hunger and awareness are on the rise, and the desire to express one's spirituality is now becoming much more commonplace among emerging generations. It really is thrilling to see so much spiritual interest surfacing. We have gone far past any "God is dead" mantras and are living in a culture in which God is very much in the thoughts of today's generations.

> *Tell me all your thoughts on God, 'cause I would really want to meet her. . . . So tell me am I very far—am I very far now?* —DISHWALLA, "COUNTING BLUE CARS"

There is good news and bad news. The good news is how fashionable it is these days to talk about God. Praying is even in. Britney Spears proudly told the press that her boyfriend at the time, 'N Sync singer Justin Timberlake, had given her a copy of the book *Conversations with God*. Deepak Chopra was featured in *Rolling Stone* magazine promoting his latest book, *How to Know God*. Visit any non-Christian bookstore and you'll find plenty of books about God, Jesus, and developing a spiritual life. We did a survey of four hundred students on a local college campus where there is hardly any Christian presence, and over 75 percent said they believe in "God." Even *Newsweek* had a cover article acknowledging that our brains are "Wired for God." God is in; spirituality is hip. A huge number of websites are dedicated to spiritual discussion and information. These are exciting times!

Now for the bad news. As often as God and Jesus are thanked in the limelight, the message being taught by the prophets of our day is not a biblical one. Often, just prior to crediting God, these same artists have performed a song that demeans women or promotes violence or glorifies sexual promiscuity. It is common to hear Christian terminology used by celebrities without any grounding in either Scripture or the person of Christ. Confusing messages are being sent to emerging generations who are learning these theological terms and having God and Jesus defined and described differently than the Bible does.

> We need to stay true to who God is and what God has done as revealed to us in Scripture. But doctrine alone is not enough; lived doctrine will make the difference between effectiveness and ineffectiveness in this spiritual landscape, whether we're wanting to reach adults or teens. The postmodern, post-Christian world is relational to the core. It is much more interested in matters of being than simply knowing. As Christians, the most difficult thing about this new world is that we are no longer going to be able to impact the world by just spouting our theology. We're going to have to live it out—radically.
>
> —SALLY MORGENTHALER

✠ Spiritual but not religious

We also see that while there is a genuine openness to spirituality, the attraction is usually to a mix of religious faiths, a piecing together of various spiritual beliefs. When exiled Tibetan Buddhist leader the Dalai Lama came to California, he drew an audience in the tens of thousands, including a significant number of young people.

One evening I was visiting the University of California–Santa Cruz campus when I heard drums in the woods nearby. I wandered down a path to find a circle of six or seven guys playing conga drums and other percussion instruments—stark naked! The clotheless drummers greeted me with great friendliness and invited me to sit with them. I had been a drummer in a band for many years, so I could appreciate the variety of rhythms they were producing. I sat down with them (clothes on!), and as we chatted, I learned that they considered the drum circle a very spiritual event. They seemed wide open to discussing the topic and were knowledgeable about the various beats and their origins in African tribal drumming. Their beliefs were a far cry from the doctrines of Christianity, but the fact remains that they were seeking a spiritual experience.

There's a God-shaped vacuum in every man that only God can fill.
—BLAISE PASCAL, FRENCH MATHEMATICIAN (1623–62)

✠ The hole only God can fill: a final note of hope

Ancient, medieval, modern, or postmodern—emerged or emerging—when it comes down to it, we still have the same basic human needs. We all want to be accepted. We all want to know that we are loved. We all long for purpose. We also long for spiritual fulfillment and meaning. We long to know our Creator and are born with a hole in our hearts that only he can fill. These things will never change this side of heaven. This means Jesus will be the only answer to fill this eternal longing created in us, whether we're ravers, gothics, or Wiccans, twenty-year-olds or ninety-year-olds, Madonna or Marilyn Manson, Elton John or Eminem. The early church was birthed into an environment of sorcerers, gods, goddesses, and many spiritual cults and religions. We are not facing anything new. We are not facing anything that the Holy Spirit of God moving in the emerging church cannot overcome.

He has also set eternity in the hearts of men. *—ECCLESIASTES 3:11*

I believe we are living in times of incredible promise and hope. What a wonderful and adventurous privilege to live in this moment of history when emerging generations are so open spiritually. My prayer is that we will have the courage to stay true to the Scriptures while radically rethinking the way we do ministry. May we seize this moment in history and become missionaries again, being sensitive to post-Christian culture, living lives of intense dependence on the Spirit, and rethinking what the emerging church will be like for new generations.

EMERGING THOUGHTS

1. Suppose you went to your local university and asked students, "What comes to mind when you hear the name Jesus?" and "What comes to mind when you hear the word Christian?" What do you think you would hear? Why? (You might want to actually conduct these interviews and then show the video to your church for its teaching impact.)

2. What are some ways the popular culture is teaching people in your church or community about theology, or who God is?

3. Could you identify with the observations of the writer who attended the "Christapalooza" event? Have you ever tried to view an event like this through the eyes of someone like him? Explain.

4. How do you think a post-Christian would view your church, your logos, your mission statements, the wording in your bulletin? Are there things your church should consider changing to communicate to the culture without altering the essential meaning?

What Is "Church?"

The Second Most Important Chapter in This Book

8

> **Be shepherds of the church of God, which he bought with his own blood.**
>
> —Acts 20:28

While teaching a series from the book of Acts, I made a statement that provoked a lot of confused looks. "There is not one verse in the New Testament that says they 'went to church.'" I could almost read their minds. "What do you mean, they didn't go to church? Of course they went to church."

"According to the Bible," I continued, "it is actually impossible to 'go to church.'" Again, I could tell what they were thinking by their expressions: "What do you mean by that? I am in church right now! How can you tell me it is impossible to do what I am doing?" I then capped it off by saying, "If you woke up this morning and said I'm going to church today, you would actually be making a theologically incorrect statement."

✚ Nowhere in the New Testament does it say they "went to church"

I was trying to get the point across that the church is not the building, nor is it the meeting. The church is the people of God who gather together with a sense of mission (Acts 14:27). We can't *go* to church because *we are* the church.

If you are a pastor or leader, you likely understand this basic theological truth. Maybe even if you are an informed attender you understand.

But I would guess that to many attending our worship services, the word church refers to the Sunday meeting during which the pastor speaks, the worship leader leads some songs, the choir sings, and the offering is taken. Then "church" is over, and they go home.

I may be pressing an issue that's merely semantical here, but I am coming to the conclusion that perhaps a great part of why our modern contemporary churches have become increasingly consumeristic and are having less impact is due to the way we use the word church. The way we use the word could be one of the most important factors in shaping the culture and ethos of the emerging church.

✠ Whatever happened to the word church?

Words have power. A. W. Tozer makes this provocative statement at the beginning of his classic book *The Knowledge of the Holy:* "What comes into our minds when we think about God is the most important thing about us." I'd like to propose that, in a similar way, what comes into our minds when we think of the word church is the most important thing shaping how we function as a church. The way leaders define church will determine how they measure success, where they focus our time and energy, how they design their strategies and form their ministry philosophies. How we define church will even determine the focus of our prayers. This, then, trickles into the minds and hearts of people in the congregation, shaping how they think of church.

In the New Testament, the word church is the Greek word *ekklesia,* which means "assembly" and was used in a somewhat political sense to refer to early meetings among believers that had a purpose and a mission. We see this word also used for a nonreligious gathering (cf. Acts 19:32 and Acts 19:41).

However, the word church was used primarily to describe the followers of Jesus. In a gathering aspect, it is most used to describe the groups of people as they met in homes (Rom. 16:5; 1 Cor. 16:19). The church was "gathered" (Acts 14:27), but never do we see that people met *at* a church.

The term is used in the singular to describe several churches in a region (Acts 9:31) but also is used to describe a church which is comprised of believers everywhere on earth. We are part of a local and a universal church. The emerging church will gather in various forms, but one thing we all must have in common is a missional emphasis.

+ The missional church: sadly forgotten amid the programming, preaching, and people pleasing

Theologian Millard Erickson makes the case that the primary function of the church (the people) is her evangelistic mission. He says that "the one topic most emphasized in both accounts of Jesus' last words to His disciples is evangelism. In Matthew 28:19 He instructs them, 'Go therefore and make disciples of all nations.' In Acts 1:8 He says, 'But you shall receive power when the Holy Spirit comes upon you; and you shall be my witnesses in Jerusalem and in all Judea and Samaria and to the end of the earth.' This was the final point Jesus made to His disciples. It appears that He regarded evangelism as the very reason for their being."[1]

If this is true, then how are we doing? Do the people in your church regard evangelism as the very reason for their being as the people of God? If we took a hard look at how we spend our time and energy and resources, my guess is that the average church focuses most efforts on the quality of the programs and ministries to keep those already attending happy rather than on our biblical mission. Where have we gone astray?

The excellent book *The Missional Church,* edited by Darrell Guder, makes the case that since the time of the Reformation, the church unintentionally redefined itself. The Reformers, in their effort to raise the authority of the Bible and ensure sound doctrine, defined the marks of a true church: a place where the gospel is rightly preached, the sacraments are rightly administered, and church discipline is exercised. However, over time these marks narrowed the definition of the church itself as a "place where" idea instead of a "people who are" reality.

The word church became defined as "a place where certain things happen," such as preaching and communion. Gruder writes, "Popular grammar captures it well: you 'go to church,' much as the way you go to a store. You 'attend' a church, the way you attend a school or theater. You 'belong to a church,' much as you would a service club with its programs and activities."[2]

The words we use are critical in shaping people's expectations. Never underestimate this effect. As Guder writes, "In North America, this 'place where' orientation manifests itself in a particular form. Both members and those outside the church expect the church to be a vendor of religious services and goods."[3]

⊹ A vendor of religious goods and services?

Yikes. Those are strong words. But let's think about this. Have we, over time and with good intentions and pure motivation, turned our

93

churches into vendors of religious services and goods? In our desire to attract people to our churches, have we subtly taught that church is where you *come* to learn about how God can help you fix your problems? Where you come to have others teach your children about God for you? Where you come for your weekly feeding in the Word of God? Where you come for quality programs to help you live life better and develop a social network? Where you come to experience high quality worship music?

A foundational and critical challenge for the emerging church will be teaching people that *they are* the church and that they don't simply attend or go to one.

If the church has become the place instead of the people on a mission, leaders only naturally start focusing their efforts on what people experience when they come to the place on Sundays. In recent years, we have even added the words excellence and relevance to our value statements for church. In doing so, we naturally began spending more time focusing on the quality of the music, sound system, and bulletins. As the church grows, the pressure to continue this focus increases and the problem escalates.

The bigger the church gets, the better the preaching needs to be with more dynamic presentations and better PowerPoint slides. The music needs to be more professional with better sound systems and lighting. The children's programs and youth ministries need to be better to keep the teenagers happy and paying attention so their parents can sit in the larger gathering where religious goods and services are dispensed. Great intentions, but as a result the church can subtly lose sight of its identity and missional function, and people come to church to have their needs met by others, volunteering only if they have any time to spare. As we create a culture in which people *come* to church, people generally are content to remain spectators.

✛ Could we be guilty of creating consumer Christians?

Could our leadership be the very cause of it all? Could providing bigger and better programs and ministry services be backfiring on us? Erwin McManus, pastor of Mosaic church in Los Angeles, writes: "'We're looking for a church that meets our needs.' It seems like I've heard this one a thousand times. The phenomenon of church shoppers has profoundly shaped the contemporary church. The entire conversation is not about relevance but convenience. The focus is not in serving the world; the church itself became the focal point. Our motto degenerated from 'We are the church, here to serve the lost and broken world' to 'What does this church have to offer me?'"[4]

I believe this is the root of the problem the modern church has created. As the leadership subtly focuses on the programs and not the mission, we become known in the community for our programs, our preaching, or our music rather than for the qualities the Thessalonian church was commended for.

The emerging church must address this and shift from being consumer oriented to mission oriented. If people really see themselves as the church on a mission, everything changes. Everything!

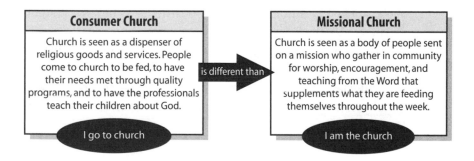

✛ Why this is the second most important chapter in this book

The emerging church must define the church scripturally again, teaching people how the church fits into the grand story of the Bible. People need to see how they as individuals and as members of the church are part of God's story. The church is God's instrument through which the Holy Spirit moves and expresses his love and as Jesus redeems the world to come under God's kingdom. Then the focus would move off of ourselves. We would then naturally break out of our consumer mindset, changing everything.

➡️ People won't "go to church" but will be the church on a mission together.

- People couldn't help but feed deeply on the Scriptures on their own to keep their hearts soft and their minds sharp and ready to give an answer for the hope they have to those they interact with (1 Peter 3:15–16).
- People will see themselves as ambassadors of Jesus (2 Cor. 5:20) and be motivated to live holy, kingdom-minded lives so that they do not dishonor the name of the King they represent.
- Parents who see themselves as the church will lead their families the way Deuteronomy 6:4–9 describes, rather than leave it only to the church.
- People will become desperately more dependent on prayer for the mission the church is on (John 15:5).
- People will more naturally see the church as family and as a community on a mission together (Acts 2:42–46).
- Our ministry designs and strategies will shift from big programs and productions to equipping people to serve on the mission (Eph. 4:11–12) and elevate the priesthood of believers again (1 Peter 2:5–9).
- Evangelism will drastically rise, since the entire church is *always* on a mission (locally and globally).
- Our churches will more naturally and eagerly be concerned with social justice, the poor, and the needy in this world because of the mission.

✠ The great opportunity to redefine the church to new generations

There's no way a missional church that understands her place in God's story can produce consumer Christians. It would go against its very nature. But becoming a missional church means more than having a mission statement or offering an occasional class. It means "rebirthing" the church from the inside out and maintaining its new psyche. It means constantly resisting the tendency to become consumer-oriented by keeping the mission at the forefront of all we do. How thrilling that we have the opportunity to redefine church to emerging generations. Because they are experiencing it for the first time, they don't think of the church as a place to get your needs met and consume religious goods and services. We have the exciting opportunity to retell the story of the church and how they are in that story today!

+ **Please remember . . .**

We need to remember this definition of the word church in coming chapters as we speak about the design of worship services, leadership, preaching, and discipleship. If we don't build everything on the biblical definition of what church is, then we will simply be fueling the consumer mindset. Walking this fine line is probably one of the bigger challenges facing the emerging church.

May God's Spirit guide us as we venture ahead and reimagine what the emerging church might be. May we approach our roles as shepherds of his emerging church with great honor and joy and yet with trembling and wonder.

EMERGING THOUGHTS

1. How would the average person in your church define the word church? How would the leaders define it?

2. Would you view your church as consumeristic? Why or why not?

3. How much of your leadership's energy is focused on putting on the weekend event compared with energy spent on training and teaching people to understand their true identity as the missional church?

4. Do you agree or disagree that how a pastor defines the word church is the most important thing about the function, strategy, and methodology of a church? Why?

Part 2

RECONSTRUCTING

Vintage Christianity
in the Emerging Church

The Dilemma of Seeker-Sensitive Services

> "Whatever type of people you already have in your congregation is the same type you are likely to attract more of. It is very unlikely that your church will attract and keep many people who are different from those who already attend.

—Rick Warren, *The Purpose-Driven Church*

What a stimulating experience I had recently, attending a worship service at a very large church. Looking around I saw thousands of people praising God to the upbeat music of a keyboard-driven band with a row of well-dressed backup singers who were every bit as professional as the *Tonight Show* crew. The room was well lit and cheery, the atmosphere celebratory and festive. I could feel excitement in the air. I could see no religious symbols—no crosses—and the stage was decorated with classy props. The preaching was excellent—exactly thirty minutes. The communicator delivered his well-thought-out four-point sermon with conviction and passion. People eagerly and enthusiastically filled in the blanks on the note sheets they were given.

But I was left with some deep concerns. Among all those thousands of worshipers, I could hardly find anyone who looked to be under thirty. I looked around pretty hard, too! As best as I could tell, apart from a very few, everyone seemed to be between the ages of thirty-five and fifty-five—mainly middle-aged and well-dressed, though casually. I knew that there were lots of younger people in this community, but they certainly were not to be found in this worship service.

This really didn't surprise me, though, because the approach, values, and methodology were almost the opposite of what I believe emerging generations are seeking. Please understand, God was doing great things there! And I thank God. This church was growing, but by attracting more of the same kind of person. Entire segments of the local population, in terms of both age and mindset, were missing. I couldn't help but think that it was because this particular style of worship service would cause many of the unchurched in the emerging generations to run and hide. Why?

✛ Values are changing in the emerging church

Differences in values are shaped by differences in worldview. As you will hear me say over and over, as long as we are biblical, there is no right or wrong way to design ministry or worship services. However, our audience does make a difference. I believe the emerging church is going to look and feel a lot different from most contemporary churches. I think there will be not just one emerging-church approach but dozens, even hundreds, of beautiful varieties of communities of faith, each unique to its context.

In the next few chapters, I will address the matter of designing the worship service for emerging generations. However, let me first state two assumptions.

✛ 1. The church must continue to meet together

Hebrews 10:25 tells us to "not give up meeting together." The believers regularly gathered as a church in smaller groups in homes (1 Cor. 16:19; Col. 4:15; Philem. 2). Community is essential to our life as disciples of Jesus. Teaching must take place (2 Tim. 4:2). However, how we meet together today is quite different from those early church gatherings. Leading a church is more complex today, and as numbers in our churches increase, the complexity increases.

Not all emerging churches are going to have meetings like the ones described in the following chapters. Some emerging churches may choose to focus on home meetings and intentionally stay small. However, if your worship gathering begins to grow larger, even larger than thirty or forty people, the following discussion should be relevant.

✛ 2. You've read the first part of this book

Whatever I say from here on needs to be read in light of what we've covered in the first part of the book so as to avoid the mistake of trying

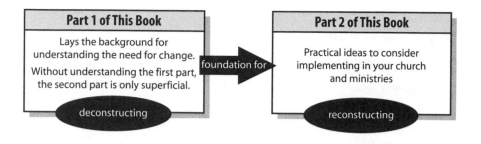

Part 1 of This Book	Part 2 of This Book
Lays the background for understanding the need for change. Without understanding the first part, the second part is only superficial.	Practical ideas to consider implementing in your church and ministries
deconstructing	reconstructing

foundation for

to make only cosmetic changes in your church. As you read through the rest of the book, remembering our definition of the word church, as well as how I'm using the term seeker-sensitive, is critical.

✢ The seeker-sensitive church faces an identity crisis in the emerging culture

In the 1970s and 1980s, God raised leaders to give new life and vision to dying churches. God used and still uses churches that employ seeker-sensitive methodology to draw hundreds of thousands of people across North America back to Jesus and his church. The values of these churches were birthed specifically out of the leaders' desire to identify with the people they were hoping to reach. Even if a church did not fully embrace a seeker-sensitive strategy, many churches at least adopted many of its contemporary approaches to ministry. The emphasis on creating a place for seekers to come meant emphasizing the weekend service as the entry point to the church. Contemporary architecture was developed for worship buildings along with new approaches to preaching and communication. Dramas, videos, and production staff were added to larger churches to help make the weekend services more professional. Even Garth Brooks-like headset microphones were used to show that we really are keeping up with the times and are hip to current culture.

Based on my observations and conversations, however, I think that many of these very things are contrary to what emerging generations value and are seeking in their spiritual experience.

We very likely could see the pattern of past generations repeated. As churches lost touch with the culture and didn't connect with younger generations, the seeker-sensitive movement was born. This time, however, it is the seeker-sensitive movement that loses touch as it grows more and more disconnected with the heart of emerging generations.

The remainder of this book will explore not only the worship service but also leadership, preaching, communication, spiritual formation, and evangelism. A cultural shift is occurring that impacts all we do. Let's take a look at some of these differences in values as they relate to the design of a worship service.

Modern seeker-sensitive churches face a dilemma as more emerging generations are born with no connection to their approach. We will soon lose our impact and influence in the emerging culture, unless we plan to reinvent ourselves for their future.

✢ Examples of values differences between services for seeker-sensitive and post-seeker-sensitive generations

The examples in the following table show some of the differences in values between a modern seeker-sensitive service and a service designed for post-Christian generations. Neither are right or wrong. They are simply different values for different mindsets. Many emerging churches will not have worship services like those I describe in later chapters. We will likely see more smaller gatherings birthed as churches in homes. I also believe we will see emerging churches form church communities in workplaces and apartment complexes. However, I assume that the bulk of churches will have a larger weekly gathering.

As our culture shifts, churches need to adapt how they function. Virtually every week I receive several emails from leaders across America who are concerned about the absence of younger people in their church services. "What should we do to see younger people become part of our church?" "Do we change our services and start trying to blend methodology?" "Do we start a new service?" "Should we plant a new church?" People are looking for options as they realize that most seeker-sensitive services are not connecting with emerging generations.

✚ Some options churches are choosing to impact the emerging culture

In terms of worship services, some try to take their current worship experience and add some new elements to create a "blended" service. My opinion is that trying to bring new styles into your existing service will end up pleasing no one, thus becoming more of a problem than if you stuck to your original approach. Besides, making a few superficial adjustments in style will not address fundamental differences in values regard-

Shifting Values in Approach to Worship Services

MODERN CHURCH (Seeker-Sensitive)	EMERGING CHURCH (Post-Seeker-Sensitive)
Worship "services" in which preaching, music, programs, etc. are *served* to the attender	Worship "gatherings," which include preaching, music, etc.
Services designed to reach those who have had bad or boring experiences in a church	Gatherings designed to include and translate to those who have no previous church experience
Services designed to be user-friendly and contemporary	Gatherings designed to be experiential and spiritual-mystical
A need to break the stereotype of what church is	A need to break the stereotype of who Christians are
Stained glass taken out and replaced with video screens	Stained glass brought back in on video screens
Crosses and other symbols removed from meeting place to avoid looking too "religious"	Crosses and other symbols brought back into meeting place to promote a sense of spiritual reverence
Room arranged so individuals are able to see the stage from comfortable theater seating while worshiping	Room arranged to focus on community, striving to feel more like a living room or coffeehouse while worshiping
Lit up and cheery sanctuary valued	Darkness valued as it displays a sense of spirituality
Focal point of the service is the sermon	Focal point of the gathering is the holistic experience
Preacher and worship leader lead the service	Preacher and worship leader lead by participating in the gathering
Uses modern technology to communicate with contemporary flare	Gathering seen as a place to experience the ancient, even mystical (and uses technology to do so)
Services designed to grow to accomodate the many people of the church	Gatherings designed to grow to accomodate many people but seen as a time when the church which meets in smaller groups gathers together

ing leadership, spiritual formation, evangelism, and so on. Churches need to make some *holistic* fundamental shifts and decisions to truly engage the emerging culture.

Some churches have started using video broadcasts of the regular sermon but have changed the music to attract a younger crowd. In my opinion, this approach doesn't address many of the fundamental issues we are facing. What is happening in our culture requires more than just changing musical styles. As I talk with church leaders who are taking this approach, the services that are working are attracting primarily baby boomers who already attend church or are associated with the church. The initial reports say they aren't seeing younger people attending who weren't raised in the church or who weren't already Christians.

Here are some options I believe are worth at least exploring for existing churches.

✠ Approach 1: Start a life-stage outreach service in your church

Your church could start a life-stage service incorporating post-seeker-sensitive values in order to attract emerging generations. Some churches market these "young adult" or "twenty-something" services to eighteen- to thirty-year-olds with the hope that when attenders mature or hit a certain age, they will move on to attend the "main services" of the church.

I don't know of many churches in which this approach is working well. In fact, in almost every case I have observed, they have eventually moved to an all-ages approach, not a life-stage service. Why? Because enforcing age restrictions creates problems. After all, if people in this age group weren't drawn to the "main" worship service in the first place, why would they suddenly develop the urge to attend because they've hit a certain age?

For several years, one very large East Coast church has been the primary flag-carrier for the life-stage approach. Their goal was to see people transition out of their young adult service into the main service when they hit age thirty. But the leadership of the church finally realized that when people hit thirty, they still didn't want to attend the other services. Who they were and how they learned and worshiped were fundamentally different. The church decided to allow people to simply grow through life together in these new gatherings, rather than being forced to "graduate" to a different service when they hit a certain age. They now focus on developing ways for the attenders of the various worship services to come together in the life of the body outside of worship.

+ Approach 2: Start a worship gathering in your church with new values and a different approach, but remain one church

You could start a worship gathering and department of your church to target a different mindset and people group than your church currently reaches. As you start the service, remember that more than just the worship gathering needs to change. Fundamental approaches in leadership, in spiritual formation, and in other values will all need to be considered as well.

While these new gatherings generally will be attended largely by younger people, a remarkable number of older worshipers will also relate to this new approach. As pastor and author Brian McLaren estimates, one-third of the baby boomers are more postmodern in their approach to God. So don't be surprised if you find many of all ages who resonate with a new worship service.

Some complain that starting a new service will divide the church, and it can, if you are not careful. It is essential to plan to integrate the entire body outside of the worship services. This can happen through mentoring programs, through overseas mission trips, on men's retreats, in prayer meetings, and by serving together. The possibilities are endless, as long as the people who go to various worship services still see themselves as one church and function as one church through the week.

This approach requires that church leaders not feel threatened by new thinking and that they relinquish the need to understand and control every aspect of these new services and ministry approaches. These new approaches will be messy! But so was the early church and every missionary work since then, as believers pioneered ways of presenting the gospel of Jesus to a new culture. You wouldn't expect to run a Chinese service like you would a modern seeker-sensitive service. The same goes for a service geared for a post-Christian mindset. You wouldn't need to start a new service in the first place if the values were all the same.

✢ Approach 3: Redesign your existing youth and college ministry

Though cultural changes are impacting more than youth and young adult ministry, these are the ministries most affected. Rather than start a new service, some churches may prefer to redesign their existing youth and college ministry. This can be a good start toward engaging the emerging culture. However, you do need to think this through longer term. As our culture continues to change, you will need to make changes beyond just your youth and college ministry.

I believe that high school ministries in particular can begin making significant changes in how they approach ministry. Of course, teenagers still need to have fun and do all the things teenagers enjoy doing. Yet in our local setting, we are seeing teenagers increasingly being drawn to a "vintage" approach to ministry. I recently attended a junior high ministry which was complete with candles and a darkened room as youth were being taught to pray silently and sit still to listen to God's voice. They had some zany junior high games to start off, but then they got really serious.

✢ Approach 4: Plant a new church to reach the emerging culture

Some churches decide either that they don't want to alter their values or that the issues involved in starting a new service in their particular church are too messy for them. But because they desire to reach the emerging culture, they choose to plant a sister church with a new culture and philosophy. This is another great way for a local church to extend its mission to the emerging culture. And because these church plants are ingrained from the beginning with the philosophy and values of emerging leaders, church planting is a great option for making change happen more quickly.

✢ However it happens, the goal is to reach the emerging culture

Whatever plan we adopt to address the dilemma faced by seeker-sensitive services, the goal is to create a culture and a church community that will impact people in the emerging culture. The future is now upon us, and the seeker-sensitive church and other modern contemporary churches must not let this moment go by. In the next few chapters, we'll consider what worship services designed for emerging generations might look like.

EMERGING THOUGHTS

1. What would you say the major values differences are between your church's worship gathering and the values that are characteristic of emerging generations?

2. Is there anything on the values table in this chapter that you resonate with or disagree with?

3. Out of the possible approaches presented in this chapter, which do you think would work best in your church? Why?

What Is This Thing We Call the "Worship Service?"

10

> " **Calling a church service a "time of worship" does not always make it so.**
>
> —George Barna

I participated on a panel at a national conference where we were discussing the design of experiential worship services for people in the emerging culture. I came hoping that I could learn from others and that some of the things we've done at our church could be helpful to people. We began by introducing ourselves and then opened it up for questions. Immediately the audience began asking about how we use videos, how we create interactive experiences, how we incorporate the arts into our services, and other related questions. We could see by their energy and enthusiasm that this was exactly what they came to hear.

✚ Experiential worship services: the next generation of consumer Christians?

The pastor to my left told how he had created an actual desert in his church by bringing in a few tons of sand. The idea was that people could walk in their bare feet, pray, and experience the desert like Jesus did. They even brought in rocks. My response was to be really impressed. I couldn't help imagining how cool that would be and was soon trying to figure out how we might do this in our church. Then the pastor to my right talked about how they present dance and art pieces while the message is being given. I was impressed again! My mind was awhirl, thinking of how we too might use that idea. I also got the chance to explain some

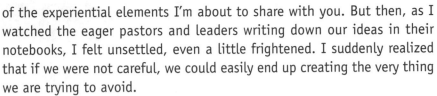

of the experiential elements I'm about to share with you. But then, as I watched the eager pastors and leaders writing down our ideas in their notebooks, I felt unsettled, even a little frightened. I suddenly realized that if we were not careful, we could easily end up creating the very thing we are trying to avoid.

Our hope is that the emerging church will break out of the consumer Christian mentality. Our aim in making a worship gathering more experiential is that people would participate in the service rather than remain spectators. Experiential and interactive worship, in addition to the teaching that occurs, is a refreshing practice that resonates with those being raised in this culture and returns to something more like what an early church gathering was like. But if we focus too much on creating cool and creative experiences for our worship gatherings—if most of our time is spent figuring out how interactive art can be incorporated in the service or what dance we can use or what meditative visuals would look good on the screens or what candlelit prayer stations we can design—we may well end up in the same consumer Christian trap. If we aren't careful, we'll soon be hearing people saying, "Well, I think I'll go to First Baptist tonight. I hear they've got sand on the floor!" Or, "I'll go to Community Bible this weekend because they have artists painting during the message." Or, "I like all those scented candles they use at that other place."

Woe to us in the emerging church if we do not keep balance and perspective. Please, as you read through the following chapters, keep this caution in mind, lest you train people to become consumers of religious goods and services.

✠ Defining the worship service or gathering

Before we look at designing a worship service or gathering for emerging generations, let's first take a look at what a worship service is. So many of us have simply adopted what we were taught in seminary or have patterned our ministries after churches we've attended. But where did all this come from? Why do we even do what we do in these worship gatherings? I want to keep questioning our presuppositions because as Albert Einstein once said, "It's impossible to get out of a problem by using the same kind of thinking that it took to get into the problem."

+ Worship gatherings in the early church

While very few documents describe the early church's first worship gatherings, it is safe to say that they probably looked quite different than what we commonly experience today. Not only were these early believers on the raw edge of a brand-new movement, they functioned in a different culture with people of a different mindset. However, it helps to recognize that certain concepts span both time and culture. We see from Scripture and from early church writings that there was an order to what they did and that their gatherings included instruction from the Word, song, prayer, celebrating the Lord's Supper, and individual participation (1 Cor. 11:17–26; 14:26). They met primarily in homes, probably in groups of less than fifty people (1 Cor. 16:19; Rom. 16:5; Col. 4:15). We do see larger numbers used in the book of Acts, such as in 2:41 where there were three thousand in the church in Jerusalem. But remember this was during Pentecost, a festival time when Jerusalem was full of visitors. There is no indication that they regularly all gathered together for a "worship service" like we have today. The religious Jews would never have allowed them to regularly meet en masse in the temple for a service which focused on a false messiah they had crucified. We do see times when preaching occurred in the temple during the time of spreading the message (Luke 19:47–48), but that is not where the church met regularly. The temple was destroyed in A.D. 70, so they could not have met there long term. Large gatherings like the ones we experience today did not occur until several hundred years later.

✣ Very Christ-centered, very community oriented, very vintage

We can determine that much of what the early church did when they gathered as a church for worship was heavily influenced by what they were used to in the Jewish synagogue. We know the early church met on Sundays, even though it was a working day in their culture. They must have met at other times when they had meals together (1 Cor. 11:17–22). Justin Martyr, in his "First Apology," written around A.D. 150 in Rome, offers us a snapshot of these early home church meetings. He tells us that they had prayer, a reading from a portion of the Scriptures "as long as time allows," followed by a discourse given by someone in the church to encourage them to imitate what was heard in the Scriptures. They would then stand, pray, and take communion. Then off to their daily work they went. Some of this order of service was probably based on the synagogue liturgy with which many of the early Christians would have been familiar. Pretty simple, nothing fancy. Very Christ-centered and very participatory and community oriented. Very vintage. This was the worship service of the early church.

> What the New Testament church did not have were buildings—for nearly three hundred years! That's why at Saddleback church we waited until we had over ten thousand in attendance before we built our first building We wanted to prove that the church is people, not a building. If you want to be a truly vintage church, don't build a building!
>
> —RICK WARREN

✠ What is worship?

We can say this for sure about the worship of the early church: They came to worship the risen Jesus through song, prayer, the Lord's Supper, and teaching. I think keeping this simple snapshot in mind helps us remember why we are gathered. Even the word worship should resonate in our thoughts as we plan each service.

Biblically, *worship* is used in two primary ways. *Proskuneo,* literally "to kiss toward," is the primary word for worship. Theologian Charles Ryrie states that kissing the earth was an act to honor the deities of the earth, as was prostrating oneself in reverence.[1] Our English word worship is a shortened form of *worthship,* which means "to attribute worth." In the Hebrew Bible, the word *hishahawah* literally means "a bowing down." This conveyed the idea of bowing down in reverence before the holy presence of God. The Greek word *proskunein* is used in the Septuagint to translate *shahah,* also having the connotation of submissive lowliness and deep respect.[2]

The other primary word for worship in the Bible is *latreuo,* meaning "to serve or minister." This conveys the idea that worship is also a priestly service and shows that worship is a participatory action of service and involvement.

+ Vintage worship is going back to the original and keeping that in mind

I wonder if in the rush of creative planning and the desire to see people enjoy our worship gatherings in the modern church, we have pushed to the sidelines what we are supposed to be doing. We need to keep these definitions of worship in the forefront of our minds as we plan our services, asking the Spirit to guide us.

> We must unlearn our program-evaluation mindset in regard to our worship gatherings. We must first ask whether God is truly encountered and worshiped and whether people are encouraged to become disciples of Jesus.

In the emerging church, we need to make sure we view our worship services as gatherings in which people come to "attribute worth to God," "to kiss toward him in reverence and lay prostrate" or "bow down" to him

either physically or in our hearts. This can be done by singing praises to God (Eph. 5:19) in community, by having God's Word taught and read and used to focus our hearts and minds on who he is, and by honoring and remembering Jesus, our shepherd (Col. 3:16–17). Worship gatherings can also include our participation in serving and in ministering to one another as an act of worship (Mark 10:43–45; James 5:16).

In our discussions about the emerging church, it is a mistake to focus more on the arts, on making organic flow, and on including experiential elements than on asking how this gathering is creating an environment in which people worship God. We should always be asking how any interactive element moves people to worship God more. Is this environment and what we do allowing us to become more intense worshipers of God?

If you are part of a staff that evaluates worship services, what do you base your evaluations on? Do you immediately discuss the music, the video, or the length of the message? Or do you ask, "Did people encounter God here? Was Jesus lifted up in honor? What have we trained people to think when they leave? Do they say 'I enjoyed that,' or 'That was a good message,' or are they thinking, 'I encountered God today,' and, 'I became more of a disciple of Jesus today'?" The emerging church must value worship over the quality of the program or of the "goods and services" we deliver.

✠ Who is the worship service for? Believers or nonbelievers?

A question that was hotly debated with the rise of the seeker-sensitive church is whether the service is for believers or nonbelievers. But this isn't much of an issue for the emerging church, since in the emerging culture, the things that seeker-sensitive churches removed from their churches are the very things nonbelievers want to experience if they attend a worship service. So I don't think there will be much controversy about bringing back all the spiritual elements and going deeper with our teaching! Vintage worship gatherings are for believers to fully worship our God and be instructed, equipped, and encouraged, even to a deeper level than ever before. This same very spiritual, experiential worship gathering can be a place where nonbelievers can come and experience God and learn about the practices and beliefs of Christians firsthand.

I've heard it said that nonbelievers don't belong in a worship gathering; they can't worship a God they don't know. I disagree. Why? For one thing, we see unbelievers present in the worship gatherings of the early

We live in a world that is looking for something, someone, worthy enough to reverence. Worship—if it is true worship—reverences. It is not primarily about who we are and what we need but about the one reverenced. And if it is true Christian worship, it reverences with unapologetic specificity: the Three-in-One who shaped the entire cosmos, invaded our history, became one of us in Jesus Christ, and was lavishly poured out for us in love. Emerging generations are drawn to reverence as never before. Like Paul in Acts 17, our task in the emerging church is not to protect post-Christian generations from their created need to reverence (see Rom. 1) or the acts of reverence (see 1 Cor. 14) but to reorient them to the one and only God who deserves their reverence.

—Sally Morgenthaler

church. Sally Morgenthaler, in her book *Worship Evangelism,* writes, "Nowhere does Scripture say that seekers do not belong in worship. Nowhere does it say that seekers cannot be moved by observing God's interaction with believers. On the contrary, worship and evangelism are conspicuously linked throughout the Old and New Testaments."[3] Throughout the Old Testament, God's people were encouraged to publicly declare his glory among pagan nations (Isa. 66:19). Moses in the tabernacle gave instruction on how to deal with the non-Israelites who were present during worship (Num. 15:14). In the New Testament, nonbelievers commonly were present at church gatherings, so Paul had to instruct believers on how to make their theology and practices clear to the unsaved among them. In fact, the goal is that "he [the unbeliever] will be convinced by all that he is a sinner and will be judged by all, and the secrets of his heart will be laid bare. So he will fall down and worship God, exclaiming, 'God is really among you!'" (1 Cor. 14:23–25).

+ Truly worshiping in a worship gathering

As I type these words from Scripture, my heart really begins pumping because this is exactly what I believe the emerging church should be about. We should be returning to a no-holds-barred approach to worship and teaching so that when we gather, there is no doubt we are in the presence of a Holy God. I believe both believers and nonbelievers in this emerging culture are hungry for this. It isn't about clever apologetics or careful exegetical and expository preaching or great worship bands. It is about believers in Jesus falling to their knees in worship, truly taking their faith seriously, and even repenting publicly in prayer. It is about the Spirit of God as an evident participant in our midst as the Holy Scriptures are read. This is what people in this emerging culture are drawn to. We no longer have to apologize for what we do. Explain ourselves and teach clearly, yes. But apologize? No longer. Emerging generations are hungering to experience God in worship.

✢ Worship "service" versus worship "gathering"

Before we close this chapter, I want to raise one more semantical issue that to me is pretty important. It used to be that when we used the term *worship service,* we were referring to the time when the church meets to offer our "services" to God in worship. Now, however, it really means something more like a time when "services"—music, preaching, etc.— are offered to the people who attend. Even our "order of service" can feel more like here's what we have for the people, like a menu, than here's what the people bring to God. We have subtly lost the meaning of a phrase we use quite often. A phrase, by the way, that you'll never find in the New Testament.

For the rest of this book, I will use the term worship gathering. It emphasizes that the church gathers together. And it emphasizes that when the church gathers, it is to worship God. Semantics, yes, but think about what we subtly teach people with our words.

Now, in the next chapter, let's talk about what a worship gathering might actually look like.

EMERGING THOUGHTS

1. Have you ever reflected on what the early church did when they gathered and how different (or not) it may be from what we do today? From the very brief description of early church gatherings given in this chapter, are there any elements missing in your church?

2. How do leaders evaluate your worship services or gatherings? By the quality of the program, or by the degree that true worship occurred and that people learned to become more mature disciples of Jesus?

3. What thoughts do you have on why you use the term worship service instead of worship gathering?

The Seeker-Sensitive Service versus the Post-Seeker Worship Gathering

> **No single church can possibly reach everyone. It takes all kinds of churches to reach all kinds of people.**
>
> —Rick Warren, *The Purpose-Driven Church*

While in Mexico for a summer missions trip, I attended a worship gathering. Over two hundred people were tightly packed into a building built for half that number. It was 90 degrees outside and at least 100 degrees inside the crowded sanctuary. This was the first Mexican worship gathering I'd ever attended, and I couldn't help but notice serious differences between the values and methodology of this congregation and those of the typical suburban American church.

For one thing, the beat of their worship music went against my natural rhythm. I actually became somewhat irritated with it. And the songs were extremely long; that bothered me even more. They used horns in the worship band, horns whose piercing sounds became very grating to me. I noticed that people didn't really sing in sync with the worship leader, which caused further frustration. And at one point we had to hold one of our hands up for a prayer exercise. I didn't particularly care to do this, although it seemed natural to everyone around me to worshipfully pray this way.

We stood for what seemed to me like forever; the intense heat made it seem even longer. The first preacher, a woman, came out and began to speak. After a full message at least forty minutes long, we sang again. I thought it was over, but I was wrong. A second preacher (a man this time) emerged from a back room and presented yet another message, almost as long as the first. The service turned out to be almost three hours long! While I sat there, unable to understand the language and incredibly bored, I became (in case you couldn't tell) very critical. I noticed how poorly they had designed their worship service, and I thought of all the things they could do differently. If I were the pastor there, I thought, things would be a heck of a lot different.

But eventually a strong conviction came upon me. I began to notice that I hadn't seen a single person (other then a few youth in my group) leave during the service. In spite of the close quarters and the heat, I never saw anyone doodling, looking bored, or checking their watches. The people were praising God and learning from the Bible; the service perfectly matched who they were. In fact, this particular village was not very large, so to have two hundred people packed in a church meant God was really at work. Of course their approach to worship would be drastically different from mine; I don't live among these people or think like they do. But their pastor and leaders did, and they had designed a gathering that suited their congregation perfectly.

✝ There isn't just one way to worship

This experience provides a good example of the way we must think when designing worship gatherings for the emerging culture. Rick Warren states that "understanding the demographics of your community is important, but understanding the culture of your community is even more important. . . . I use the word culture to refer to the lifestyle and mind-set of those who live around your church."[1]

Exactly. Unfortunately, it's often a challenge to help others understand this point. Talk about changing the way we do things here in the suburbs of America and you may find resistance, usually from older pastors or leaders who have grown attached to a certain way of doing things. If we were talking about the need for unique approaches to worship in the context of cross-cultural missions, there would be no argument. Remember how Hudson Taylor's methods and approach to ministry in China weren't understood by his British superiors? In fact, they were rather upset with him for changing the way they were used to doing things. But because he understood the new culture and worldview, he made the changes that worked for those people. I encourage you to take a look around your worship center next Sunday. If you don't see row upon row of the fresh young faces of people who weren't raised in your church, you probably need to consider making changes to your approach.

In the emerging church, we might not sing with the same beat as did generations past. We might preach differently. Our worship gatherings might have a different design and rhythm and schedule. We might do things that seem unnatural or out of order. We may want it dark instead of all lit up. We might want times of silence and reflection, perhaps more art and visuals. This is only to be expected if our approach to ministry is truly a response to new mindset.

> Absolutely everything we do when we design worship gatherings for the emerging church should have Jesus at the center as we lift up his name. May we never allow creative service design to subtly push Jesus to the sidelines.

✠ A linear versus organic worship gathering

Modern thinkers want things very orderly and systematic because they learn in a logical and progressive manner. They prefer, generally, to sit and listen. Emerging post-Christian generations, on the other hand, long to *experience* a transcendent God during a worship gathering rather than simply learn about him. They want fluidity and freedom rather than a neatly flowing set program. They want to see the arts and a sense of mystery brought into the worship service, rather than focusing on professionalism and excellence. This will shape how a worship gathering is designed.

This organic approach could be called a "vintage-faith" worship gathering. It resonates more in a post-seeker-sensitive culture and really goes back to more of a *vintage* way of expressing our *faith* during worship as believers have done throughout church history. From here on, I will use the term vintage-faith to express the approach.

Let's compare these two types of gatherings: a modern seeker-sensitive worship gathering and a more organic worship gathering for the emerging post-seeker culture.

+ Layout of a more modern linear service

Modern seeker-sensitive services are typically driven by values of excellence, professionalism, and relevance, a response to how unprofessional, sloppy, dull, and irrelevant church had become in so many places. Of course, the intent is to honor God and create a church worship experience

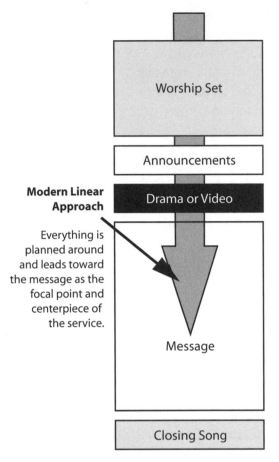

Worship Set

Announcements

Modern Linear Approach

Drama or Video

Everything is planned around and leads toward the message as the focal point and centerpiece of the service.

Message

Closing Song

that would not be out of touch with culture and technology and thus be a hindrance for effective ministry.

For people of a modern mindset, this is exactly what is needed and valued, and of course great things have happened as a result of this emphasis. Among other things, it involves a more linear approach to communication. A typical worship service consists of a few opening songs of praise, some announcements regarding church happenings, then usually a drama, a video clip, or special song, all of which set up the focal point of the worship service—the preaching message. Preaching in the modern contemporary worship service is clearly the centerpiece. Experiencing God, whether we say it outright or not, primarily comes through the preaching. In many seeker-driven services, the corporate worship through music was taken out altogether, elevating the teaching segment even further.

But people with a post-Christian mindset don't share these modern values. They aren't looking for a smoothly run, programmed worship gathering as much as one which screams of a rawer and more vintage spiritual connection.

We must not be afraid to admit that the modern contemporary form of worship services may not connect with emerging generations. We must not be afraid or too prideful to allow them to use new forms of worship.

✢ Designing a more organic worship gathering

In a more organic, vintage approach to a worship gathering, the scriptural theme is woven throughout the entire thing. This theme, which brings us into God's story of how he is moving throughout history and in our lives today, is the focal point of the gathering, instead of a central preached message. In the design of most modern worship services, the teaching (preaching) portion of the gathering is generally where we expect God to do the most work. In an organic worship gathering, however, the teaching begins even as people walk through the doors and continues by way of various elements throughout the whole gathering.

The gathering functions with a good deal of ebb and flow and is usually much more interactive and participatory than an event which is simply attended and absorbed. It is characterized by fluidity rather than by progressive steps and stages; it is more artistic than it is engineered. The visual format of scriptural teaching is equally as important as the spoken word. Of course, it still all needs to be well planned; the transitions must be thought through, worship songs selected in advance. In fact the need for such organization is even greater due to the complexity of this type of gathering. The difference is in values and structure. In an organically designed vintage-faith worship gathering, the theme is intended to flow throughout the event via multiple experiences, multiple ways to participate in the message as a community, and multiple opportunities for the Spirit to minister to those hurting and to convict those in sin.

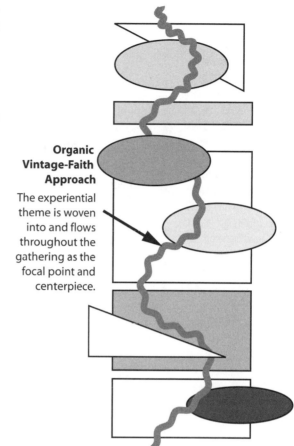

Organic Vintage-Faith Approach

The experiential theme is woven into and flows throughout the gathering as the focal point and centerpiece.

We will be giving lots of examples in the following two chapters of various worship elements and experiences. To see a layout of a vintage-faith worship gathering which took place in our local context, look at appendix A. It will give you an idea of how a worship gathering for several hundred attenders was designed.

The goal is to move from a more consumer-oriented, "sit and watch" event to a more vintage, community oriented participatory gathering which points us toward experiencing God in a transcending way. Not to just *know about* him (which, of course, is very important!) but to *experience* him as well.

I realize there will be emerging churches that do not put this much emphasis on the gathering itself. Smaller gatherings probably won't require as much detail in its planning. However, as a gathering grows, it will eventually come to a point where more attention to layout and thinking through the design of the gathering is needed.

☩ Forgetting the Spirit: a danger for both designs

Both of these approaches to designing a worship gathering can lose their effectiveness if they rely too heavily on programming and technique. In spite of good intentions, quality production and multisensory experiential elements can subtly become the primary values, and we can lose sight of what is most important. Jim Cymbala, in his book *Fresh Faith,* offers us a good reminder, whether we are designing a linear or an organic worship gathering: "Pastors today operate church services that are so regimented there is no place for any spontaneous leading of the Holy Spirit. Events are programmed right down to the minute. Song selections are cast in stone for days in advance. There is no allowance for God to lead anyone in another direction—certainly not during the meeting itself. We aim rather at being 'smooth' and 'slick.' What we value most are great organization and having our act together."[2]

☩ The true designer of our worship gatherings

I'm assuming that we all, as we plan our worship gatherings, spend time on our knees asking God what to do, asking his Spirit to move in us to create a gathering that honors him and accomplishes his purposes. This book is not a study of the Spirit's role in worship, but I cannot close this chapter without a reminder that we are not just putting on a program. The worship gathering you plan each week is a holy event. We must never forget the Holy Spirit's role as the true designer, the one who convicts and moves. We would do well to heed Cymbala's warning.

Lord, no matter what approach we use for worship services, may we never see ourselves as simply designing a program. Lord, may we never rely on human engineering or creative artistry as a substitute for what only your Spirit can do. Jesus, please help us to know how to think about and create gatherings for the people you purchased with your blood and entrusted to our care. May we honor you always and have you at the center of our worship services, whether modern, contemporary, seeker-sensitive or post-seeker-sensitive.

EMERGING THOUGHTS

1. Bearing in mind the analogy of the worship service in Mexico, why are some people with modern mindsets uncomfortable with an emerging church approach to worship?

2. Does your worship gathering lean more to a modern linear approach or an organic vintage-faith approach? Explain.

3. What concerns you about moving toward a more organic approach? What excites you?

4. How can you make sure in the planning of any worship gathering that you rely on the Spirit and not just human methodology?

Overcoming the Fear of Multisensory Worship and Teaching

12

> **"That which was from the beginning, which we have heard, which we have seen with our eyes, which we have looked at and our hands have touched—this we proclaim.**

—1 John 1:1

an, why did you use incense? I'm not sure I like walking over to those prayer stations with all those props; can't we just pray from our seats? Why aren't you just preaching the Bible? I wasn't too comfortable when you had those times of silence, and it's a little too dark in there for me." These were the gentle and concerned comments of a very dear man in his seventies who had just attended our vintage-faith worship gathering. He had spent most of his life in a Baptist church culture. To him, the worship service is singing four songs followed by the preaching of the Bible. He didn't have much experience with multisensory elements in a worship service. I fully understood his concerns. His experience was shaped and formed by modernity and the Reformation. But we need to rethink whether it's okay to appeal to the senses in worship, not only because the Scriptures are pretty clear that worship involves more than just the sense of hearing but also because emerging generations desire a multisensory worship experience.

John 1:1 indicates that in the beginning was the Word, and the Word was with God, and the Word was God. Jesus was the Word; not the Word who became facts or knowledge but the Word who became flesh (John

1:14). The Word became three-dimensional, living, breathing, able to hear, to see, and to touch. The Word himself ate, drank, tasted, had a sense of smell, felt emotion. The Scriptures present a multisensory, multidimensional Word, but some evangelicals in the modern church have reduced him to mere words and facts to learn.

The modern church (in particular the theologically conservative and seeker-sensitive church) has forgotten the multisensory aspects of who God is and the multisensory dimensions of worship.

✛ God created us as multisensory beings

God created us as multisensory creatures and chose to reveal himself to us through all of our senses. Therefore, it's only natural that we worship him using all of our senses. Worship in the temple in Jerusalem was much more than just listening to the words of a sermon. Every sense was involved. You could smell the burning sacrifices and incense, hear the trumpets and temple choirs, and see transcendent architecture of soaring pillars and expansive courtyards. Even the texture and colors of the priests' clothing communicated specific things about God and his covenant with Israel.

Couldn't our worship involve much more of our senses than are allowed in a typical modern contemporary worship service? What does Scripture say about multisensory worship?

Sense of smell. Throughout the Old Testament, the use of incense was common in worship (Exod. 25:6; Mal. 1:11). In the New Testament, we see the Magi presenting Jesus with multisensory gifts (Matt. 2:11). Philippians 4:18 refers to offerings which were "a fragrant offering . . . pleasing

Periodically the offering is taken at stations where incense is lit to symbolically show that financial giving is a direct way of presenting sacrificial worship before God's throne (Rev. 5:8).

to God." Even the church itself is metaphorically to be the "fragrance of the knowledge of him . . . the aroma of Christ" (2 Cor. 2:14–15). Incense is used in the worship described in Revelation 8:4.

Sense of touch. We also know that in worship, the sense of touch was involved in all forms and practices of worship. They laid hands on others when they prayed (Acts 6:6), they clapped their hands (Ps. 47:1), they felt water as they were baptized (Acts 8:38), and they touched the bread in communion (1 Cor. 11:23–24).

Sense of taste. The sense of taste is acknowledged quite often in Scripture. Psalm 34:8 says, "Taste and see that the LORD is good." Psalm 119:103 says, "How sweet are your words to my taste, sweeter than honey to my mouth!" The taste of bread and wine are involved in communion (1 Cor. 11: 23–26). In Revelation 10:10, John writes, "I took the little scroll from the angel's hand and ate it. It tasted as sweet as honey in my mouth, but when I had eaten it, my stomach turned sour."

Sense of hearing. Music was involved in worship, employing all types of praise and musical instruments (Ps. 150). Jesus sang with his disciples (Matt. 26:30). The Scriptures were preached to crowds (Acts 2:14).

Sense of sight. Throughout the Scriptures we see great emphasis on the visual in worship. God valued the visual beauty of worship in the tabernacle (Exod. 25:3–7; 26:1–2) and in the temple (1 Kings 6:29–30) where we see detailed descriptions of color, texture, and design.

Notice the place of senses in the table on page 130.[1]

God created the senses, so why shouldn't we use them?
—HOWARD HENDRICKS

God communicated in a multisensory way and received multisensory worship. In the emerging church, we must revisit a holistic multisensory approach to worship, an approach which is biblical.

✠ God uses multisensory teaching

In Scripture, from Genesis through Revelation, we see displays not only of multisensory worship but even of multisensory teaching. God uses object lessons, miraculous events, and supernatural displays of his power to help people learn about him and respond in worship. He didn't just speak; he spoke out of a burning bush. He didn't just dictate the law; he wrote it with his own finger. He didn't just lead Israel through the desert; he led them with a pillar of smoke and a pillar of fire. Jesus didn't simply heal the blind man; he made mud with his spit and smeared it over his eyelids.

Senses Involved	Mt. Sinai (Exod. 19)	Isaiah's vision in the Temple (Isa. 6)	The Last Supper (Matt. 26)	Heavenly Worship (Rev. 4–5, 19)
Hearing	Thunder Trumpet blast Voice of God	Voice of God Singing of cherubim	Voice of Jesus Singing together	Singing of angels and heavenly hosts Lightning
Seeing	Lightning Cloud of Glory	Lord seated on throne Six-winged cherubim House filled with smoke	Bread, cup Incarnate presence of Christ	Jesus on a Throne Rainbow Four living creatures Angelic beings Powerful visuals described
Touching	Ground quaking	Lips touched with live coal	Disciples leaning on one another Bread and wine to lips	Casting crowns Bowing to the ground
Smelling	Smoke and fire in the air	Smell of smoke	Aroma of wine, bread, and meal	Golden bowls of incense
Tasting		Coal in mouth	Eating bread and drinking wine	Marriage supper of the Lamb

God's prophets did outlandish things to communicate his truth with more than words. Isaiah walked around town naked for three years; Ezekiel lay on his side for weeks on end, building little miniature villages out of mud. Jeremiah carried around rotten fruit. Even if people refused to obey the prophets' instructions, they certainly wouldn't forget what they had heard, seen, and smelled. Teaching as well as worship can be multisensory, as God has clearly demonstrated.

+ Now we can move ahead . . .

I needed to address the issue of multisensory worship because the next several chapters will be talking a lot about multisensory, experiential worship and teaching. We will discuss various ways that we can incorporate hearing, seeing, smelling, and touching into a worship gathering with the goal of broadening how we worship God. This isn't just about clever tricks or trendy new ideas. These are ancient ways of worship demonstrated throughout the Scriptures.

The danger, of course, is focusing so much on experience that we teach people to respond only by feelings and emotions. The goal is not to manipulate people's emotions through experiences or preaching or use of multisensory experiences. We need discernment. I believe the more the emerging church uses multisensory worship and teaching, the stronger and deeper our use of Scripture needs to be. Those of us who are emerging leaders need to make sure we are using Scripture to guide and teach as we worship. This will put Jesus all the more at the center of our worship gatherings, not move him away! More on this in the following chapters. But now let's take a creative look at worship gatherings.

EMERGING THOUGHTS

1. Have you ever considered that multisensory worship and communication are actually biblical? Why don't we hear much about this topic? Are there other examples from the Scriptures you can think of?

2. What are some benefits to using multisensory worship? What are some dangers or cautions?

3. Do we in leadership need to look at how we currently define worship and perhaps redefine it?

Chapter 13

Creating a Sacred Space for Vintage Worship

> **It is an essential condition of any traditional religious service that the space in which it is conducted must be invested with some measure of sacrality.... If an audience is not immersed in an aura of mystery and symbolic otherworldliness, then it is unlikely that it can call forth the state of mind required for a nontrivial religious experience.**
>
> —Neil Postman, *Amusing Ourselves to Death*

Neil Postman, in his insightful book *Amusing Ourselves to Death*, warns that television and media are dumbing down our capacity to think and process truth. Postman alerts us that religion itself is losing its transcendence and reverence as we have moved into an era of communicating our faith via media. He claims that we have forgotten how important it is to create a sacred space in which to worship. Now, I know that we can worship anytime and don't need any special environment. But when it comes to our regular place to gather for worship, Postman's point is nevertheless valid.

In the next few chapters, we will look at various aspects of designing and thinking through a worship gathering. Since the first thing people experience as they attend a worship gathering is the worship space, let's look at that first.

sa·cred

adj. associated with or dedicated to God or a god, or regarded with reverence because of this[1]

✛ Sacred space: the importance of aesthetics and environment

When we first considered starting a worship gathering for emerging generations at Santa Cruz Bible Church, I took a mixed group of nonbelievers and believers in their early twenties to an excellent, seeker-sensitive contemporary worship service. We even visited the service which was geared to reach a younger crowd. Afterward we gathered, almost like a focus group, so I could listen to them talk about the experience. It proved to be a memorable and insightful session. What's interesting is that most of their early comments were about what they *visually* experienced. Let's walk through their comments together and think about how they might relate to your context. Remember, their comments were about an excellent seeker-sensitive contemporary service that was reaching people whom I would consider to have a modern mindset.

✛ "It didn't look like a church in there; it looked like a Wal-Mart."

This comment caught me totally off guard. A Wal-Mart? It was a brand-new building with state-of-the-art equipment—great lighting, nice video screens, and contemporary architecture. Most pastors would absolutely love to have a worship center like this. But my "focus group" friends said the building had the air of a chain church, somewhat corporate and unspiritual.

So I asked what they would like in a church building. "Architecture that shows a respect for God," was one reply. "I like churches like the ones I saw when I was in Europe." "Gothic cathedrals are very cool," said another. Emerging generations are definitely attracted to architecture and to an atmosphere that shows that there is truly something spiritual happening. I was surprised at how strongly they felt about these things. What do you think they might say about the worship space you meet in?

Examine your building through the eyes of someone from the emerging culture and decorate accordingly. Consider forming a team of people in their teens to late twenties and anyone else you feel represents the mindset of the emerging culture. Ask nonbelievers to give you input on how to design a sacred space that will best relate to them and their peers.

Although the worship gatherings I lead currently meet in a modern contemporary building, we wanted it to have a vintage-faith feel. We may not be able to meet in a gothic cathedral, but we can creatively and without much cost bring a sense of the ancient into a contemporary room. We began by purchasing eight-foot-high black curtains like those used in trade shows. Each week we place them in an arch around the outer rim of chairs. On the curtains we display the artwork of people from the church community. I have seen churches who have hung bed sheets for dividers to create a more intimate space. It doesn't have to be expensive. When creating a sacred space becomes a value, cost is not a factor and creativity can solve a lot of problems.

Because we wanted people to have a visual experience from the moment they walked into the room, the first thing people see is a table, behind which several people are stationed to greet people and answer questions. This table is draped with velvet and tapestries and has a backdrop of art. Scattered on the table are Celtic crosses and candles. The volunteer team in charge of our decor is led by an artist and has found ways to incorporate texture, light, fabric, and various unusual materials around the room at minimal cost. They take great pride in what they do and look on their work and ministry as designing sacred space.

We've even used old props from Easter musicals on the stage. Roman pillars communicate that something ancient is being discussed here. Remember, the point is not just to look cool but to do anything that helps convey the fact that Christianity is a nonmodern religion. I personally would love to meet in a medieval cathedral with pews—with cushions on the pews and a heated sanctuary!

We want the aesthetics to scream out who we are and what we are about the moment people walk in the doors. If you were to enter the stairway that leads up to the meeting space at Solomon's Porch, an emerging church in Minneapolis, you would probably be instantly taken with the artwork on the walls and ceiling. It is beautifully painted with the words *shalom, peace, justice,* and *love* above a mural of the city landscape, along with an American Indian and a grouping of people representing cultures around the world. Placing artwork in the main entry of the church makes a powerful statement.

It's ironic, and importantly so, that as we spend more and more time in virtual reality, we take "actual reality" more (not less) seriously. We care more and more about aesthetics, color, feel, ambience, quality, history, uniqueness in our physical surroundings. I think that the more time we spend in virtual reality—online, in theaters, watching screens of all sorts, even having our heads in books (which are just a lower-tech form of virtual reality, aren't they?)—the more time we need to decompress, defragment, and debug as human beings with bodies, senses, in space and time—in real places, places with a feel, with gravity, with actual atmosphere. Of course, God's creation is the ultimate arena of "real reality," but our churches should be wonderful sanctuaries within and in harmony with God's creation.

—Brian McLaren

Do not underestimate the differing aesthetic values of different people groups. What feels like sacred space to one mindset may be ugly or repellent to another.

True, we can worship anywhere, anytime—in an igloo, a palace, or a cardboard shack. I have had powerful worship experiences in a shabby cold basement with ugly cinderblock walls. So aesthetics is not an end in itself. But in our culture, which is becoming more multisensory and less respectful of God, we have a responsibility to pay attention to the design of the space where we assemble regularly.

+ "It was too bright in there; I thought church would be darker."

In the emerging culture, darkness represents spirituality. We see this in Buddhist temples, as well as in Catholic and Orthodox churches. Darkness communicates that something serious is happening. Rick Warren, in *The Purpose-Driven Church,* makes a case for the importance of lighting from the opposite perspective. "Lighting has a profound effect on people's moods," he writes. "Most churches are too dark. Maybe it's conditioning from all those years Christians spent worshipping in the catacombs. . . . Somehow, churches have gotten the idea that dimming the lights creates a more spiritual mood. I completely disagree. I believe that church buildings should be full of light."[2]

However, Rick advises at the beginning of his chapter, "Plan the service with your target in mind." For his Orange County, California, baby boomer audience, what he says about light and darkness is exactly right! But to emerging generations who are seeking a spiritual experience in church and a different kind of reverence in their approach to worship, darkness is more desirable. Different audiences have different values.

Lighting should reflect who you are and who attends your church. Time and time again I hear how important the darker environment is to those at our vintage-faith worship gathering. Attenders feel they can freely pray in a corner by themselves without feeling that everyone is staring at them. Not that it's pitch black! We brighten the lights during the message so people can see their Bibles and read the notes we hand to them as they enter. We make sure there is adequate lighting on the faces of those speaking. Perhaps in some way the whole concert scene, where the lights go out as the band plays, has had some influence on emerging generations' desire for a sense of darkness in worship. Whatever the reason, people all across America are noticing this shift and turning down the lights in their services.

I had the privilege of attending a Tuesday night prayer service at the Brooklyn Tabernacle church where Jim Cymbala is pastor. Guess what? On the night I was there, the lights were kept really dim. So low I could barely read. This communicated the message: "This is a prayer service. This is a spiritual event." Have you realized that Jesus' most intense moments of prayer took place in the darkness of night? He went up on a mountainside all night to pray in the dark (Luke 6:12). He spent time praying at night in the Garden of Gethsemane. Conversely, I know that many New Age meetings and even some Wiccan meetings take place in very bright, well-lit rooms, with the participants all wearing white. I don't think we can make too much of a case that darkness is a bad thing. After all, we can sin just as easily in the daylight as in the dark.

✢ "Why does the band disappear behind a curtain? It feels like a performance."

At the church our focus group visited, curtains on the stage would close when the worship band finished playing, and the speaker would address the audience from the front portion of the stage. It worked great for the large crowd attending, but it backfired with our group of twenty-somethings. To them, this felt like the band was there to perform, rather than to worship God.

At our vintage-faith worship gathering, we try to avoid doing anything that suggests that the band or the speaker are there to perform or that hints that they are "above" those who attend. We try to bring the band and the speaker as close to the people as possible. This means taking the extra effort to build an extended stage out into the audience, but it's worth it, since such efforts are valued in today's culture. The band U2, on their Elevation Tour, created a huge heart-shaped walkway that extended far into the crowd. In fact, quite a few bands are doing this sort of thing today. Even the over-the-top band KISS, which is known for their productions, moved to having a ministage out among the crowd to break the barrier down between them and the people. Why? Because bands increasingly value being with the people instead of being far above them.

Worship gathering at Grace, in London, England. This particular gathering focused on Rembrandt's painting The Return of the Prodigal Son *and was based on Henri Nouwen's book about the painting. (Photo © Steve Collins. Used with permission.)*

To take this a step further, who says we even need to see the worship band? Shouldn't the focus of worship be on God, not on the leader and the musicians? Have we modeled ourselves after rock concerts in this respect, without even realizing it?

Obviously, the leader needs to be able to give direction. To some degree the worship leader serves as a priest before the people, leading them in worship to God. But I am becoming uneasy with the way we call attention to our worship leaders or bands as they face the congregation, usually with colored lighting highlighting their presence. In the ancient temple in Jerusalem, the musicians and choir would place themselves on top of a platform in the Court of Israel facing the altar just inside the Nikanor Gates. They would pause several times in their worship, and the priests would sound silver trumpets and all the people in the court would prostrate themselves before God's presence. This shows how they were intentionally not the focus of the people as they sang. In fact, although their music was loud enough to carry all around the temple itself, most people could not even see them in the inner court. Likewise, in church architecture in the past, the choir was often placed in the rear of the building, which elminates any sense of performance or focus on the singers.

Josh Fox, the worship leader at our vintage-faith gatherings, often sets up the worship band in the back of the room in which we gather for worship. He may start from up front at the beginning of the service, but after a transition, he will continue leading from the rear. Not only does this keep the band from being the focus of attention, it also adds to the sense that we are all worshiping together as a community without any of us being more significant than the others. We set up an empty cross on the stage to direct our focus to the fact that we are here to praise God and worship the crucified and risen Jesus. I believe in this so much that I imagine we will eventually place the worship band and leader in the back of the meeting space every week. I know of one church that, to eliminate the focus on the band, even uses back-lighting so the band is totally in shadow. However we do it, I think we need to get away from making the worship leader and band the unintentional focal point when we worship.

✛ "Where were the crosses? It seemed more like a theater than a church."

So many newly built modern churches, in order to avoid appearing too churchy, have no crosses or other religious symbols. Ironically, people in emerging generations, even nonreligious people, often wear crosses,

Egyptian ankhs, and other religious symbols. Our worship facilities should clearly communicate a sense of spirituality. So even though we meet in a brand-new, warehouselike worship center, we bring in large wooden crosses to put up on the stage and often place smaller crosses around the room. Many of the paintings we display incorporate Christian scenes and symbols. Most of our PowerPoint slides incorporate ancient art, stained glass, and Christian symbols.

We also use a lot of candles, not just because they are trendy but because they symbolize sobriety, spirituality, simplicity, quietude, and contemplation. It's not surprising that the set of a nationally televised fundraiser following the September 11th tragedy was barren except for celebrities and candles. Why? Because the mellow, flickering light of candles creates a mood that speaks of the serious, somber purpose of such an event.

The early church used a lot of candles, but not just because they didn't have electricity! They used them symbolically too. When it was time to pray, they often would light a lamp to symbolize the light of Christ shining among them. When someone was baptized, they would be given a candle or a lamp as they walked out of the water, symbolizing that they possessed the light of Christ. Religious Jews today still light candles weekly for Sabbath. Everyone likes the mood that candlelight sets in a Christmas Eve service. Why shouldn't they be an ongoing part of who we

Spaces such as this one are created to show how important prayer is in worship gatherings and are set up in various places around the room. In this photo, worshipers, surrounded by candles, write out their prayers.

are and what we try to communicate throughout the year? The great richness in the symbolism of candles speaks volumes to the emerging culture.

Remember how Jacob in Genesis 28:10–22 set up a pillar of stones and anointed it with oil as a memorial of where he had dreamed of the stairway to heaven? In parallel fashion, you might consider creating memorial symbols with artwork or props that represent the theme of a series of messages or a communal experience. We had people dip their hands in paint and leave their handprints on a large canvas to show how we are all one body. Because of the colors and the quality of the work, it really looked like a nice piece of artwork. We hung it on our walls afterward, and it served as a memorial of that biblical teaching and of that event.

Many of our modern churches have woefully neglected thoughtful architectural beauty in the design of their buildings. Most of our buildings no longer have stained glass, or if they do, quite often it is of the tacky 1970s variety. This is unfortunate because our emerging culture highly values art. Stained glass can communicate the story of our faith, just as it did in centuries past when people were unable to read the Scriptures for themselves. We often use video projectors to project stained-glass images as a focal point during worship, Scripture reading, or even during the sermon. Your building may not be a cathedral, but you can convey that sense of timeless beauty, order, and sacred space by finding ways to use architectural or stained-glass images on your screens.

No matter where you gather, if you are creative and value beauty, you can transform any meeting place into a sacred sanctuary of ancient faith. I have seen this accomplished in a rented senior citizen's center, in a giant church with hideous out-of-date architecture and ugly carpet, and in very modern and contemporary buildings. It can even happen in a high-school gym.

✛ "Why is the speaker way up on that stage? It feels like he is talking down at us."

My focus group immediately noticed that the speaker stood on a platform about four feet higher than their seats. Now, you and I know that this is so people can see him or her clearly. But remember, this group likely mistrusts Christians, especially leaders. Anything that feels like a performance or communicates hierarchical spiritual leadership is suspect.

So here we are in the church putting our leaders up on a stage, while pop-culture performers are trying to put themselves closer to the people. In our worship gatherings, we have built a lower platform which extends into the seating so I am with the people instead of way above them. We arrange the seating in a curved fashion so people are looking at each other too and not just the stage. We also set up some round tables, to provide a community feel. We used to use mainly all tables until we had too many people to do that. Of course, the room and the number of people determine what you can do, but try to avoid the "stage and audience" feel as best you can. Interestingly, in the early church, the speaker actually sat down when he spoke, following the pattern practiced in the synagogue at that time.

Just this week, I met with a nonbelieving college student who is an anthropology major and chose to study our church for a class project. She has been attending our vintage-faith Sunday night services and interviewing our staff. When she came into the office to interview me, I ended up interviewing her, asking questions about what she liked, what she didn't, what she noticed, and what her beliefs are. One of the first things she said was that she noticed immediately that I was not on a stage when I spoke. She thought that "all preachers speak from a platform" and said she really appreciated that I was down at her level.

Two things I think we can conclude about aesthetics and environment for the emerging church:

1. *Aesthetics and environment are important.* I can't begin to count the number of times visitors have commented first on the atmosphere. "I really loved the candles." "It was great to see the artwork on the walls." "I loved the decor." "I'm so glad it was dark in there; it allowed me to pray." You might find it helpful to survey people, specifically about your worship building, but don't ask just those who regularly attend your church! If the atmosphere were a problem for them, they wouldn't be there. If your church is serious about engaging the post-Christian culture, remember that people are highly sensitive to anything that looks or feels corporate or points to a modern institution or organized religion. I know of a church that has two-hundred-plus people when they gather, and 90 percent of their seating is couches! Think of what that communicates. And when the pastor speaks, he stands among them instead of in front.

2. *Aesthetics and environment should reflect who you are and who you are trying to reach in your community. Don't just copy someone else.* The emerging church is not a McDonald's chain church in which all churches look alike. Each community needs to reflect

who they are. The more your worshiping community is producing and creating the space themselves, the more it will reflect who you are. I hope examples in this chapter stimulate ideas for what would be right for your community.

The website www.vintagefaith.com offers further examples of visuals used in worship services, as well as links to other sites where you can see how other churches are incorporating some of these concepts.

EMERGING THOUGHTS

1. What do you think a focus group of nonchurched people in their twenties would say if they attended one of your worship services? What observations do you think they would make about the visual experience?

2. Why should visual objects such as candles, crosses, and decor be used? Can you explain any biblical reasons for this?

Expecting the Spiritual, Expressing the Arts

> " **If you can't go to church and at least for a moment be given transcendence, if you can't pass briefly from this life into the next, then I can't see why anyone should go. Just a brief moment of transcendence causes you to come out of church a changed person.**
>
> —Garrison Keillor

My wife and I were visiting a major city. We had heard about a 9:30 Sunday evening compline service at an Episcopal church and that there were a lot of younger people attending, so we decided to visit. Arriving a few minutes late, we were surprised to find no parking places left; we ended up parking on the grass. We made our way through large wooden doors into this cathedral-like, gothic old building built in the 1930s. The service was already underway. The sanctuary was crowded with over four hundred people, many of whom were even sitting on the cold cement floor. We ended up sitting on the floor with them.

The average age of the worshipers seemed to be early twenties and late teens, although there were also sprinklings of other ages. It definitely felt like a youth service. However, there was no loud music, no Delirious or Matt Redman pop songs. In fact, it was quite the opposite. In the front of the church, ten or twelve men dressed in robes sang chantlike choir songs in English, none of which were familiar to me except for the Apostles' Creed. Yet the songs were scriptural and God-focused. Though there were plenty of teenagers, there was no rustling, jokes, or whispered comments from the back row. Everyone simply sat, totally quiet, listening.

Many had their eyes shut in meditation; others looked toward the ceiling. I saw no Christian T-shirts or WWJD bracelets. Instead, I saw many punkish teens, a lot of college students who, judging from their dress, looked more artistic, and, of course, average younger people as well. But what was fascinating was that the whole experience didn't reek of the contemporary evangelical form of Christianity. There were absolutely no gimmicks, no hype, no cheerleading. After an hour it just ended. No big send-off or wrap-up song or applause. We simply all walked silently into the night.

Now, from a pastor's standpoint, I couldn't help but wonder whether any discipleship was happening through this church. Did people ever open their Bibles? Where were they serving in ministry? After just one visit, I had no way of knowing. But what I did know was that this had been a flat-out, unapologetic, Christ-focused event and that young people had come in droves to be a part of it. I had seen them praying, listening to the quiet soothing voices of the choir singing scriptural lyrics, and meditating.

✛ Expecting and expressing the spiritual in the emerging church

Since emerging generations really want to experience the spiritual, shouldn't our worship gatherings provide that for which they crave? Shouldn't it be a place to connect with God, to breathe, to slow down and experience some peace as they focus on God and lift up the name of Jesus?

> *My soul is lost, my friend. Tell me how do I begin again? . . .*
> *With these hands, I pray for the faith, Lord. . . . I pray for your*
> *love, Lord.* —BRUCE SPRINGSTEEN, "MY CITY OF RUINS"

I have heard a great deal about the ecumenical community of Taizé in a small village in eastern France. In the summer, three to six thousand young people stay there each week for prayer, meditative singing, and spiritual renewal. These young people come from post-Christian Europe—Germany, Italy, England, and elsewhere. And they are drawn by the tens of thousands not to a hyped Christian concert or revved-up summer camp with games and swimming pools and ropes courses but to a weeklong

Christ-centered contemplative experience. They gather in a worship space that's darkened and filled with symbols; they sit on the floor and enjoy extended periods of worshipful silence.

What an incredible thing that post-Christian generations desire a real encounter with God, rather than entertainment or a lighter version of a spiritual experience. As we think through what to do in our own contexts, let's not be content to fill every minute of our gatherings with noise, videos, and talking, only to send people away disillusioned and still hungering to connect with their maker. Or worse yet, let's not let them leave thinking that what they just experienced is all there is to Christianity.

✠ But our younger people think being serious is boring

Many times as I have spoken around the country, I have been told that many churches are only just now incorporating more programmed pop worship songs and moving away from liturgical elements to a more revved-up program. They think that to do some of the things I am suggesting in these chapters is a step backward! They say, "Our younger people think being serious in church is boring!"

Even though I absolutely believe that Christians need to have fun, my assumption is that leaders of youth or young adult ministries are already providing the people they serve lots of fun things to do as a community. By no means am I saying to stop having crazy games for junior highers or to stop taking college students on water-skiing retreats. By no means am I saying not to use humor or to laugh together in your worship gathering (I personally use a lot of humor when I speak—sometimes too much!) What I am saying is that we cannot shortchange the reason we are gathering in worship; we also need to get serious about God. We are seeking his presence, and we had better not take that lightly. We do need to encounter God, to take communion, to sit in the quiet, to hear his voice. It may vary depending on the age and maturity of who you are gathering in your church to worship, but even in junior high, elements of serious worship can be brought in and experienced.

✠ A horrible and boring church experience

One Sunday while I was an undergraduate student at Colorado State University, I decided to go to church. I was not a regular church attender at the time; this was my attempt to walk in from the street and try to meet God. As I entered the building, I immediately felt weird and out of place. It was dead silent except for a droning organ. I didn't get a friendly greeting as I sat down in the pew, and I felt very alone. People around me talked only in whispers. I also couldn't help but be distracted by this very ugly, horrible orange carpet on the floor. It must have recently been cleaned, because it smelled strongly of some chemical that was making me dizzy. The service started with some liturgical elements, including a time of silence and some repeated creeds. (Many of the very things I am going to say to do in these chapters!) But it was lifeless and routine. Nothing was explained, so I was totally lost. The pastor used no humor and exhibited no joy. On top of that, the organ made me feel like I was in a funeral. No wonder I left as soon as I could.

This experience is not a good example of what I am talking about doing. Rather, employ some of the things this church did with life, explanation, joy, better music, and without that horrible smell coming from an exceptionally clean carpet. (I do think an orange carpet should be avoided if possible!) As you read these chapters, think of bringing new life to your current service. You may need to change the music style. But don't give up on the "serious" things in a worship service for emerging generations. Instead bring new life to ancient beauty.

✠ Incorporating arts and the visual into worship

I confess that I am not a sports fan. I haven't even watched the Super Bowl in the last ten years and don't remember the last time I sat down to watch an Olympic event. For me sports is bowling and shooting pool. I have lots of friends who love sports, of course, and I do appreciate athletic skill. But I am much more enthused about comics art or music than sports. My background is in drawing presentational graphics for architects. So for me, fun is attending a comics art convention, listening to one of my favorite bands in a local club, or walking through an art exhibit.

When I first entered the evangelical world, I discovered that virtually every pastor I met was into sports. Since most of their sermon illustrations were sports related, I somehow felt a bit lonely and very uncoordinated at church—like a misfit. In staff meetings, as they rattled off names of sports celebrities and teams I had never heard of, I would politely nod and smile as my mind drifted off to think about the latest Brian Setzer CD, which innovatively and eclectically combined rockabilly guitar with sixteen horns for a version of a Glenn Miller big-band song, and to wonder who the graphic artist was who drew the cartoonlike CD cover and if the retro-lounge fonts he used could be incorporated into our church bulletin design.

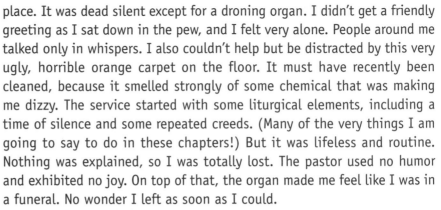

Of course, even the most hyped up and exciting Pentecostal worship can become rote in time. After five or twenty-five years of shouting, dancing, clapping, or even writhing on the floor, these rituals (they are rituals—after a while, at least) become as much an expected and customary part of worship as crossing oneself or fingering a rosary. These kinds of services may not seem like a funeral (as the service Dan refers to did), but they can seem like a sales rally for plastics, or like a professional wrestling event, or like a three ring circus. Exciting may be better than boring, but meaningful and authentic trumps both, I think.

—BRIAN MCLAREN

I usually felt I was in a different world in that respect, and I never heard the arts discussed, unless someone was thinking of using a Willow Creek drama to illustrate a sermon point. That was about as artsy as the talk would get. It seemed as though churches all across America had volleyball nights and softball leagues but gave little attention to artists. But then a fresh wind for artists began blowing in the church.

✝ Encouraging the artistic community in your church

Over the past couple of years, I have met more and more pastors and leaders (usually from the emerging church movement) who are actually into the arts. I have been hearing how emerging churches are incorporating paintings in their preaching as illustrations. Some churches even allowed artists to paint during the worship time as an expression of worship. After all, doesn't God value creativity? God's Spirit filled Bezalel and Oholiab in Exodus 31:1–11 to have "skill, ability and knowledge in all kinds of crafts—to make artistic designs." Great attention was given to the artistic design of holy instruments used in worship, designs that God himself gave instructions for. Our values in culture are now shifting, allowing the arts back into the church.

Thank you so much for sharing your background, Dan. It always helps to know where an author is coming from. God wired you to be a champion for the arts in the church.
Go for it.

—RICK WARREN

> The emerging church must be 100 percent about worshiping God when we gather. No matter what creative form it takes, worship cannot be merely a meeting, a presentation, or a program. We must worship or we cheat God and those who come to our gatherings.

A few years ago, as we began our Sunday-night worship gatherings with a vintage-faith approach, we saw more and more artists attending and becoming part of our community. As we talked about the arts and paid attention to how we used them, a grassroots group of artists formed and started meeting monthly in our church. After some discussion it was decided that we should host an exhibit to give Christian artists the opportunity to express themselves. Our first event, called Frames, attracted over fifty artists who displayed fantastic creative expressions of all types. And they had been sitting in our midst the whole time! Over six hundred people attended. We had to expand it to two nights the following year, as over eighty artists participated and over eight hundred people attended. We even added a children's art section.

Since the emerging culture highly values the arts, shouldn't the church embrace and encourage artists and art enthusiasts just as much as it does athletes and sports fans?

+ Creative expression in worship

When we design worship gatherings, we look for ways to incorporate the arts. One of the ways we do this is to use art consistently in all of our PowerPoint presentations during the musical worship, teaching, and prayer meditations. So many wonderful artistic depictions of biblical stories are available. For example, Gustave Doré is an incredible French artist from the 1800s who created amazing biblical scenes. Instead of using some of the more cheesy backgrounds included in the PowerPoint software, why not use art from Doré or other great artists? Watch out for the rather goofy or funky Christian clip-art stuff. If you search, there is plenty of beautiful art out there. Or even better, what about the artists in your church? It is becoming fairly easy to take a digital photo of a painting or to scan photographs. Display the art of people from your church on the walls. If you have curtains in your meeting place, try hanging paintings and light sculptures on them.

Using powerful visuals while you teach is another wonderful way to incorporate art into your gathering. Or overlay art with Scripture quotations during meditation or poetry readings. You might set aside times for silence, accented only by painted scenes of biblical events or various depictions of the face of Christ.

Drama is another art form that can be fantastically effective—or embarrassingly horrible. In our gatherings, we rarely use a Willow Creek–type sketch in which a conflict is dramatized before the message is given. But we do use a lot of dramatic Scripture and poetry readings, or we'll have actors express various emotions while a script is being read. During a series on the Ten Commandments, we had a running drama in which a few actors briefly represented each commandment through a dramatic exchange. They didn't speak; they simply acted out how they felt the commandment could be portrayed. We've had actors present monologues in which we hear their prayer to or dialogue with God about some struggle. The point is to use drama in ways that resonate with our culture.

Just last week I was teaching about Abraham and the covenant God made with him. I used two actors, a male and a female dressed in ancient garb, to dramatically read the long narratives from Genesis. This proved to work really well to convey that we were telling a story using the Scriptures themselves.

✠ Incorporating the ancient into worship gatherings

A major criticism of the church today is that it is a modern, Americanized, organized religion that has lost its ancient roots and sense of mystery. But what do emerging generations value? The ancient—the mystery of religious faiths of old. But what do they see when they come to our churches?

In the emerging church we need to bring back the ancient symbols and talk about the Jewish roots of our faith. For example, our church once asked a Jewish believer to talk to us about Passover and walk us through a messianic Seder dinner. Another time, he presented a Jewish perspective on the Messiah and his return.

We also have what we call Hymn Times. We place a large velvet chair on the stage, and before we sing each hymn, someone sits in the chair to read about that hymn, explaining why, when, and by whom it was written. Good hymns go over really well in a post-Christian culture because they are fresh, unknown, and reek of history. They teach deep theological truth and focus on God and his attributes. As long as people can relate to the musical accompaniment we use, we could easily incorporate numerous hymns into our services. Younger generations seem to love hymns, and we sing many of them. Even a couple in their seventies attend our worship gathering because we do more hymns than the service they had been attending.

The "Hymn Chair" on one side of the stage is a place where the stories behind the hymns are read. Scripture is also often read from this chair.

+ Honoring older generations in front of younger ones

Emerging generations need and actually are seeking individuals who have been down the road of life before them. So even in worship gatherings which are mainly composed of younger people, you can bring in older people who have walked with God for forty or fifty years to share their testimonies and tell stories relating to the sermon topic. When we were teaching on Ecclesiastes 12, we asked a couple in their eighties to talk about what it is like to face death. During a series on personal worship, we brought in a man in his midseventies to tell how his friendship with God has developed over the years. Another time, we asked a couple to talk about how they've kept their marriage alive for more than fifty years. Most of these people did not regularly attend our vintage-faith service but came to offer the wisdom and knowledge they'd gleaned over the years.

> *One generation will commend your works*
> *to another.* —PSALM 145:4

A group of mostly retired people at Santa Cruz Bible Church gathers once a month for a hymn sing. One time they came into the Graceland service, twenty of them, and stood on stage and led us in several hymns. It was great! I don't know if they appreciated the dim lighting, and I think they were caught off guard by having to squeeze in between all the candles, but it was a wonderful experience for everyone as a way to honor older generations in front of younger generations.

✢ Males *and* females in roles up front

In the emerging culture, the role of women in the church is a huge issue. People in the emerging generations think of churches as male-dominated and oppressive of females. So whatever your theology may be about the role of women in the church, I would still highly encourage you to have females in up-front roles as much as possible, whether it is teaching, giving announcements, leading worship, sharing testimonies, or reading Scripture. This is critical for the emerging church.

✢ Children and families in worship gatherings

We need to rethink how we tend to separate the members of families, who come to worship. We usually put the children in Sunday school during the worship gathering, even when they're in junior high and high school, so some families never actually attend a worship gathering together.

Perhaps the modern church has been responsible for subtly teaching parents that the church, rather than the parents, is responsible for the spiritual formation of their children. But Scripture indicates it's the parents' responsibility to teach their children the things of God (Deut. 11:19). The church should supplement rather than replace the parents' role.

That's why we work hard to find ways to incorporate children and families into our worship services. The parents in emerging generations are protective of their families, perhaps in response to what they've observed in previous generations with so many families splitting up or raising their children poorly. We invite children to be part of the first twenty minutes of our gathering, occasionally asking one or two to read Scripture. On occasion we have asked children to sing in the worship band. After the first part of the gathering is over, the children are dismissed into classes where they receive age-appropriate teaching. Why not occasionally design entire worship gatherings specifically for families? Even child dedications can provide occasions to show the importance of the parents' role in the upbringing and spiritual formation of their children. Perhaps the church needs to spend more time teaching parents how to teach their children the ways of God and kingdom living.

✛ The use and abuse of technology

Although technology is a wonderful ally for ministry, it has great potential for abuse and distraction as well. I have attended worship services in which I've actually become dizzy from all the flashy effects on the screen. This may be news to some, but people really are not impressed anymore with fancy PowerPoint special effects and videos.

Video clips can be effective if used tastefully, especially to tell a story. In our church we use video clips from movies only every few months, both to avoid bringing too much modern culture into our services and so that when we do use them, they are a refreshing and effective tool. We never use a clip from a movie that we wouldn't recommend in its entirety. Though this might appear to be legalistic, I feel a responsibility to use only films that I believe would honor God (Phil. 4:8).

The use of street interviews conducted at local campuses and malls can help Christians gain insights on the thoughts of nonbelievers and enable nonbelievers sitting in the pews to hear their thoughts voiced. And conducting the interviews can prompt those you interview to think a little deeper, or at least differently, than they would have if you hadn't come along with your questions and camera. They may even visit your service just to see themselves on the big screen. I know of one person we interviewed who ended up attending and eventually became a believer.

Additionally, it can be effective to use video looping of images or colors, or to use video for the purpose of slowing down and focusing on Scripture or prayer.

I believe we'll see a huge increase in this sort of use of video in worship.

✛ Using the arts through technology in worship

Here are some examples of how you could use projected images of ancient or modern art in your services. These are all done by nonprofessionals using simple methods. The first PowerPoint slide shown incorporates art by Doré which powerfully illustrates scriptural stories. It could be used for meditation, for musical interludes, or to illustrate the main point while the preacher talks.

Another way of reminding worshipers that Christianity is not a modern religion is to use stained-glass images as backgrounds for song lyrics or Scripture readings, as shown in the second slide.

The use of photographs taken by church members to illustrate the lyrics of a worship song or Scripture text also emphasizes the value of local artists. The third slide shows an example.

I think you can see the difference between these slides and the Power-Point slides usually used in business presentations. Keep it simple. Avoid words that move quickly and flashy graphics. (Check out the website www.vintagefaith.com for links to sites with art resources.)

+ **We cannot afford this! We don't have the staff to pull this off!**

I can proudly say that in our church, we have carried out virtually all of the ideas I have discussed so far with volunteers. Volunteers get the song list by Wednesday, put all the PowerPoint slides together, and email the presentation or bring it to us on Sunday. If you don't use PowerPoint in your church, you can do almost the same thing with an overhead projector. Our volunteers also put together any videos we use. The decor and atmosphere are also handled by a volunteer team. If a team grasps the vision of being a ministry, it is a wonderful way for them to serve God using their creative talents and passion (1 Cor. 12:1–31; Rom. 12:3–8; Eph. 4:11–12). You don't have to spend a lot of money. For example, you could use cheap bedsheets for drapery effects, or for dividers, if needed. Look for props and candle holders at garage sales and flea markets. Even old slide projectors will work fine for projecting colors or still images.

Creativity, however, does take planning. As you include creative and artistic elements, your volunteer team should be meeting, brainstorming, and assigning responsibilities several weeks ahead of time so they won't be rushed. Our volunteer team meets weekly to plan the creative elements, just like the worship band rehearses weekly for their part in the worship gathering. The greater the number of people who are involved, the more ownership they tend to take. The more your teams capture the vision, the more excitement they will have for creating a worship experience in which people meet with God in a mighty and memorable way.

EMERGING THOUGHTS

1. Do you agree or disagree that post-Christian generations are seeking a spiritual encounter with God when they gather for a worship gathering? Can you give examples to illustrate?

2. Why do we need a balance of using liturgical elements and silence but still providing for fun and life?

3. Can you give some examples of art and drama done well and done poorly? Do you have an untapped community of artists in your area? How could you encourage them to become part of your worship?

Creating Experiential, Multisensory Worship Gatherings

> **The problem is, we are living in a culture that breeds spectators. . . . Spectator worship has been and always will be an oxymoron.**
>
> —Sally Morgenthaler, *Worship Evangelism*

ometimes I try to picture what it would have been like to participate in a worship gathering of the early church. First Corinthians 14:26 indicates that when the early church came together, perhaps in a group of twenty to forty people, their worship was very experiential and participatory: "When you come together, *everyone* has a hymn, or a word of instruction, a revelation, a tongue or an interpretation. All of these must be done for the strengthening of the church." It doesn't say that only the preacher and the worship leader has these things; *everyone* has. The early church was not comprised of spectators who sat down in a building, passively listened, watched, and then left. Yet aren't many of our worship services a spectator event?

Of course, our culture today is different, and designing a meeting for forty worshipers is a lot different than for four hundred or fourteen hundred worshipers. Still, worshiping God together in community should be a participatory and experiential event.

Participation and experience are very important to people in emerging generations, in all areas of life. They prefer to learn through interactive and participatory experiences. People don't just visit museums anymore; in places like Seattle's Experience Music Project, San Francisco's Exploratorium, and Silicon Valley's Tech Museum, they *interact* with them. Gone are the days of monotone tour guides and passive visual displays; people are eager to *experience* truth and knowledge. Home audiences participate in television game shows, news programs, and sitcoms by logging onto websites and giving their unique input, sometimes even emailing comments that run along the bottom of the screen during the program. Live audiences on MTV's *Total Request Live* (*TRL*) are encouraged to participate in the program, interacting with VJs and guest celebrities.

> *During the last decade, many have discovered the limits of the intellect. More and more people have realized that what they need is much more than interesting sermons and prayers. They wonder how they might really experience God.* —HENRI NOUWEN

The business world has also noticed this shift. In the past, modern world, simply giving people information about a product was enough to sell it. But Joe Pine and James Gilmore, in *The Experience Economy,* make a case for how important it is to sell an *experience* of a product. It's the experience of the product that "creates a memorable and lasting impression that ultimately creates transformation within individuals."[1] Of course, God is not a product, so please don't think that I am imposing business principles on the church. But we need to recognize how important experience is in transforming someone's opinions in today's culture.

> *It is one thing to talk about God. It is quite another thing to experience God.* —LEONARD SWEET, *POSTMODERN PILGRIMS*

✝ Consumer watch!

In chapter 8 I warned about the dangers of creating consumers of spiritual goods and services. Likewise the emerging church shouldn't be so focused on creating cool multisensory worship services that we end up creating consumers of another kind. After all, it's the Spirit of God who transforms lives, not the programming that we do. We have nothing but a show or a program if our services don't point to Jesus and produce true disciples and if worshipers don't encounter God when we gather.

✠ Singing is an obvious way to be experiential and participatory

When we praise and worship through song, people participate in the service. As they are drawn toward truth by the lyrics, they begin to focus their hearts and minds on God. They begin to interact with the truth, responding to it as the Holy Spirit leads them. They have become part of the worship experience, not just observers.

In a typical contemporary worship service, the bulk of the musical worship precedes the message, after which everyone gets up and goes home. But does it have to be this way? Why do we sing primarily at the beginning of the service? At our vintage-faith services, we place the bulk of the participatory worship (at least twenty-five minutes) after the message. I am finding that many emerging churches are extending the musical worship after the message. This post-sermon time is an opportunity to respond to how the Word of God has encouraged, convicted, confronted, or challenged us (Heb. 4:12).

After a sermon, we really want to give time for people to breathe, interact with God, pray, search their hearts, and not just rush out the door after hearing a verbal message. It doesn't seem natural to send them off immediately. Perhaps in such a rush to get folks out the door after the message, we don't give them time to interact with God. Isn't this when the Holy Spirit seems to do the most work in hearts and lives?

+ The incredible importance of experiential musical worship, plus a word of caution

Madonna sings on her *Music* album, "Music makes the people come together." True! Music does allow people to somehow feel united, to share in community. Whether it is a rock concert or a worship service, music is a powerful influence. In a church service, though, the lyrics and music have the ability to direct our hearts and minds toward God and to draw us into worship.

> *I always left before the sermon. I loved singing, even about Jesus, but I didn't want to be preached at about him. . . . it was the singing that pulled me in and split me wide open.* —ANNE LAMOTT, *TRAVELING MERCIES*

Even nonbelievers watching and listening to Christians sing about God can be impacted by the power of this experience. It may be foreign to them, but it is also very attractive. On more than one occasion I've heard new believers say that a crucial role in their consideration of Christianity was seeing the passion on the faces of worshiping believers as they sang and prayed.

You may have noticed an incredible increase over the past several years in the number and popularity of worship CDs. This is great! But I'd like to offer a few words of caution, especially for leaders.

Worship is not just singing. Unfortunately many have come to define the act of worship solely by music. So leaders need to redefine worship and explain that singing is but one form of worship expression. Music is not the third sacrament!

Guard against addiction to musical worship. Immature hearts and minds in particular can become accustomed to thinking they haven't worshiped unless they have experienced the power and emotional rush of an all-church or large-group praise session. We must be careful that we are not just working people into an emotional frenzy with what we do musically. I believe we should be using upbeat joyous songs but also meditative ones. I believe we need to think through the power of music and be sure we don't subtly manipulate people emotionally rather than allowing the Spirit to do that.

Guard the content of what we sing. Too often while sitting in a church service, I'm asked to sing lyrics that are not theologically sound, that are me-focused rather than God-focused, or that are so metaphorical that the true meaning has been lost. We need to be careful how self-focused our lyrics are so that nonbelievers don't get the wrong message about our faith. I pray that the emerging church will bring back strong integrity in what we sing. Don't forget that many hymns have strong God-focused lyrics and are beautiful songs to teach emerging generations. I also believe we need to encourage songwriters in our churches to write worship songs. Don't always look to the outside; you may have great worship songs within your church community waiting to be sung.

✥ Worship leader-*teacher*

In our services, worship leader Josh Fox will often read from the Scriptures before we sing, offering insight and background to the words. Or he may quiet down a song in the middle and read the Scripture it is based

> What's even worse is that now the term worship is used for a style of music. If it is loud and fast, they call it praise, and if it is slow and intimate, they call it worship. Worship is far more than music. It is a lifestyle (Rom. 12:2). Worship is anything that brings pleasure to God.
>
> —RICK WARREN

> The most common mistake Christians make in worship today is seeking an experience, rather than seeking God. They look for a feeling, and if it happens, they conclude that they have worshiped. Wrong. In fact, God often removes our feelings so we won't depend on them. Seeking a feeling, even the feeling of closeness to Christ, is not worship.
>
> —RICK WARREN

In vintage-faith worship, Josh Fox and the worship band often lead from the back of the building instead of the front. This way the focus is on the empty cross and the lyrics of the songs instead of on the band and worship leader.

upon. In this way, scriptural truth, historical context, and right theology are woven into the worship experience, making the songs all the more powerful and rich. I strongly feel that worship leaders should be guides and teachers as they explain and teach from Scripture about theologically sound songs. How much more powerful it is when we engage the heart through song and the mind through the lyrics.

The quality of musical worship is even more important to the emerging culture than the oratorical skill of the preacher. Music is such a major part of the lives of people in emerging generations that how we incorporate it into a worship service is absolutely critical. We need to be discriminating when it comes to the talents and abilities of those we allow to play and lead; musicians should be of a certain level of quality, but at the same time we need to guard against any hint of performance on the part of the band or the leader. In fact, part of my personal evaluation of a worship band is how well they disappear as they lead.

☩ Times of silence are a way for people to worship experientially

A pastor of a large seeker-sensitive church once visited our worship service and asked me, "Are those times of silence planned? Do you allow those on purpose? They drove me crazy! I need everything to fall like dominos in our worship services, one after another with no gaps in between." He made falling-domino motions with his hand. "To just stop and sit like that drives me nuts!"

I wasn't particularly surprised by his comment. Several times I have visited his very large church where programming is so well organized that every transition is made smoothly. Every gap is filled in a tight one hour and fifteen minutes of very professional and slick production. God does seem to be using this church tremendously to reach people who value smooth programming. But contrast that with our vintage-faith service, in which it's not uncommon for our worship leader to come to the end of a song and simply stop for a while before moving on to the next. Led by the Holy Spirit and his intuition, he pauses to allow the truth of what we've just been singing to sink in. Sometimes this is planned; most times it is not. Sometimes, he'll quietly ask us to just think about the words of the last song; sometimes he'll ask us to sit quietly and pray for a minute or two.

Be still, and know that I am God. —PSALM 46:10

Understand why this makes sense. Kalle Lasn in *Culture Jam* writes, "Every day, an estimated 12 billion display ads, 3 million radio commercials, and more than 200,000 TV commercials are dumped into North America's collective unconscious. . . . Quiet feels foreign now, but quiet may be just what we need. Quiet may be to a healthy mind what clean air and water and a chemical-free diet are to a healthy body. . . . Poet Marianne Moore contends that the deepest feeling always shows itself in silence."[2] People move at a frantic pace all week long. When do they have time to just stop and be quiet? When do newer or less mature Christians, who do not yet have a practice of personal worship throughout the week, stop to hear the still small voice of God speaking to them? It's not likely to happen through all of our programmed noise and talking. Silent pauses may be uncomfortable for some, but as it becomes the norm in the culture of your worship services, it will become a highlight. I am amazed at how many teenagers always say they like the times of silence.

Another thing you can do is plan times of quiet while Scripture is projected on screens. For example, after a message about our identity in Christ, we ended with eight minutes of silence while one Scripture after another appeared on the screen. No noise. No fancy moving words on the screen, either. Just slow fades of white text through a black background. While the truth of God's Word quietly worked in that room, I watched people get on their knees. Some people wept. Others simply sat and soaked in the reality of what it means to be a child of God. There were no voices, no special songs—just quiet and Scripture on the screens.

Isn't silence a lost aspect in our worship today? Where else are people to learn the beauty of being quiet? Where do we allow the Spirit to speak? Where do we teach emerging generations the importance of slowing down and listening for God's voice? This is a powerful way to include an experiential element in our worship gatherings.

✠ Offering can be an experience of worship

Have you ever attended a service (perhaps in your own church) in which you felt that people were embarrassed about the offering time, as if they were trying to get it over as quickly as possible?

When we first started the Graceland services at Santa Cruz Bible Church, I was afraid of taking the offering, not wanting to offend anyone or make anyone think we were just after money. So we initially just had a box in the back. Then we went to passing bags around. But I've since learned that by failing to present the offering time as a legitimate practice of worship, I was actually doing these people a disservice, even cheating them of the opportunity to worship through giving.

Since giving is an act of worship, we need to teach it as such to generations who never viewed worship this way. We did a teaching series on worshipful giving, explaining that our worship is like incense rising to the throne of God and that what we give supports the ministry, both locally and globally.

That night, instead of just passing the bags as usual, we set up tables in the front of the room, just off to the sides so they wouldn't be directly in view. On these tables we placed large woven baskets draped in cloth. We also decoratively wrote Scripture verses about worship on cards that we placed around the baskets, which were tall enough so that no one could see what anyone put in them. At offering time, we lit incense on the tables as a reminder that as we give our offering, its scent goes up before God (Rev. 8:3–4; Ps. 141:2). I asked people to leave their chairs to place their offerings, along with their prayer requests, in the baskets while we worshiped through song. I asked them to pause as they did so, to look at the incense and realize that their prayers and offerings were actually rising up to God as a fragrant aroma.

I had no idea what to expect, but I was amazed at what happened.

While the band softly played and led some contemplative worship, people began getting out of their chairs at random and making their way

In my travels, I've met a lot of folks from high-intensity worshiping churches who (though they are often embarrassed to admit it) are getting bored and tired. More is not always better. Louder is not always better. More intense is not always better. The human mind and imagination (not to mention body) need a balance of consistency and order with variety and novelty, and those of us who plan public worship need to attune ourselves to that fact. We also need to get in sync with the rhythms of community life, which may also be the rhythms of the Holy Spirit. A community may need a latency, a rest period, a time of calm; we're actually out of step with the Spirit if we're trying to keep everyone at least as excited as they were last week—if the Spirit is seeking to lead the community "to lie down in green pastures, beside still waters" to restore their soul. And the converse is also true: there is a time and season for everything—rejoicing, repenting, relaxing, celebrating, grieving, questioning, asserting, and more.

—BRIAN MCLAREN

toward the front. Two huge lines began to form, one behind each table. Some of the people kneeled before they placed their cards and offerings in the baskets. I eventually got in line, holding my offering envelope in my hands with a very real awareness that I was about to offer a portion of my earnings, entrusted to me by God, back to him. My turn at the table was the most powerful giving experience I have ever had. I approached the table and smelled the incense, watched it rise into the air, and then read the verses about worship. I placed the envelope in the basket, and for the first time, all the things that I knew cognitively about giving and worship I now actually experienced. I wasn't just giving to the church; my financial offering was truly going up before the throne. It really was a holy moment for me.

The amount of the regular offering that night more than doubled, even though we were making it harder for people to give because they needed to leave their seats. I did not hear one single complaint—only the opposite. Imagine what a powerful statement it made to nonbelievers that night as they watched their peers get out of their chairs and walk forward with their offerings. I am sure many people will never view offering time the same after that night.

We do this as an experiential act of worship only about every four or five weeks, because we don't ever want it to become cliche or lose its impact. But don't ever think that you can't talk to those in the emerging church about money.

✠ Communion as the ultimate experiential act of worship

The Lord's Supper is one of the most beautiful and central corporate expressions of our faith (1 Cor. 11:17–30). To me, nothing is more powerful or more naturally and beautifully designed for experiential participation than communion. Depending on your denomination, the ideas I am going to share may not be new to you. However, in many seeker-sensitive churches and in the more conservative churches, communion is conducted in a very controlled manner. Tiny bits of cracker and tiny cups of juice or wine are passed up and down the rows in golden trays. Everyone waits for the signal, someone leads in prayer, and it's over. It can be very meaningful, of course, but I always felt like something was missing, that communion was tacked on at the end or done quickly to get it out of the way so the sermon could be preached. I felt locked in my chair, sometimes wanting to kneel but feeling I couldn't. Many times I needed more time to contemplate and do some self-examination. Nonbelievers and those living openly in sin were instructed to let the tray pass by, which may be scriptural, but it also left the abstainer feeling very conspicuous.

But my perspective changed when I attended a communion service at St. Paul's Cathedral in London. People were asked to come forward row by row to take the elements. With my American Bible church background, this act of coming forward made a strong impression as I observed how people had time to reflect and to pray before leaving their seats. This made so much sense! So back in California we began to set up communion near the front of the room.

Remembering the importance of the visual, we place large wooden crosses behind each table, lay velvet cloth around the tables and place lit candles off to the sides. Depending on the teaching topic, we'll sometimes place Scripture verses or other symbols or props on the tables. Instead of telling people to come forward row by row, we allow people to come up and take communion any time they want to during the twenty-five to thirty minute worship period following the message, similar to the way we take the offering. Thus, people not taking communion don't feel as conspicuous. We offer clear instruction about what communion is and ask nonbelievers to quietly observe believers in this act. Communion also helps us remember Jesus in a multisensory way, as we eat, drink, touch, and smell the bread and wine or juice. Pay attention to what you use. To me, some communion bread looks and feels more like Chiclets gum than the bread described in the Bible. We've chosen to use matzo (unleavened) bread. Matzo can be broken beforehand into pieces or people can break it themselves.

After we explain what communion is, the worship team softly plays, and we give people time to pray, prepare their hearts, confess sin, and make their way to the front when they're ready. Many go off to the side to kneel in prayer before walking to the front. It is common to see married couples serving communion to one another off to the side while kneeling together. As a variation, occasionally we'll set up tables more centrally and take the elements as a gathered community where we can see one another more.

Everything about these communion services puts Jesus front and center. Because of the sacredness of these nights, we always remove everything but the cross from the stage. The worship band always plays from the rear of the room so that the focus can be on the empty cross, which reminds us that the crucified Jesus has risen.

Imagine the impact on nonbelievers! We always share the gospel during these nights and very clearly explain that communion is for believers.

Along with Dan, I too believe that communion is a critical and central part of our worship gatherings. Regardless of a congregation's official stance on how God is or is not present during communion (i.e., does something immediate and miraculous happen or is it just a matter of memorializing Christ's life, death, and resurrection), I continue to hear how God has used the celebration of the Lord's table to evangelize and transform postmoderns. And I have heard these stories for over a decade. Perhaps we need to rethink the way we have so often relegated communion to the status of an obligatory ecclesiastical act. The New Testament church's worship was organized around the Word (Scripture read, sung, interpreted, and discussed in light of the risen Messiah) and the table (participation in Christ's redemption through the distribution of bread and wine). If communion was that central to the early Christians' experience of God, why is it not central in our worship experiences?

—SALLY MORGENTHALER

163

But imagine being invited by a friend to church, hearing about the meaning of Christ's sacrifice on the cross, and then seeing your friend go forward and drop to his knees. No matter how you felt about religion, you would probably think your friend must really love this God he talks about. You'd be struck by how seriously the people around you seem to take their faith. It's no wonder that in our church far more people have become believers on communion nights than on any other night. It really is a beautiful thing seeing people make decisions at a service that is probably more flat-out unapologetically spiritual than anything else we ever do.

✛ Open sharing as experiential worship

Many times we'll plan an open-mike time in the service as an opportunity for people to share and respond. This always feels a little risky, since it's impossible to know what people will say, but it's usually well worth it. We make sure the time is clearly explained and firmly directed so that no one is able to monopolize the time or preach his or her personal agenda. We send roving mikes out into the congregation rather than have people come forward.

From time to time during worship and prayer, we invite people to speak out (loudly) a word or two that comes to their minds about God or to say something they are thankful for that ties into the evening's topic. Other times we ask people to read a verse or two that is meaningful to them. We've found that these moments of open sharing are great ways to promote the values of community and individual expression.

✛ Reading verses or creeds out loud together

You may already be reading verses or creeds aloud as part of your denominational culture, but for others, this is a new idea. It's a valuable way to involve everyone at once in the same way singing does. Words can be printed in the bulletin or projected on the screen so that everyone is able to read from the same translation.

✛ *Lectio divina*

The early monks utilized a practice called *lectio divina,* which means "divine reading" or "sacred reading." In addition to their routine of prayer and reading, they would set aside time to repeat out loud a passage from Scripture. When they came upon a word or a phrase which stood out from the rest, they would stop to ponder it and pray about it in relation to the rest of the passage. This would go on as the passage was repeated and prayed through in-depth, and the Holy Spirit would bring things to mind.

In typical worship services, we rarely pause to reflect on Scripture. God's Word is spoken, taught, even sung, but we don't stop to contemplate it. This is what *lectio divina* is about. In a worship gathering, you can lead people in this by:

- *Reading a selected passage slowly out loud.* The passage can be projected on the screen or printed on a handout, or people can read from their own Bibles, if most of them have the same translation.
- *Meditating on a passage.* Instead of rushing from one verse to the next, ask the people to silently read a passage over, or the leader can read it to them several times. While it is being read, people can ask the Spirit to allow a word or part of the passage to really stand out to them. The goal is to chew on and experience the passage.
- *Praying.* After reading a passage several times, allow people to sit quietly, asking the Spirit to guide them in prayer.

This ancient practice is very powerful when done during a worship gathering, sometimes in as little as five to ten minutes.

✝ Prayer as a way to worship experientially

When do we really pray as a community? Not counting the opening prayer, closing prayer, and offering prayer, what time is really set aside for talking to God during a service? Lengthier times of prayer are typically reserved for prayer meetings, which are lightly attended at best or nonexistent in many churches.

> *He went to the house of Mary the mother of John, also called Mark, where many people had gathered and were praying.* —ACTS 12:12

Prayer is one of the most important ways to worship experientially. It is personally encountering God as we pray and listen and worship. But strangely enough, prayer is not the easiest thing to incorporate into the culture of worship services. It takes effort. In our worship gatherings, we try to make prayer such a normal part of every week that it simply becomes part of the fabric of who we are instead of something we add on. Consider the wide variety of ways to include prayer in services. We

> In case you haven't noticed, worship is on the rise.... You hear stuff like "wow ... 800 students come to worship each week!" To that I say incredible! But are our songs wed with tears? Trust me, I'm into worship ... but there must be more than songs of praise.... Oh, for the day when someone could spend an hour on our campus and quickly know where the praying takes place.
>
> —LOUIE GIGLIO, FOUNDER OF
> PASSION AND ONE DAY

have a trained team that is always available to pray for people. They have a table off to the side of the platform with free Bibles to give out. At any point after the message is over, during the extended musical worship and afterward, people are free to pray with someone on the team, ask questions, or receive a free Bible.

We also provide times of silence for prayer. People are allowed to stay in their seats or get on their knees or even go behind the curtains that surround our seating area if they want privacy. During the longer worship times that are typical of communion nights, it is normal to see hundreds of young people flat on their faces or on their knees praying as they confess sin or just do business with God before taking communion. These times are clearly explained for the benefit of visitors or nonbelievers, and those not comfortable praying on their knees are given permission to stay seated, and many do.

We frequently conclude the worship service by asking people to pray with the person they came with. Sometimes this is planned, and other times it is the result of the Spirit's prompting. I always make sure I tell people they can slip out of the room if they want to and that those sitting by themselves are free to pray alone or with a member of the band or prayer team. Nonbelievers can just sit and watch or join in and pray with us. (They generally don't have a problem with letting someone pray for them.)

This is a great way to help those in the body break through the discomfort they may feel about praying with their friends. I let them know it's fine just to say a few words, like, "Please let whatever we just talked about from the Scriptures happen in my friend's life." However we do it, we must model the value of prayer for the emerging culture, for both believers and nonbelievers, and bring this discipline into our worship services.

Another way we have imaginatively incorporated prayer into our services is by using prayer stations. It's amazing to me how sometimes just getting up out of your seat at a time of conviction or to receive some encouragement can cement a moment in your mind. It is worth spending time, energy, and whatever other resources we can spare to encourage people to respond to God's work in their hearts. We have had nights when there was barely any message given from up front. We simply set up prayer stations and allowed the Scripture on the tables to do the talking, giving people extended time to respond in prayer.

In our services, a prayer station usually consists of a round table draped with cloth and holding various props related to a central theme. For instance, we once did a series on the portrait of a disciple. For the

Spaces such as this one emphasize the importance of prayer as well as encourage people to write out prayers or ask others to pray for them during the service.

final night of the series, we set up prayer stations representing each of the disciplines or aspects of a healthy Christian life. To the far left of the stage was a station dedicated to community. That table was set as though for an evening meal, with family photos and Scripture verses on cards scattered across the tablecloth. I had taught that being a part of a church is to be a member of a family, and during the worship time, people were invited to spend a few moments at this table, asking God to work in this area of their lives.

Another station represented discipleship. On this table we had placed a baton like those used in relay races and surrounded it with verses that had to do with passing on the faith. Questions laid on the table were, "Are you discipling and mentoring another to be an apprentice of Jesus?" and, "Who are you passing your faith along to?" We had a prayer station with a lifesaver prop in the center, representing the need to be sharing with others the rescue we experienced through Jesus. As people stopped at this table, some would get on their knees and ask God to put people in their lives with whom to share the news of the gospel and the kingdom.

Prayer stations allow people to experientially interact with the message or theme in a variety of ways: they can pray about it, read Scriptures about it, be challenged, encouraged, even simply learn about it. You can even involve more of the senses by adding elements to touch and interact with in some way. For one evening on which the theme was being seen as righteous in God's sight through Christ, we set up prayer stations with bowls of water. Those who wanted to could dip their hands into the bowls before they prayed to symbolize and remember their cleanliness before God. Another time, we had people press their hands into a box of sand to symbolize that they leave imprints on other people and had them pray that the imprints they leave are Christlike. There are all types of things you can do. Activity at the prayer stations usually occurs during a musical worship set so people can feel free to participate or not.

Sometimes people are asked to leave a bit of themselves at the station as well. We've covered tables with butcher paper and invited people to write their prayer requests or the names of those they hope would become believers. We have set up large crosses with bowls beneath them and invited people to write down their prayers and confessions and leave them there at the foot of the cross. Our prayer team later prays for these requests and concerns. We have laid out a huge map of the world and had people pray for a specific place and then mark its location on the map. Just walking up to that station and finding a map covered with marks representing the prayers of the saints is a powerfully moving experience that can't help but broaden a person's perspective.

One time during our annual art event, we set up a prayer labyrinth, which was really a series of experiential prayer stations. A labyrinth is a

The focus of this prayer station is a large cross made out of a mirror. The message that evening explained how Jesus took all of our sin upon the cross. The prayer station allowed people to see themselves reflected in the cross as they wrote out prayers of thanksgiving.

mazelike path similar to those designed into the floors of European cathedrals during the Middle Ages. Christians of that time would slowly walk the labyrinth as an aid to contemplative prayer and reflection. Ours took an hour to go through, and it was incredible to see so many people waiting their turn and then spending such an extended amount of time in prayer.

However it is done, I believe that emerging generations need to see prayer modeled and valued, because they are hungering for it. Prayer is a natural and beautiful way to see the worship service become much more interactive and participatory. The more we can incorporate personal communication with God, the better. Even nonbelievers, if they have any belief in a "God" or a higher power at all, believe in prayer. In a worship gathering such as this, we have the holy privilege of helping them understand what it means to pray to the one true God and how to have a relationship with him.

✠ The new cutting edge, or simply back to the basics?

I had an amusing experience recently while talking with a friend of mine who is on staff at a contemporary church. He leads a vintage-faith worship service which uses many of the things I have been talking about in this chapter. He told me that the senior pastor of the church once said in a staff meeting that my friend and his team were really "pushing the envelope" and doing some really "cutting edge" things. "Crazy things happen in that service," he said. You may be wondering what was going on in that church. Well my friend told me, "Dan, we aren't cutting edge at all. All we are doing is praying more in the service. We might get on our knees more. We have times of silence. We read creeds together. This is what my senior pastor says is cutting edge!"

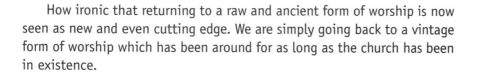

Worship in the emerging church is less about looking out for what is on the cutting edge and more about moving back into our spiritual center with Jesus as our sole focus.

How ironic that returning to a raw and ancient form of worship is now seen as new and even cutting edge. We are simply going back to a vintage form of worship which has been around for as long as the church has been in existence.

+ A final note on experiential worship elements

Experiential worship, as opposed to spectator-oriented worship, does not require a large budget or staff. It only requires a good deal of planning and a team which understands the goal, the heart, and vision behind what you do in your worship gatherings. The point is to help people stay focused on Jesus, not on the experience; to offer scripturally based worship and learning, not just trendy tricks and gimmicks. I would form a team and plan a minimum of three or four weeks in advance of each service.

There are so many ways one can be creative in expressing our worship. However we worship, let's make sure Jesus is in the center and that we help people maintain a high, holy view of God. May we never create experiential worship services that end up drawing more attention to the experience than to Jesus. Jesus must be the center of all our worship gatherings, whether they are post-seeker-sensitive or seeker-sensitive, ancient or modern, vintage or contemporary.

EMERGING THOUGHTS

1. **How would you rate your current worship gathering? Is it more of a spectator event, or is it a participatory and experiential one? What makes it such?**

2. **How would the average person in your church define worship? Would they think of worship as primarily the musical portion of the service?**

3. **How much is prayer a part of your worship gatherings now? How might it be incorporated more?**

4. **Are any of the ideas about multisensory worship in this chapter possibilities for your church?**

   For more photos and links to other websites with examples of experimental worship, go to: www.vintagefaith.com.

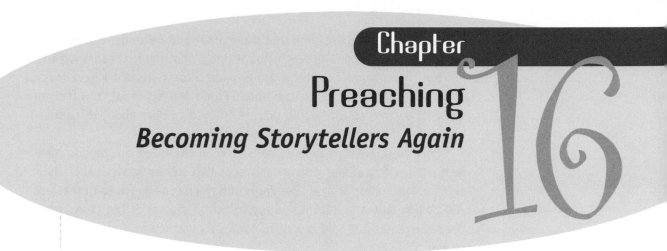
> "In the past . . . preachers have been able to assume
> the basic building blocks of a Christian worldview. . . .
> You could take texts like John 3:16 or Romans 5:8 or
> Isaiah 53:4–6 and hang them on the "clothesline" of
> a Judeo-Christian worldview. The problem in trying to
> reach postmodern people is that there is no clothes-
> line. . . . the great challenge of the preacher is to put
> up the clothesline.

—Colin S. Smith, *Telling the Truth*

Imagine you're part of a group being addressed by an excited speaker who says, "I have some really good news! No longer do you need to fear the evil Shelob. Her hypnotizing presence is weakened significantly by the Phial of Galadriel. Although the wickedness of Sauron still builds in the east, your mission to carry the Ring to Mount Doom is secure, and as long as you cling to Sting and wisely use the glittering Phial, you will be safe. Keep following Smeagol, for now, and make your way past Cirith Ungol. Isn't this great news?"

If you've read J. R. R. Tolkien's *The Lord of the Rings,* you likely understand what the speaker has said. You may have even felt recognition and wonder spring up within you as some of the names and places were mentioned. Knowing the story, you understand what a relief it was for Frodo to hold that gift of Galadriel and ward off the huge spider Shelob. You understand the mission to reach Mount Doom and why it is so important.

But if you haven't read this 1,085-page trilogy, you don't have much of a clue, nor do you care much about Frodo and his Phial. You feel no sense of danger, so why would you be relieved to hear about this possibility of escape or your need for a weapon?

Or if you haven't read the books or seen the films, maybe you have heard something of the story from one or two Tolkien fanatics, but their extreme fascination with Middle Earth minutia has managed to disinterest you completely. And because you've heard only parts of the story, what the speaker has just said is a little confusing and seems pretty irrelevant to you.

✛ The thrilling and amazing story needs to be told again

Why this *Lord of the Rings* diversion? Because isn't the experience of someone who knows little or nothing about *The Lord of the Rings* similar to that of many post-Christian younger people when they hear explanations of biblical teaching, including the gospel of Jesus? We start in the middle of a story that they don't know or that they know very little about mainly through negative experiences. We offer them escape from a peril they don't know they face, and we use words that either aren't part of their vocabulary or that they don't correctly understand. Because people in the emerging culture don't know the story, preachers must become storytellers again.

✛ The storybook is not viewed the same way anymore

But we encounter a new problem as we try to tell this story. At one time Billy Graham could hold up his black leather Bible and say, "The Bible says . . ." and people would listen and respect his words from the "storybook." After all, the Bible was known to be God's Word. In a modern world, he was speaking primarily to a Judeo-Christian audience. Even if this audience didn't believe in God, they still had a general understanding of and respect for the Bible and for preachers.

Today as we hold up our Bibles in the emerging culture and say, "The Bible says . . ." we are likely to get a very different response. "What makes that book any different from all the other religious books out there?" "I learned in college that the Bible is entirely man-made and is simply a variation on other mythical religions of the ancient Near East." "The Bible? So much pain and hatred has been caused by that book." Even people's view of preachers has changed. What once was a respectable role in society is now unfavorably stereotyped. Even the word preach is now a negative one: "Don't you preach at me!"

You might not hear comments like these from the average person in your church because they have already accepted the Bible as a source of truth. And if the younger people in your church aren't stating these opinions, chances are they grew up in Christian homes that have shaped their worldviews. But if you are engaged in conversations in the emerging culture outside of Christian circles, comments like these are the norm. We need to rethink some aspects of how we go about our preaching and communicating.

+ Values differences in preaching and communicating

The Bible commands us to preach and communicate the scriptural news about the kingdom. Let's look at some of the words used in the Bible for *preach:*

1. *Kerugma* means "to proclaim" (Matt. 12:41; Luke 11:32; Rom. 16:25).
2. *Euangelizo* means "to bring or show good tidings or news" (Acts 13:32; Rom. 10:15; Heb. 4:2).
3. *Kerusso* means "to be a herald" (Luke 12:3; Acts 10:37; Rom. 2:21).

Preaching is "proclaiming" the story of God and humans, the good news of the kingdom. It is a central and critical part of our mission, and we cannot push it to the sidelines in the emerging church. First Timothy 4:13 reminds us that we should "devote" ourselves "to the public reading of Scripture, to preaching and to teaching." In the Old Testament, "they read from the Book of the Law of God, making it clear and giving the meaning so that the people could understand what was being read" (Neh. 8:8). The emerging church needs to elevate public reading, preaching, and teaching. In a culture void of truth and lacking understanding of the scriptural story, we need to proclaim, herald, and preach all the more. But the way we do this needs to change because the audience has changed.

The following comparative table provides perspective (employing some hyperbole) on our assumptions about how to preach to modern audiences and to post-Christian audiences. I'm not saying one methodology is

We can help our preaching task tremendously if the grand story is also being woven into other parts of the service. One way is to dig into the past. Our ancient liturgies were not only modes of worship but delivery systems for the grand story. From beginning to end, worshipers sang, chanted, and antiphonally narrated this story: the God who creates out of nothing, who patiently cares for his people, who becomes one of us, redeems and, in the fullness of time, will restore the entire universe. Before we go back to our old preaching ruts—planning thematic, moralistic services—perhaps we need to reestablish the most crucial theme of all: the works and historical presence of God the creator, redeemer, and sanctifier.

—SALLY MORGENTHALER

better than the other; they simply represent different values for different audiences with different worldviews.

Before we continue this discussion of preaching to emerging generations, let me clarify my assumptions:

1. That you will prayerfully study and exegete the Scriptures to accurately communicate their meaning. More than ever, we need to "correctly handle the word of truth" (2 Tim. 2:15).
2. That when you preach, Jesus will be the ultimate focus of your sermons, and that you will not just be giving information about him but also tell people how to relate to and experience Jesus as his disciples (John 5:39).
3. That no matter what preaching style or method you may use, your goal is to see listeners' lives change so they can truly be ambassadors for Jesus (2 Cor. 5:20) and messengers of kingdom living.

✠ Haircut homiletics

I get my hair cut twice a month, mainly because of how much I learn about preaching and communicating each time I go. At my local salon almost all the stylists are young and represent today's culture. To my knowledge none of them attends church or has anything to do with it. But over the past two years, I have developed a friendship with the girl who cuts my hair—a twenty-five-year-old who's into the psychobilly music scene.

Each visit, I have the privilege of sitting and talking with her for nearly an hour. Often our conversation turns to whatever I'm preaching about in church for the following few weeks. She loves giving her viewpoint and has no trouble at all talking about spiritual things. Her insightful comments help me think through how members of a post-Christian generation view the world, biblical topics, church, and Christians. This biweekly haircut-homiletics class has really given me more practical insight on preaching and communicating than any seminary class I have ever taken. If you are serious about understanding those you hope to reach, I strongly encourage you to have an ongoing relationship with someone like this to gain insight. Hairstylists or barbers in the church ask me all the time if I want them to cut my hair. But after thanking them, I always turn them down because I want every opportunity to be around nonbelievers. I have vowed never to have my hair cut by a Christian again!

Shifting Values in Approach to Preaching

Modern Church	Emerging Church
The sermon is the focal point of the worship service.	The sermon is one part of the experience of the worship gathering.
The preacher serves as a dispenser of biblical truths to help solve personal problems in modern life.	The preacher teaches how the ancient wisdom of Scripture applies to kingdom living as a disciple of Jesus.
Emphasizes the explanation of what truth is.	Emphasizes the explanation and experience of who truth is.
The starting point is with the Judeo-Christian worldview (Acts 17:1–3).	The starting point is the Garden of Eden and the retelling of the story of creation and of the origins of man and sin (Acts 17:22–34).
Biblical terms like *gospel* and *Armageddon* don't need definition.	Biblical terms like *gospel* and *Armageddon* need to be deconstructed and redefined.
The scriptural message is communicated primarily with words.	The scriptural message is communicated through a mix of words, visuals, art, silence, testimony, and story.
Preaching in a worship service is the primary way one learns from the Scriptures during the week.	Preaching in a worship gathering is a motivator to encourage people to learn from the Scriptures throughout the week.
Preaching takes place within the church building during a worship service.	A lot of the preaching takes place outside of the church building in the context of community and relationship.

During one of these homiletics sessions, I bumped into someone from church. As we talked, this person happened to make a comment about being saved. My stylists' confusion about the way the word was used precipitated a conversation in which I learned she had no idea what salvation is or why it might be needed. Virtually the entire story of the Bible and its characters were unknown to her. Her idea of "God" was totally different from the God of the Bible. In fact, she had heard that the Bible had two different "Gods," one in the Old Testament and one in the New Testament. As it turns out, she is actually open to the idea of many gods; her worldview is very far from a Judeo-Christian worldview. So when communicating with her, I need to start at a different point than I would if I were talking to a "churched" individual.

✝ Different starting points for different worldviews

A portion of Scripture essential to the discussion of preaching in the emerging church is Acts 17. Paul entered the synagogue in Thessalonica and "reasoned with them from the Scriptures, explaining and proving that the Christ had to suffer and rise from the dead" (Acts 17:2–3). Paul's audience respected the Hebrew Bible and accepted that its authors were inspired by God. The synagogue attenders already knew the big story of God and man. They knew the story of creation and the fall. They knew about Noah, Abraham, Moses, David, and Daniel. Paul was able to simply open the scrolls and prove from the Scriptures that Jesus was the Messiah.

But we see a much different approach in Acts 17:16–32. Paul arrived in Athens and was distressed to find a city "full of idols." The people were not familiar with the Hebrew Bible and probably didn't know the story of creation and the fall. They didn't know the overarching biblical story; they had a different set of beliefs and stories which shaped their way of thinking.

No wonder Paul used a different approach in his preaching at the meeting of the Areopagus court. This meeting most likely involved a group of men who supervised religious and educational matters on Mars Hill. So instead of starting with the Scriptures, Paul began by acknowledging that his listeners were spiritual people (Acts 17:22). He didn't start his message by pointing out how they were wrong, nor did he assume that they agreed with him and shared his belief in one God. Instead, Paul went back and told the grand story about a God who created everything (Acts 17:24). He then talked about how close this God was to them, even using words from a Cretan poet named Epimenides to illustrate his point. He also referred to the poet Aratus from his own country, Cilicia (Acts 17:27–28). Paul relationally brought his teaching into their world, eventually bringing his message to a point of challenge and decision, explaining that man would one day face this God in judgment and that the only answer to this situation is found in Jesus and his resurrection from the dead (Acts 17:31).

Paul used two different starting points for two different audiences, based on their worldview and knowledge of Scripture. He provides a model for how we should preach to and communicate with a mix of people who, with one major difference, are very much like those at the meeting of Areopagus.

+ Gaining our voice and trust back before we can speak into lives

The major difference between the challenges Paul faced in preaching and those we face today is that Paul's Greek audience was interested in listening to him. Christians were new on the scene, and the Greeks welcomed fresh ideas as fodder for discussion. Most post-Christians, on the other hand, have a vague sense of what Christianity is and represents, and they want no part of it. So it doesn't work anymore to just stand up and start talking to a group of people who don't think they want to hear what you have to say.

The girl who cuts my hair had pretty much rejected Christianity before she even knew what it was. She's had some negative run-ins with Christians, and the Bible means nothing to her. Telling her "this is what the Bible says" doesn't hold much weight. If her trust in Christians is broken, it can be restored only through relationship.

Just last week in my haircut-homiletics class we spoke about her breakup with her boyfriend. Because I have a relationship with her, speaking about spiritual things has become normal. I was able to speak of God's design for men and women and what it means to be one flesh. She suddenly stopped cutting my hair, spun the chair around, and jerked it to a stop. She looked me in the eye, with the razor still buzzing in her hand, and said, "Say that again. I want to hear more about that." Because she trusted me, I was able to say some very strong words about God's design for sex and relationships. As I spoke, she was about as wide-eyed and open to questions as one could ever hope for. Her eyes even welled up with tears as she expressed how she could relate to some of what I said. You see, hearing about God's guidelines for sex and relationships was not a negative thing at all to her. It truly was good news because for the very first time, she was hearing the story of God and his love and how our sexuality was designed by him. I didn't just talk about sin, but I told the story and how relationships and sexuality fit in that story. She never would have listened to that while sitting in a worship service. (She still hasn't gone yet.) It took friendship to get the opportunity to speak those biblical truths to her.

So our first big challenge in preaching to emerging generations is to regain our voice by earning the trust of our hearers. (We will talk about this in chapter 20.)

As we prepare messages for the emerging culture, think like Paul did. When we preach, we must never assume everyone shares our presuppositions. You can speak to believers and nonbelievers at the same time, provided you make the extra effort to do some redefining and to rethink your approach when you preach.

Continually tell the story of God and humans. Tell the grand wonderful story, over and over again. We cannot assume that people know the whole thing. We must constantly paint the big picture of the Bible story and tell it in as many ways as possible through our preaching.

Dan's emphasis on the story couldn't be more important. What would happen if we dropped all of our categories of systematic theology and in their place structured our thinking and living around our grand story of creation, alienation, and new creation? Systematic theologies are wonderful late-medieval–modern constructions; to me, they are like the cathedrals of the Middle Ages. Even though few of us worship in cathedrals anymore, we value them and know they should be preserved for their beauty. The intellectual symmetry and grand arching structures of systematic theologies similarly should be preserved and appreciated. But my guess (and hope) is that we will not live by systematic theologies alone in the future but rather will learn how to inhabit the biblical story ... and extend it through our lives.

—Brian McLaren

Deconstruct, reconstruct, and redefine biblical terms. Most people outside of the church think the word gospel simply refers to a musical style. Their definitions of biblical terms come from movies, songs, and other media. Most people have no idea how many disciples there were, or what a disciple even is, for that matter.

✢ A new hunger for depth and theology

We can no longer simply give messages on "three easy steps" to solve a problem. I sense a renewed hunger for theology and an interest in discussing the mysteries of God. Emerging generations are starving for depth in our teaching and preaching and will not settle for shallow answers.

Allow God to still be God. In the modern church, we tried to systematize God in order to understand and explain him. Too often we have turned our theology into mathematics and taken all the mystery away. We need to celebrate his mystery and worship him all the more because of it. We mustn't be afraid to say "we don't know." This goes against the very fabric of modernity, but unless we admit that spiritual mysteries exist, we will not sustain a voice in our culture for very long.

Make preaching theocentric rather than anthropocentric. The seeker-sensitive movement brought great attention to the benefits of topical, felt-need messages. Granted, this approach has value. Jesus himself appealed to felt needs. Some of God's names reflect felt needs (Yahweh-Jireh, the God who provides). But in many cases, unfortunately, we've made ourselves, rather than God, the focus of our preaching. We gather on Sundays to learn how *we* can have a happy family, how *we* can have our finances right, how *we* can live a peaceful life, or how *we* can have a better marriage. A strong theocentric approach to preaching is exactly what emerging generations are starving for.

Don't insult people's intelligence or desire for spiritual depth. If I went to a Buddhist temple to have a deep spiritual experience and upon walking in received a fill-in-the-blank sheet with an easy-to-remember acrostic for three steps on how to "M-E-D-I-T-A-T-E," I imagine it would catch me off guard. If I were then subjected to an upbeat, seminar-style teaching message with a flashy PowerPoint presentation, I'd feel a little confused and let down.

Likewise, people in emerging generations attending a worship service hunger for a deep experience of God's wisdom. If we distribute sermon notes, they should be comprehensive and give the historical context for the Scripture passages we use.

One time, when preaching on Romans 6–8, I felt like I was teaching an English class, because I walked the audience through the definitions of *sanctification, condemnation, imputed righteousness,* and other terms. I put together extensive sermon notes to hand out, and that night, we actually ran out of them and had to print extra sheets for several weeks afterward because the demand was so great. Emerging generations are starving for deeper teaching, and our job is to respect them enough to give it to them.

We don't have to limit sermons to twenty-minute quickies. Should messages always be under thirty minutes? On occasion you may want to limit them to that, depending on the worship service design for that night. But I know of several large churches drawing hundreds and thousands of younger people in which the message is forty to fifty minutes long.

Use complete sections of Scripture from both Old and New Testaments. It's important, as we're constantly retelling the story, to remember to tell the complete story from Genesis to Revelation. Using just one verse here and there isn't enough.

Teaching the Jewish roots of the faith. I mentioned earlier the importance of restoring the Jewish roots of our faith in worship gatherings, and this includes our preaching. More than ever we need to reveal the ancient Jewish roots of the faith. Philip Yancey raises this point in his book *The Jesus I Never Knew.* He writes, "I can no more understand Jesus apart from his Jewishness than I can understand Gandhi apart from his Indianness. I need to go back, way back, and picture Jesus as a first-century Jew with a phylactery on his wrist and Palestinian dust on his sandals."[2] It is strange that the modern seeker-sensitive church almost completely ignores this, yet emerging generations crave to know Jesus in this way.

+ "Theotopical" preaching: retelling the story to shape a worldview

I have heard topical preaching blasted by some pastors who say that we should only employ expository sermons. Likewise I have heard rebuttals by those who point out that neither in Jesus' example nor anywhere in the New Testament do we see the modern form of expository preaching. While there are good cases for both perspectives, we can get so caught up in arguments about methods that perhaps we miss the point of preaching. I don't think you'll hear anyone from the emerging culture complain about what method of preaching we are using. They don't know the difference and haven't the church background to form opinions. They will complain,

As the famous pastor R. G. Lee used to joke, "Sermonettes produce Christianettes who smoke cigarettes." Saddleback pastors regularly teach for fifty minutes or more. But you'd better have something to say. Like the oil drillers say, "If you don't hit oil after thirty minutes, stop boring."

—RICK WARREN

however, if they aren't deeply learning about the God they seek to encounter.

Preaching is a beautiful way of showing people in emerging generations not only that there is truth in a world of relativism but also that there is a Truth who personally loves them (John 14:6). This is what the girl who cuts my hair needs the most. Not just teaching that she shouldn't have sex before marriage because it is sin but also teaching on the grand story of the Bible so she sees herself as God does and sees how her sexuality fits within that story. So much of our modern preaching jumps straight to the issue of sin and then attempts to solve it by giving people "action steps" to take or "four principles" to follow.

I just talked to a pastor who was teaching a Sunday school class of retired people. They ended up in a discussion about the whole Bible, and he was amazed that even though the people in his class had attended church their entire lives, they could not explain the big story of the Bible. They knew about sin, and they knew the Bible stories, but they didn't know how it all fit together.

I use a mix of both expository and topical preaching, a type of preaching I call "theotopical." We should be expository in terms of doing the right exegetical work for biblically rooted messages. But at the same time preaching is an opportunity to shape a theological worldview for people by telling the story. Every time I preach I clearly know what theological concept I am trying to teach and how it fits into the story of the Bible.

For example, I recently taught a Christmas series in which my goal was to theologically teach how each person of the triune God of eternity was involved in the Christmas narrative. My goal in a series on dating and relationships was to teach on sanctification as well as to tell the story in Genesis of how we were created in God's image. In a series on Israel and Palestine, my goal was to teach on the Abrahamic covenant and eschatology as well as to tell the big picture story of the land of Israel and the future Jerusalem. (See appendix B for lists of theotopical teaching series and what my theological and story goals were.)

I want my post-Christian listeners to see the world through a theological, big-picture, scriptural story lens.

✢ Message selection and critical topics to address

No matter who you are preaching to, it is essential to understand the spiritual climate, worldview, and major life-concerns of your audience. I am constantly taking surveys, reading through prayer requests, and in general keeping my ear to the ground to learn what the questions and issues of the church might be. In a post-Christian culture, I've found the need for regular and repeated clarity on the following issues.

All preaching should somehow teach on kingdom living as a disciple of Jesus. We need to refocus our application, no matter what the topic, to this critical awareness of living as a disciple, or an apprentice, of Jesus.

Regularly preach and teach about the triune God. We need to regularly teach the mystery of the Trinity and how God himself exists in community as Father, Son, and Holy Spirit. We need to teach emerging generations a healthy fear and awe of God again (Prov. 1:7). Our teaching needs to include his character and the need to reverence him.

Regularly teach what it means that Jesus is the only way to God. The motto of the emerging, highly pluralistic culture is "all religions lead to God." Therefore the truth of Jesus as the sole mediator between man and God (1 Tim. 2:5; Acts 4:12) should regularly be taught from the Bible. However, if we address this without prayer and a gentle heart, we can easily lose the respect and trust of the emerging generations. Instead of attacking other faiths and their beliefs, immediately discrediting our message, I believe we should preach as Paul did when speaking to the Athenian Greeks in Acts 17. This requires knowledge of other faiths so we don't perpetuate the stereotype of Christians as closed-minded and ignorantly dogmatic. I've learned never to make comments about another religion until I have studied it or talked with someone from that faith. Although this wasn't a large issue in past generations, it certainly is a huge issue for today's emerging culture.

> *One of the biggest mistakes we make is to believe that there is only one way. There are many diverse paths leading to God.* —OPRAH WINFREY

Address human sexuality regularly. With so much confusion regarding sexuality today, it's important that we regularly teach the biblical pattern for human sexuality, including the story of Adam and Eve and how God created us as sexual beings, but that sin tainted this and every other area of our lives. We need to address homosexuality, on a regular basis, in a spirit of gentleness and compassion rather than in attack mode. We need to have our hearts broken for those who, not having understood the way God designed us sexually, have been broken and beaten by the world.

Woe to us if we simply blast away at sin in our preaching without considering that some of our listeners may be finally checking out church for the first time, bringing with them all sorts of confusion about their sexuality. We get to teach them, perhaps for the very first time, the biblical picture.

Redefining marriage and family to new generations. Most of those growing up today have never experienced God's design for the family or marriage as a holy covenant. We must make it a point to preach and teach what a biblical family looks like and what the biblical view of marriage is.

Teach on hell more than ever. Some people may have come to the conclusion that the seeker-sensitive church has removed hell from its vocabulary. That's not necessarily true. But I frequently search various church websites and tape catalogs as I gather ideas for message series and rarely find a message on hell. Heaven, yes. Hell, no. And it's no wonder. I can hardly think of any more offensive doctrine of the Christian faith. But if hell is a reality, and Jesus sure talked about it a *lot,* shouldn't we be warning people about it? Not with vengeance, anger, or manipulation but through tears. Our hearts should be so broken by the horrible reality of an eternity apart from God that our listeners can easily sense our compassion as we speak about it.

Preaching is more important and holier than ever as we exercise the sacred privilege of opening the Scriptures and teaching the divine story of God to people who are hearing it for the very first time. Woe to us if we take this incredible privilege lightly.

Teach the trustworthiness of Scripture. Because the Bible does not hold the respect it once did in our culture, so we must lovingly and intelligently offer reasons why we believe the Bible is trustworthy and point out what makes it different from other religious books. I use the word trustworthiness because that's what we need to be reinforcing about the Scriptures. If we read from the Scriptures, how do our listeners know they can trust what they hear? Remember how trust has been broken with the church and Christians. How refreshing it is to emerging generations, floating in relativism, to hear that they can intellectually trust and believe in God's inspired Scriptures.

Regularly preach and teach how our spirituality will be messy. I like the title of Mike Yaconelli's recent book: *Messy Spirituality.* We need to admit that life and our spirituality will be messy because we are flawed, sinful human beings. We need to make people in emerging generations understand this so we don't produce Christians who end up feeling self-defeated and guilty. We need to admit that though we as human beings are messy, we have a God of grace and compassion.

☩ I love to tell the story

I watched a scene from Robert Duvall's movie *The Apostle* in which the characters sang the hymn "I Love to Tell the Story." Quite honestly, because I come from an unchurched background, I had never sung that song or even heard it in a church before. It was written by a woman named Catherine Hankey, who lived in London in the 1800s. Catherine loved to lead Bible studies, but she became too sick to continue teaching and had to take time off to heal. While she was bedridden for a year, she began to write poems instead, and one of them became the words to this hymn.

You see, Catherine couldn't preach and teach like she used to, but she couldn't help but tell the story about the Jesus she loved, so she taught from her bed through poetry. In the emerging culture, we might not be able to preach as we've been used to, using entirely modern methods, but we can tell the story in wonderfully colorful ways to generations that have never heard it before. And when we do it with heart and in a way that communicates to them, eager ears are ready to listen.

I love to tell the story, 'tis pleasant to repeat
What seems, each time I tell it, more wonderfully sweet.
I love to tell the story, for some have never heard
The message of salvation from God's own holy Word.

I love to tell the story, 'twill be my theme in glory,
To tell the old, old story of Jesus and His love.

EMERGING THOUGHTS

1. In your church, how does the values-differences chart on page 175 reflect your preaching approach? Is the preaching more of a modern approach or an emerging-church approach?

2. Do you have a post-Christian in your life right now from whom you are taking a haircut-homiletics class? If not, how might you make that kind of contact?

3. Do you agree or disagree that emerging generations are hungry for depth in spiritual learning? Can you give any examples?

4. Would you agree that the topics mentioned in this chapter need to be addressed more than ever in the emerging church? What other topics would you add?

Preaching
without Words

17

> **Preach the gospel at all times.
> If necessary, use words.**
>
> —attributed to St. Francis of Assisi

I didn't come to this place to be lectured at by a Tony Robbins clone. I thought I was going to meet God here." These rather blunt words came from a girl in her twenties whom I had found pacing the hallway of a contemporary church building during the worship service. She was obviously not happy, so I had approached to ask if she was okay. It turned out that she had come to the worship service at the invitation of a friend but hadn't realized that "church" was going to be a long talk that reminded her of the self-help motivator Tony Robbins. After about twenty or thirty minutes, she was both bored and disillusioned. I asked her what she had been hoping for. "To pray," she told me. "To hear some encouraging music. To quiet my heart and connect with God."

Even though I could sense she was probably not a church-attending believer, I could see how badly she truly wanted to connect with God. She explained how this worship service felt more like a cross between a pep rally and a business presentation, and although she wanted to learn, this was not what she thought a Christian worship service would be. So she left her friend inside and waited in the hallway until the service was over.

Now, of course preaching and communicating must take place in a worship service, but don't just brush off this girl's words. Think about what she was hoping for—to "connect with God"—and then what she experienced—a lecture.

185

It's commonly held that St. Francis of Assisi once said, "Preach the gospel at all times. If necessary, use words." In his context, he was primarily referring to social action, making an effort to live out the kingdom in practical, everyday ways. In other words, one can proclaim Jesus and the kingdom by actions as well as through words. This happens mainly outside of the worship service, but it can happen inside a worship service as well. With our current culture's ever-changing forms of communication and the way emerging generations are accustomed to learning, his words of inspiration are as timely as ever.

Please don't assume I'm dismissing the need for preaching with words. I usually preach with words thirty-five to forty-five minutes every week. In the previous chapter we built a strong case for using words and teaching with more biblical depth than ever for emerging generations. What I am saying is that in communicating to emerging generations, we must not limit our mode of communicating truth merely to the use of words.

✛ Wordless preaching in a world which bases truth on experience

Our culture is producing people who prefer to learn experientially. Listen to what Leadership Network said about this shift in an online issue of *Explorer:*

> *The shift from knowledge to experience.* Experience is the new currency of our culture. In the past we gained knowledge of a subject or issue and then later validated that knowledge. Today, people have an experience that is later validated by knowledge.... This shift has implications in the way we learn, communicate and interact. For churches it impacts the design of worship, liturgy and the shape of and content of educational ministries, the process of spiritual formation, the design of sacred space, and programming.[1]

In chapters 12 through 15 we addressed the implications of this change for worship services, specifically the need for services to be multisensory and interactive and the need to create a sacred space. I gave scriptural examples of how God used more than just words to communicate truth. Through various experiential elements as well as through the space itself, we can actually preach biblical truth. Art preaches. Scripture preaches. Music preaches. Even silence preaches.

The article also shows how communication in today's culture has shifted from one-way expression to dialogue:

> *A shift from broadcast to interactive.* We are living in a time of revolutionary change in communications. The print world that had been dominant for 500 years began to give way in the 1950s to a visual or broadcast world dominated by radio and television. In the last ten years, the shift from a broadcast to an interactive world has accelerated rapidly.[2]

In the modern church, most of our preaching focused on the logical presentation of facts to move people toward a decision, which worked great for a modern mindset. But because of the shift in communications in the last decade, our form of preaching needs to go beyond words and be interactive.

Of course, no matter how we teach or preach, it is the Spirit of God who does the convicting (John 16:8) and guides people to all truth (John 16:13). But our job is to take into consideration how we present truth to the people we hope to see transformed. If the goal of our preaching is to bring about behavioral change as people learn to become disciples of Jesus, and if we focus only on preaching with words to the exclusion of experiential teaching, we will not have the impact we are hoping for in our emerging culture. We need to give people truthful experiences along with truthful teaching.

✠ Isn't propositional truth the way the Bible teaches?

A number of evangelicals are very uncomfortable even questioning propositional teaching as the only way to teach. But we can make a biblical case that God does preach without words. Leith Anderson, pastor of a large, modern church, hits the nail squarely on the head in his book *A Church for the Twenty-First Century*.

> The old paradigm taught that if you had the right teaching, you will experience God. The new paradigm says that if you experience God, you will have the right teaching. This may be disturbing for many who assume propositional truth must always precede and dictate religious experience. That mindset is the product of systematic theology and has much to contribute.... However, biblical theology looks to the Bible for a pattern of experience followed by proposition. The experience of the Exodus from Egypt preceded the recording of Exodus in the Bible. The experiences of the crucifixion, the resurrection and Pentecost all predate the propositional declaration of those events in the New Testament. It is not so much that one is right and the other is wrong; it is more of a matter of the perspective one takes on God's touch and God's truth.[3]

Hasn't the modern church neglected the fact that we can experience and learn about God in a variety of ways? Most of the time haven't we put our chips on propositional teaching as the driving force of one's conversion and worship experience? We need to approach Scripture in a holistic way, thinking through how the sermon fits within the worship experience. We need to blend our propositions of truth with experiences of truth.

+ The importance of the visual in preaching

Throughout Scripture, we see God using the visual to enhance verbal teaching. He used the heavens to declare his glory (Ps. 19:1). He spoke verbally to Moses using the burning bush (Exod. 3). Jesus, the master teacher, time and again did not restrict his teaching methods to the use of words alone but also used visuals and experiences (ie., Matt. 18:24–27; 21:18–22; John 2:1–11; 9:1–7; 13:1–17; 21:1–6). God used a dove to show the Spirit descending on Jesus at his baptism (Luke 3:22). God's voice was heard through a cloud at the Transfiguration (Luke 9:28–36). Peter, John, and James saw how Jesus' clothes became "bright as a flash of lightning." The book of Revelation is filled with visuals to communicate a divine message. Because our culture is producing emerging generations who learn visually via television, films, and the internet, we must become three-dimensional in our preaching, incorporating visual elements not as a replacement for words but in addition to words.

✢ How can we use visuals with Scripture?

Project photos, art, or graphics with Scripture text on screens. Using ancient art with Scripture provides another opportunity not only to reenforce the value of the visual but also to convey that Christianity is not a modern religion. For example, if you mention a geographical place, such as the Sea of Galilee, you could include a photograph for visual reference. The possibilities are endless, provided we stay away from flashy graphics or the standard businesslike graphics that come with most computer presentation programs. And again, consider using artwork from those in your church.

This photograph was taken by Spencer Burke of *The Ooze*. It shows the remains of a poster found on a streetside wall. It lends an added layer of meaning and impact to the Scripture quotation above it.

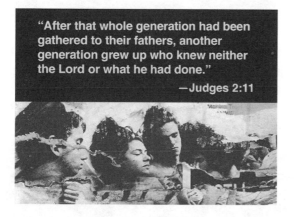

"After that whole generation had been gathered to their fathers, another generation grew up who knew neither the Lord or what he had done."

—Judges 2:11

Another idea is to photograph stained glass in churches or find photos of stained-glass images which depict the emotions of Christ or scenes from the Bible.

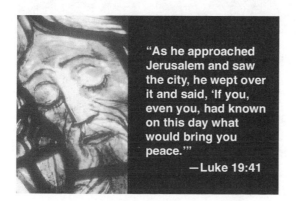

"As he approached Jerusalem and saw the city, he wept over it and said, 'If you, even you, had known on this day what would bring you peace.'"

—Luke 19:41

The work of Gustave Doré is a wonderful source of biblical images. His work is detailed, reverent, classy, and depicts a huge variety of scriptural scenes.

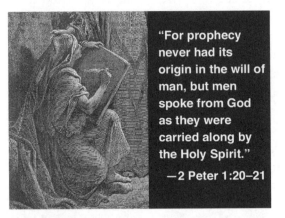

"For prophecy never had its origin in the will of man, but men spoke from God as they were carried along by the Holy Spirit."
—2 Peter 1:20–21

Use visuals to make a point. Visuals are a great way to reenforce a major point; just choose an image that illustrates your idea and project it in the background as you speak. Many images powerfully communicate biblical truth on their own without any text on the slides. As you speak on the crucifixion, art can depict a scene that words could not capture.

Man rebelled against God and **sin** entered the world

The possibilities are limitless, as long as you maintain a high standard of excellence in all you do. And this type of visual enhancement doesn't have to cost a lot or require lots of technical know how. Overhead projectors or slide projectors will work fine.

✝ Getting the focus off the preacher to tell the story

A friend of mine recently changed churches, leaving a great Bible-based fellowship with terrific teaching to attend a service that focused more on liturgy. When I asked him why he changed, he told me he realized he wanted a church that revolved around the Scriptures themselves, not the personality of the preacher. His new church has a pastor, but the focal point of the service is the reading of Scripture (lots of it). He said he wasn't distracted by the preacher or tempted to become addicted to his charisma as a substitute for the Scriptures themselves.

Although I would not consider my friend's opinion a good one for everybody, I wonder if his comments don't reflect some insight on how to reach post-Christians.

Shouldn't we begin to think of how we can draw people more to the Scriptures than to ourselves? Shouldn't we begin to think of how we can encourage people to depend on the Scriptures on their own throughout the week to learn and grow in maturity? Yes, the role of preachers is to teach the Bible, and the Spirit gives some people this gift (Eph. 4:11). We need to proclaim the Word of God, but preachers can also set an ethos in a church for people to become diligent students themselves and not be so dependent on the preacher to do the work for them. We have so many Bible study helps available today, including commentaries and computer programs which were not available earlier in history. We must create a culture in our churches for people to be deep students of the Bible, and this will happen only if it's the goal of preachers and teachers to teach others to feed themselves from the Scriptures.

Bringing Bibles back into the church can encourage a scriptural focus. While attending a large seeker-sensitive church, I noticed with great sadness that there was hardly a Bible in sight. How common is this? In the seeker-sensitive church we brought Scripture onto the screens and the

A prayer station set up not only for prayer but for reading Scripture.

191

focus onto the preacher, but in doing so, we subtly taught people that they didn't need to bring their Bibles to church. I know from experience that people in emerging generations, once they are in community and have come to trust Christians, the church, and the Bible, hunger to know what is in the Bible.

I repeatedly tell people to bring their own Bibles to services so they can become familiar with where things are found. I try every possible way to put the focus on the words of Scripture as I speak, rather than on me. I constantly encourage people to look at their Bibles as we read certain passages, hoping that by doing so, they are being trained to read and study the Bible on their own throughout the week.

Allow other people to read the Scriptures publicly. We rarely have a worship service in which I am the one reading the central passage. As often as possible, someone from the congregation presents the Scripture for the evening. Sometimes this is done through dramatic reading. Sometimes we have someone read Scripture from the stage; sometimes they read through a microphone offstage. Many times, to show that these are ancient writings, we have someone read in ancient dress. (Sounds hokey, and I wouldn't blame you if you thought so, but if it's done in the right context, it does work!) I find these ways of reading Scripture publicly valuable for the emerging culture because they take the attention off the preacher and places it more on the community.

Have everyone read the verses together. Many churches already do this, but I think in many seeker-sensitive churches, it is rarely done.

+ The importance of developing a culture which encourages questions and thinking

One of my favorite verses in the New Testament is Acts 17:11, in which God gives approval to those who were willing to question what they were being taught, using the Scriptures as a plumbline for truth. "The Bereans were of more noble character than the Thessalonians, for they received the message with great eagerness and examined the Scriptures every day to see if what Paul said was true." What a model for us today!

Why do people with closed minds always open their mouths?
—STICKER SOLD IN A POPULAR YOUTH CLOTHING STORE

We must cultivate a culture that allows dialogue. Evangelicals have been criticized—many times rightly so—for being dogmatic and closed-minded. For too long we have been doing all the talking, without any dialogue. We are now serving new generations that have serious trust issues, and trust is not earned by talking just one-way. We must disarm this criticism and regain trust. We need to encourage, not discourage, people to think, to question, to discover. Why are we so afraid of encouraging people to think for themselves? We may need to set up open forums in which people can engage in deeper dialogue about the message. I'm sure Paul the apostle used dialogue in certain preaching settings. At the very least, we need to constantly encourage our listeners to check out our teaching for themselves, measuring them against Scripture. We must avoid, at all costs, giving the impression that we have all the answers and they don't. We may indeed have answers, but if we appear to be arrogant about it, we'll lose our voice. We need to encourage people to think. We need to encourage dialogue, even to encourage people to challenge what we say. This can disarm people and prompt them to study more to see if what we are saying is true, like the Bereans did. Preachers need to be known as good listeners in dialogue, as well as good communicators. We must be creative and have dialogue as a core value for how we communicate to and teach emerging generations. This is a huge necessity for being a missional leader in the emerging culture.

> *My problem with Christianity was that they never allowed you to look into any other religions. It is like, "This is the book. This is the way. Believe it or go to hell."* —SULLY ERNA, LEAD SINGER OF GODSMACK

Learning to "struggle with the Scriptures" through the example of midrash. Midrash (Hebrew for "examine" or "investigate") is the Jewish tradition which emphasizes struggling with numerous possible interpretations of the Scriptures. To a modern mindset this might sound dangerous, but I believe this is healthy and sharpens our thinking. It also admits that we may not have all the answers about God neatly packaged. In preaching, the one speaking can share about places in the Scriptures he or she may be wrestling with. Consider setting up occasional "think tanks"; invite people to gather in a separate room during a worship service or at some other time to ask questions and have open discussion. In our church, we have an email discussion group for people to engage in theological discussion or to ask questions. I monitor it so I can give guidance as well as explain our church's stance on issues, but I allow people to express whatever they want. I always ask for questions that I can address in sermons. This approach is refreshing to people in emerging generations because it expresses an openness from church leaders who don't fear questions, dialogue, and discussion.

✠ The preacher as shepherd and fellow journeyer instead of as message giver and problem solver

I was a little nervous when a reporter from a major local newspaper indicated she was going to attend a Graceland service one Sunday night. Why? I knew from initial phone conversations that she was not a believer and had some problems with church in general. Her assignment was to write an article about why so many younger people were attending our service. It was a normal night. In fact I was speaking about our mission as believers, which made me even more uncomfortable. I was afraid she would think we were targeting people like her in order to convert them.

After the service was over, we met for an interview. In my usual fashion, I ended up asking her a lot of questions about what she believed and what she thought of the service. She said what impressed her most was that she never heard me say, "You should do this," or, "You need to share your faith." She said that every time I gave an instruction it was always in the plural to include myself. "We should do this," or, "We should share the faith." She asked me if I realized I did that, which I honestly hadn't. She told me that whenever she has attended church, the preacher was always telling "them" what to do. He had all the answers for other people. She said this was the first time she had ever heard a preacher say, "We need to do this," and she was greatly encouraged by it. She said she truly felt I was on the journey with those in the church. In today's emerging culture, the role of the preacher really needs to come across much more as a caring shepherd who is on the journey with his flock than as a dispenser of information and knowledge telling people what to do.

Preaching in the emerging church involves our hearts, marriages, singleness, families, friends, creativity, speech, attitudes, bodies, actions, jokes, whispers, shouts, glances, secrets, thoughts, and yes, our sermons too.

Our lives will preach better than anything we can say. When we preach, our attitudes will speak more loudly than our words. Our little comments

about our opinions on issues will surely be remembered more than our message outlines (Col. 4:6). May we never abuse our privilege as a preacher or teacher by spouting off about our personal preferences or by pointing fingers in an un-Christlike way. There will be a great backlash from emerging generations if they sense loftiness or arrogance. The fact that our hearts are broken over those who don't know Jesus will preach far more loudly than our words. Our admissions of our failures and joys as disciples of Jesus will carry much weight. People in emerging generations look at our hearts more than at the words we speak. Never underestimate this.

+ Preaching that goes way beyond the worship service

The way our church members live throughout the week is our best litmus test of the effectiveness of our preaching. It doesn't matter if we preach three times a day or have three thousand people listening. What matters is what type of church our preaching is producing. Is the Spirit using our words to change lives? How well are families "preaching" what a family is supposed to look like under the Spirit's control? Are the holiness and love of those in our churches obvious to their neighbors and friends? What is your church's response to the poor and needy in your town? This type of preaching (and it is preaching) in a post-Christian culture will go far beyond what our words from a stage or pulpit could ever communicate. We need to see preaching in our worship services as the first step toward what our churches preach with their lives in our communities.

✢ A model for vintage preaching for the emerging church

When all is said and done, Paul offers the ultimate model for preaching. In 1 Corinthians 2:1–5, he says: "When I came to you, brothers, I did not come with eloquence or superior wisdom as I proclaimed to you the testimony about God. For I resolved to know nothing while I was with you except Jesus Christ and him crucified. I came to you in weakness and fear, and with much trembling. My message and my preaching were not with wise and persuasive words, but with a demonstration of the Spirit's power, so that your faith might not rest on men's wisdom, but on God's power."

We would do well to have Paul's heart, approaching the awesome privilege of preaching with weakness, fear, and much trembling.

Almost every time before I preach, I retreat to a private room off to the side of the worship center to pray. If you were to see me there, you'd think I looked a bit odd, walking around in circles with both my arms in the air. I am basically praying, "Lord, I surrender everything to you. I cannot do this without you. May your Spirit speak through me. Your will, not mine. I cannot do this without you, please speak through me." I cannot possibly preach without surrendering all I have to the Spirit of God and asking him to speak through me. The Spirit is the true source of preaching that has power. Because we are faced with an even greater challenge for preaching than in generations past, may we remember this all the more.

Reflect on these words from E. M. Bounds, which speak to preachers of any time period and which reflect the key to vintage preaching for the emerging church: "The preacher must pre-eminently be a man of prayer. His heart must graduate in the school of prayer. In the school of prayer only can the heart learn to preach. No learning can make up for the failure to pray. No earnestness, no diligence, no study, no gifts will supply its lack."[4]

EMERGING THOUGHTS

1. **What is the primary form of preaching used at your church and who is it connecting with?**

2. **How can your church enhance its form of preaching to reach emerging generations more effectively?**

3. **Do you agree or disagree with Leith Anderson's statement about propositional teaching. Why?**

4. **How would you rate your church attenders? Are they "self-feeders" of Scripture? Or are they dependent on the charisma and preaching skills of the preacher for their feeding?**

Chapter

Evangelism

Beyond the Prayer to Get into Heaven

18

> **" *Out:* Evangelism as sales pitch, as conquest, as warfare, as ultimatum, as threat, as proof, as argument, as entertainment, as show, as monologue, as something you have to do.**
>
> *In:* **Disciple-making as conversation, as friendship, as influence, as invitation, as companionship, as challenge, as opportunity, as conversation, as dance, as something you get to do.**
>
> —Brian McLaren, *More Ready Than You Realize*

The unspoken motto of the seeker-sensitive movement has been a line from the Kevin Costner movie *Field of Dreams*. "If you build it, they will come." And they came. Hundreds of thousands of people now attend churches which used the strategy of producing a seeker-sensitive service with great preaching, great music, great dramas, and using great modern facilities. Some leaders shifted much of their evangelistic focus in the church to putting on a production-heavy worship service, believing that if one produces a relevant, quality service, seekers will come. However, this evangelism strategy, which works great for a modern mindset, will need to be rethought when it comes to reaching emerging generations.

197

If we scan the land, we will see that even churches that have had tremendous success with this approach are now changing their strategy to reach the emerging culture. Why? Because modern Christians may be coming, but the post-Christians aren't.

✛ The Starbucks Priest from Willow Creek

One of my favorite friends within the emerging church conversation is Daniel Hill, a pastor on the Axis team staff at Willow Creek Community Church. Axis was started several years ago when Willow Creek noticed that their weekend seeker-services were not drawing younger generations. So they started a weekend seeker-service specifically for "twenty-somethings," as they call it.

Daniel has an interesting perspective because he also works part-time at a Starbucks. His coworkers have nicknamed him the Starbucks Priest because they know he is a pastor. He took the job not because he needs the extra money but because he wanted to be around nonbelievers for evangelistic purposes. He initially thought he would work at Starbucks for around six weeks, develop some friendships, invite his workmates to their Axis services, and see them become Christians—the normal seeker-sensitive evangelism strategy. However, things went somewhat differently. How? He's now been working at Starbucks for over two years, but hasn't yet seen one person become a Christian. And apart from one girl who will attend Axis only every now and then, none of his coworkers will even go to the Axis services.

✛ If you build it, they won't come . . . yet

What is happening here? An educated, intelligent pastor from the premier seeker-sensitive church in America with great facilities and staff to make the Axis services happen is not seeing his post-Christian coworkers at Starbucks respond to the strategy of evangelism that worked in the modern seeker-sensitive church with previous generations.

With his permission, I am going to let him explain this to you through excerpts from some of our email correspondence about how evangelism is changing in the emerging culture.

? *you work at willow creek, which places an extremely high value on evangelism with great seeker-services and ministry designed for younger nonchristians to go to. so why did you feel you needed to take a job at starbucks?*

As I was teaching training and vision sessions on postmodern evangelism, I realized my stories were always in the past tense. I was regularly saying things like, "I once had a friend who . . ." or "I once had a conversation about . . ." It was at that point that the Holy Spirit really convicted me.

Here I was working at a church which focused on evangelism and I didn't even know any non-Christians. The only question was, Where can I find people from my generation that don't go to church? I remember pondering this question on a cold December evening while sitting at the Starbucks down the street from where I lived. As I sipped my latte, I suddenly had an epiphany.

They work here at Starbucks.

? *you took the job at starbucks and then proceeded with your normal evangelism strategy, which at willow is to befriend and then invite non-believers to a seeker-service. are there any "success" stories seeing them attend Axis and then become christians?*

Well, I celebrated my two-year anniversary at Starbucks this January, and the experience has been a fascinating one for me and full of lessons learned. At the beginning, I naively assumed that the only thing standing between these Starbucks employees and Jesus Christ was the absence of someone who could clearly explain the message of Christianity to them or to invite them to a relevant church service.

That has not been the case.

? *so what did you discover about evangelism by working at starbucks?*

At Starbucks, I ended up encountering a community full of post-Christian people who had little trust in organized religion and couldn't care less what I had to say. I learned that there was absolutely no interest whatsoever from them in attending a church. No matter how relevant the service was or how great the preaching, they did not have any desire to go. They don't trust Christians and usually have had only negative encounters with them. The ironic thing is that they are profoundly spiritual people. They believe in God and believe it is important to live off of a values- and morals-based system. They just won't go to a Christian church.

? *what do you think are the reasons that changes are happening in terms of evangelism strategy?*

After developing a number of friendships at Starbucks, a new distinction has emerged in my understanding: pre-Christian versus post-Christian, and this distinction has radically altered my approach to evangelism.

A pre-Christian is someone who does not have a clear understanding of Christianity but with the right approach could be convinced of its validity. If most people in today's generation were pre-Christian, I don't think the distinctions between emerging generations and the boomers would be felt nearly as strong. I think most boomers were pre-Christians because they had a Judeo-Christian worldview already. They are still open to dialogue and even invitation to a church. This isn't the case for emerging generations.

I have sensed for a long time that most of my friends were not pre-Christians but were post-Christians. By *post* I simply mean the generations born *after* pre-Christians, who were the last generations born into a Judeo-Christian worldview.

Post-Christians have already encountered Christianity at some level (i.e., as an institution or organized religion, through a Christian they know, a family member, or even media portrayal) and have decided on the answer, "Thanks, but no thanks." In other words, you are starting in a very deep hole. This makes our strategy of evangelism a whole lot different for post-Christians since it means we are starting in an extremely more difficult place than with generations past. You can't just invite them to a church or give a four-step easy gospel explanation like we used to.

+ Changing values, changing strategies for evangelism

Daniel now concentrates his evangelistic efforts on more of an incarnational apostolic ("sent out") approach. He is designing various events and gatherings to simply build friendships outside of any seeker-sensitive service. Inviting people to come to a relevant church service is not working like it did with baby boomers. He is now training people to think that evangelism to post-Christians is going to take a lot more time, effort, trust-building, and prayer than ever before. Daniel also says we are starting in a deep hole with post-seeker-sensitive generations, so we need to put a lot of effort into getting them out of the hole before we can evangelize like we used to. He is even in the planning stage of starting a new church in the city of Chicago with this philosophy of outreach.

Pre-Christian:
Most boomers, those who were the last born into a Judeo-Christian worldview.

Post-Christian:
Ones born after pre-Christians and have decided, "thanks, but no thanks."

In past years many churches have concentrated their evangelistic efforts on getting people (pre-Christians) to attend events such as Easter musicals, seeker-sensitive services, evangelistic concerts, and related gatherings. However, if post-Christians are not interested in coming to our events, then we need radical changes in our evangelistic strategy. Let me summarize some of these changes:

Shifting Values in Approach to Evangelism

Modern Church	Emerging Church
Evangelism is an event that you invite people to.	Evangelism is a process that occurs through relationship, trust, and example.
Evangelism is primarily concerned with getting people into heaven.	Evangelism is concerned with people's experiencing the reality of living under the reign of his kingdom now.
Evangelism is focused on pre-Christians.	Evangelism is focused on post-Christians.
Evangelism is done by evangelists.	Evangelism is done by disciples.
Evangelism is something you do in addition to discipleship.	Evangelism is part of being a disciple.
Evangelism is a message.	Evangelism is a conversation.
Evangelism uses reason and proofs for apologetics.	Evangelism uses the church being the church as the primary apologetic.
Missions is a department of the church.	The church is a mission.

You can see there are shifting values in how we approach our evangelism for the post-seeker church. But in addition it's helpful to rethink what our message is.

✛ Rethinking our message

I just listened to a modern, propositional presentation of the gospel given at an evangelistic event by a communicator who was precise and scriptural. He clearly communicated that God loves us (John 3:16) and that sin separates us from God (Rom. 3:23). We were told that the free gift of God is eternal life in Jesus (Rom. 6:23) and that faith in Jesus by grace will allow us to have our sins forgiven and to enter heaven when we die. He then wrapped it up, said a prayer, and asked for a show of hands from those who had prayed the prayer. This is a good example of how we explain the good news of the gospel message (1 Cor. 15:1–8). But what I think we have subtly done is actually stopped short of explaining the full beauty of what the gospel is. I don't mean we need to add anything to it (Gal. 1:8)! But we need to explain not only what it means in the future when we get to heaven but also what it means now. Are we explaining and emphasizing what might be most attractive to those in the emerging culture? And could we yet again be guilty of teaching people a consumeristic form of Christianity?

✞ Living in the kingdom now, not just when we get to heaven

Of course, the thought of the gracious free gift of being with God in person in heaven is more thrilling than we possibly can imagine. But it seems that the modern church has focused only on the problem of fixing sin (which absolutely needs fixing) through the death and resurrection of Christ. Yet heaven is not necessarily the goal post-seekers are thinking of, and their idea of sin is not the same as we would think of it. Instead, emerging generations are connecting with the idea of living in tune with Jesus, placing yourself under God's reign and being a participant in the kingdom now.

Modern church focus of the gospel message:	Emerging church focus of the gospel message:
Jesus died for your sins so that you can go to heaven when you die.	Jesus died for your sins so that you can be his redeemed coworker *now* in what he is doing in this world and can spend eternity with the one you are giving your life to in heaven when you die.

How often do we hear the kingdom talked about in evangelistic messages? How often do we hear it announced that the reign of God is present and available to us to participate in now through Jesus? Jesus told his disciples to pray "your kingdom come, your will be done on earth as it is in heaven" (Matt. 6:10).

✛ Could this be part of the reason we are seeing so many consumer-Christians?

I wonder if the way the modern church has presented the gospel by focusing on life after death has subtly helped produce a consumer mindset. Dallas Willard suggests we have basically taught in the modern church that people get a bar code, like on a supermarket product, which guarantees our salvation. With that mindset, Willard explains, "the payoff for having faith and being 'scanned' comes at death and after. Life now being lived has no necessary connection with being a Christian as long as the bar code does its job."[1]

Willard suggests that our preaching and teaching simply become focused on "sin-management" rather than on kingdom living and becoming a disciple of Jesus now, learning to live as he lived. We thus fall into a cycle of producing consumer Christians who wait to go to heaven and in the meantime turn to God simply to learn how to manage sin in this life. And it all starts with our evangelism!

We must speak about the kingdom in our evangelism because post-Christians are more concerned with the kingdom in this life than with the kingdom in the next life.

Darrell Gruder, in *The Missional Church,* describes what he feels needs to change: "Evangelism would move from an act of recruiting or co-opting those outside the church to an invitation of companionship.... To those invited, the church would offer itself to assist their entrance into the reign of God and to travel with them as co-pilgrims. Here lies a path for the renewal of the heart of the church and its evangelism."[2]

What a contrast between this approach to presenting the gospel and bringing in some well-known Christian bands to draw a primarily Christian audience for an evangelistic event. We can't just rev people up with music and then share a ten-minute message on the fact that Jesus died for your sins to get you into heaven. We have to present a life-altering, soul-changing message that invites people through Jesus' death to be participants in the kingdom of God now.

✛ So what does evangelism look like in the emerging church?

1. Evangelism offers an invitation into the kingdom instead of a way to get to heaven

We emphasize being a student, coworker, apprentice, and disciple of Jesus in his kingdom as the fruit the gospel produces. Repentance is a natural part of this type of evangelistic approach, as people align themselves with kingdom living and become students of Jesus.

2. Evangelism is less of an invitation to an event and more of an invitation to enter into community

As we learned from Daniel Hill, post-Christian generations are not as interested in attending an evangelistic event or a relevant church service. However, after they have come to trust Christians, they are highly interested in becoming part of a community of faith. We have to go back to being more incarnational, living out the message of Jesus. Our communities of faith should draw nonbelievers. Like Jesus prayed in John 17:15, "My prayer is not that you take them out of the world but that you protect them from the evil one." We cannot become an enclosed, protected community.

George Hunter, in his book *The Celtic Way of Evangelism,* has his finger on the pulse of what is happening in the emerging world of evangelism. He builds a case for how the evangelistic method of the Roman world was not effective in a Celtic culture. In past decades, evangelicals used a Roman method of evangelism because we were living in a culture that had a Roman mindset. But today, our culture is producing people more like the Celts, a pagan culture which favored a more sensory approach to learning. Hunter writes: "Bluntly stated, the Roman model for reaching people (who are 'civilized' enough) is: (1) Present the Christian message; (2) Invite them to decide to believe in Christ and become Christians; (3) If they decide positively, welcome them into the church and its fellowship. The Roman model seems very logical to us because most American evangelists are scripted by it! We explain the gospel, they accept Christ, we welcome them into the church! Presentation, Decision, Assimilation. What could be more logical than that?"[3]

But you already know enough to infer the contrasting Celtic model for reaching people:

1. You first establish community with people or bring them into the fellowship of your community of faith.
2. Within fellowship, you engage in conversation, ministry, prayer, and worship.
3. In time, as they discover what you believe, you invite them to commit.

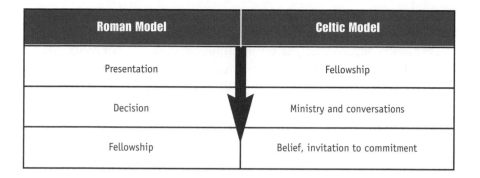

Roman Model	Celtic Model
Presentation	Fellowship
Decision	Ministry and conversations
Fellowship	Belief, invitation to commitment

We can learn from the Celtic approach. We are not facing naked, screaming, howling Celtic barbarians running toward us with swords, as St. Patrick may have faced. Yet we still have issues similar to those faced by those who communicated with the Celtic people in the fifth century.

We need to admit that our strategy of evangelism needs rethinking. If we are honest, most people attending Christian events for evangelism are Christians seeking a fun time or Christians who have strayed from church. At your evangelistic events, are you seeing not only pre-Christians but also post-Christians? People from post-seeker-sensitive generations? Have you studied the lasting impact of your events? Do you know the names of nonbelievers who now are believers and are part of your church community as a result of your events? How many are there, and how old are they? Evangelism for those of a modern mindset may not work for emerging generations. Don't be afraid to do a tough examination of what is really happening as a result of your current strategy.

We need to realize that our primary form of evangelism will be the church's simply being what the church should be. My wife, Becky, disciples and meets weekly with Ashley, who is in her early twenties. Although Ashley is now a believer and is very much part of our church community, for a long time she had typically horrible impressions of Christians and Christianity. In particular she was disturbed that Christians believed that they had the only true religion. She believed we should never make judgments about another faith until we studied it just as thoroughly as we would Christianity. Ashley's close friend Julie was a Christian but wasn't walking with God. However, Julie heard about our worship gatherings and started attending. She got back on track with God, and Ashley, still a nonbeliever, noticed her changing. Ashley was intrigued and started getting involved with a group from our church that would go to downtown Santa Cruz every Friday night and feed and befriend the homeless. Ashley became part of that group

We need to understand that the "if we build it, they will come" mentality couldn't be farther from the Great Commission. We are told explicitly to go, not to marinate in our subcultures. Second, church-shopping habits have changed. Until about 1995, a fair percentage of the unchurched seemed willing to darken our doors on a Sunday morning. Now, the percentage of non-Christian, unchurched faith-shoppers has plummeted. Which means the Sunday service is no longer the front door for seekers. The new front door is relationship—offsite connections that include sacrifice, service, and a whole bunch of time. This is where following Christ gets real.

—SALLY MORGENTHALER

of Christians. I got to know Ashley during this time, and it turned out that she became a Christian one night while serving the homeless in the name of Jesus. She experienced the gospel through kingdom living, serving in community, and being assimilated into a group of Christians who truly were living out what the church should be. This way of coming to faith is what I believe will become the norm in the future.

We need to shift the focus of our evangelistic efforts away from events and onto community. As the Roman model becomes less effective, the back to the basics approach of first seeing nonbelievers enter community with Christians becomes more effective. Rather than Christians creating a strange subculture that alienates non-Christians, believers need to seriously include those who aren't Christians into their lives, their social outings, and their regular prayers. We need to establish community in deep ways to build trust.

A problem with event evangelism—having bands and great speakers and fancy musicals—as a person's entry experience of Christianity is that when the person attends the church's regular worship service, they discover a whole different experience. There are no flashy bands and special speakers, just normal pastors and a normal church experience. Could this be one reason why we see such a drastic fall-out rate from those who make "decisions" at these events? Could it be that for emerging generations, our efforts need to focus more on connecting them into community life than on getting them to attend an event?

We need to move our strategy to outside the church walls again. With the Celts, evangelism really occurred through people entering community. In similar fashion, we need to see people become part of our community of faith before we put any pressure on them to make a decision. We can bring people into our community in so many ways. We can host social events for Christians to invite their non-Christian friends to simply for fun. We can start Bible studies in which people can be part of "talking about Jesus." These gatherings can take place naturally in homes and coffeehouses, rather than in the church building.

3. Evangelism is more dialogue and listening than preaching and telling

I have yet to be turned down when I ask a non-Christian with whom I have a relationship to go to lunch and answer questions about what they believe about Jesus and church. There is a big difference between inviting someone to listen to you share your opinions and inviting them to tell you their opinions. As George Barna comments: "You cannot effectively evangelize most of them by preaching at them. Effective evangelism with this group requires relationships, dialogue and a willingness to journey together. A Socratic form of evangelism — questions-based rather than didactic; long-term rather than hit-and-run; conversational rather than confrontational; backed up by personal modeling rather than institutional traditions and dogma — works best."[4]

Just think what might happen if the majority of people in our churches repeatedly had conversations like this with people they know and have built trust with. Do you realize how much thinking and processing would be going on as followers of Jesus lovingly listen, care, build trust, and gain understanding? Think of all the post-Christian nonbelievers who would be surprised that we care about what they think rather than just wanting to thrust our beliefs on them. Just think.

4. Evangelism is part of discipleship and the church culture rather than something you do on the side

Evangelism in the post-seeker-sensitive emerging church must be part of the lifeblood of the church and its mission, not just something that you do every now and then. A church doesn't need a missions department if its people think of everyone in the church as being on a mission, both locally and globally. Just the fact that a church has a missions department can signal that the real mission field is "way over there someplace," rather than also being all around us. If the church puts on events as the primary time when evangelism occurs, don't we then teach that the job of the people is to bring people to the leaders? If we surveyed the people of your church right now and asked them where evangelism happens and they say "at the church's events," then you are probably not reaching post-Christians. If asked, would the individuals of your church be able to clearly state how they are on an evangelistic mission? What would their evangelistic temperature be? And if it's low, could you as a church leader be the cause by not emphasizing the mission of the church or by not providing adequate training or teaching?

5. Evangelism is "discipleship-evangelism" rather than entertainment-based

No longer do we need to water anything down or do a bait-and-switch through an entertaining event. Evangelism in the emerging church means being bold and loving about what we believe. Not arrogant bold or know-it-all bold or pointing-fingers bold but relationally bold, sharing the good news of Jesus and of kingdom living with others. Emerging generations are craving spiritual meaning. Let's not hide Jesus anymore behind strobe lights and loud music. Let's show Jesus in us. Let's respect the intelligence of nonbelievers and be prepared to lovingly but intellectually speak about what we believe rather than just throw out a quick verse. Let's evangelize through making disciples.

6. Evangelism may take a lot more time and trust-building today

Don't forget that with emerging generations, we have a lot more trust to rebuild before we have a voice. Also, conversion and sanctification may be a lot messier and take a lot longer than in previous generations. In past generations, when a non-Christian converted, they generally already had a biblical worldview. Their sexuality, their view of God, their sense of right and wrong were in line with the teachings of Jesus. But with emerging generations, many times we are dealing with a total change of their concept of God, morals, sexuality, and so on.

✣ Missions is not just overseas

Emerging church leaders must create a missional culture in their churches. I believe the desire lies within people to impact the kingdom, but church leaders need to spark this passion.

Several years ago, when I was a high school pastor, I saw how excited youth would get about going on missions trips to Mexico. They would be bold sharing their faith on the streets, doing dramas in public settings, but as soon as they got home, they would be much more passive and not retain their evangelistic fervor.

It puzzled me until I realized that most of them did not view missions to be a local thing. They associated missions with other countries only. So I began creating a culture of missions that included our very own town of Santa Cruz. I gave a message in which I talked about a village called Zurcatnas, which was looking for missionaries. I told them it was right on the ocean with good surfing. They would each have a family who hosts them, and they would get a room in a house and meals, and some would even have a car. Since English was spoken there, they would be able to continue their education as well as communicate in the language of the natives. They could fairly easily get part-time jobs if they needed some spending money. And I shared how 90 percent of the teenagers in Zurcatnas are unevangelized.

When I asked how many people would want to go there, almost every hand went up. Then I explained that the village of Zurcatnas was Santa Cruz; the name was simply spelled backward. I told them that everything I said about the mission field, everything they were excited about, was the very situation that they were already in. This was a turning point, and we furthered the missional emphasis with the high schoolers by doing summer prayer walks at their schools, emphasizing that they are ambassadors of Jesus and missionaries there.

✝ Pastors and leaders leading a church of missionaries

Every disciple is an evangelist to some degree. Being a pastor means leading a community of not just disciples but mission-minded disciples. Evangelism needs to bleed from your entire church's being and should motivate Christians to be more hardcore disciples. A truly evangelistic church is a church that knows its Bible all the more, prays all the more, and loves people all the more.

We need to be training people to share with others who Jesus is. We need to be hosting nontypical evangelistic opportunities for discussion, such as film events and art exhibits that promote conversation about Jesus. We need to be thinking strategically about evangelism in everything we do.

> *While Jesus was having dinner at Matthew's house, many tax collectors and "sinners" came and ate with him and his disciples. When the Pharisees saw this, they asked his disciples, "Why does your teacher eat with tax collectors and 'sinners'?" On hearing this, Jesus said, "It is not the healthy who need a doctor, but the sick."* —MATTHEW 9:10–12

✝ Do you know any post-Christians? Do you pray for any by name?

Leaders set the pace for how evangelistic our churches are. I have the privilege of talking to many non-Christians. I try to meet with them, and I also have prayed with them. They are post-Christians who through time and trusting relationships with people in our church may eventually come to a worship event. Through this, I have personally seen many trust in Jesus. But it is not an easy or quick process anymore.

I carry a 3 x 5 card in my Daytimer, on which I have written the names of seven post-Christians who right now do not go to any church. I pray for them daily, try to make contact with them through the week, and get out of the church office as much as I can to study in places where I can make contact with them. This isn't easy because it takes time, love, and care, whether or not they ever go to a worship gathering.

> In the emerging church, evangelism is not something a disciple does; it is something that a disciple is.

Immediately following the terrorist attacks of September 11, 2001, our churches were packed. You could hear talk of revival. However, it didn't last too long. Mainly our churches were packed with fearful straying Christians who came back for a little while. All seven of the post-Christians I know did not go to church on the Sundays after that ominous attack. They got scared and turned to one another, but why would they go to church? They have never been there, and they don't trust it.

Although evangelism will not be easy, I hold out hope that emerging generations will come to know Jesus in numbers beyond our imagination. I believe that if we in leadership grasp evangelism as our mission, if we take prayer seriously, if we set the culture of our churches as one of disciples who evangelize, if we present a holistic gospel, if we don't rely simply on events to present evangelistic messages, much could happen. The potential is incredible. Perhaps the next time there is a tragic event (God forbid), or if a tragic event occurs in the life of a post-Christian, more post-Christians will know Christians and turn to them for help and comfort. Perhaps the tide will turn and non-Christians will be drawn to us instead of being turned off by us.

An outstanding chapter, Dan!

—RICK WARREN

EMERGING THOUGHTS

1. Is the primary way your church approaches evangelism a Celtic model or a Roman model? Do you need to make any changes to reach the emerging generations in your community?

2. What are some ways you could present the gospel as more than a guarantee of heaven in the future?

3. Do you agree or disagree that the days of "build it and they will come" are ending as an effective approach to evangelism? Why or why not?

4. What are some specific ways that your church could build the trust of non-Christians through dialogue and community?

5. Do you personally know any post-Christians? What has your experience been with them in talking about Jesus or inviting them to an event or a worship service?

Spiritual Formation

Becoming a Vintage Christian

" **Nondiscipleship is the elephant in the church.**

—Dallas Willard, *The Divine Conspiracy*

We filmed a Jay Leno–like interview on a high school campus, intending to show that most teenagers today know more about the popular music scene than they do about the life of Christ, being careful not to make fun of anyone. So we started by asking questions such as, "Can you name the members of 'N Sync?" Even teenagers who hated the band remembered at least a few names. Then we thought we'd ask, "What are the names of the disciples?" figuring most would be able to name only one or two. But what we found was even more disturbing. Not only could no one name even one disciple, but almost everyone wanted to know, "What is a disciple?"

In retrospect, I really should have expected that, but it got me thinking. How many people in our churches know what the word disciple means? In fact, I wondered how many pastors and church leaders could answer the question. Yet this is probably the most important question—after asking, What is the church?—that we need to be asking.

✛ Being a disciple of Jesus in the emerging culture

In Greek, the word disciple is the noun *mathetes,* which is found 269 times in the New Testament and means "a pupil, an apprentice, an adherent." The verb form, *matheteuo,* occurs four times in the Gospels and once in Acts. It means "to be or become a pupil or a disciple."[1] If our mission is to make disciples of Jesus (Matt. 28:19) and the word disciple means to be a student, pupil, or apprentice of Jesus, how will we approach this role in the emerging culture? Dallas Willard, in his book *The Divine Conspiracy,* explores the shift away from a subtle works-based form of discipleship, which focuses on modern methodology, and draws us toward a whole new level of kingdom living that is based on being a student and an apprentice of Jesus. In a conversation with me once, he explained that "a disciple of Jesus is one who practices his presence and arranges his or her life in such a way as to live as Christ would live if he were them."

The ultimate challenge is making and being a disciple.
—HOWARD HENDRICKS

Willard further explains this definition in his book *Renovation of the Heart,* in which he states that a disciple is "one of those who have trusted Jesus with their whole life, so far as they understand it. Because they have done so, they want to learn everything He has to teach them about life in the Kingdom of God now and forever, and they are constantly with Him to learn this. Disciples of Jesus are those learning to be like Him."[2]

In the emerging church, our mission is evangelism, but evangelism includes making disciples. Becoming an apprentice of Jesus is the whole process of our sanctification. Sanctification is our spiritual formation as the Spirit of God shapes and forms us from the inside out.

✠ The bottom line of spiritual formation for all generations

While we cannot treat spiritual formation and discipleship in any depth in this chapter, we can raise issues that the emerging church needs to grapple with. But we do so understanding that the ultimate goal of discipleship, no matter how it is done, should be measured by what Jesus taught in Matthew 22:37–40:

- ➡ Love the Lord with all your heart, mind, and soul. Are we loving him more?
- ➡ Love others as yourself. Are we loving people more?

With this in mind, let's consider two different ways of approaching discipleship and spiritual formation with different types of people:

+ The emerging church needs to put everything into the primary goal of discipleship

The seeker-sensitive movement put a lot of emphasis on programming and presentation for the purpose of evangelism. In many cases, once a large number of people had been drawn to the church, leaders then scram-

Shifting Values in Approach to Spiritual Formation

Modern Church	Emerging Church
Discipleship is compartmentalized.	Discipleship is holistic.
Systems are set in place for the spiritual journey.	Systems are set in place to guide the journey but not to be the journey itself.
The vision for small groups is to fill the "empty chair," develop leadership, and divide groups to reproduce.	Small groups provide a place of stability for those who have experienced divided families and instability in their world.
The Bible is a book to help solve problems and a means to know God.	The Bible is a compass for direction and a means to experience God.
Discipleship is an individual experience.	Discipleship is a communal experience.
Discipleship is based on modern methodology and helps.	Discipleship is based on ancient disciplines.
Discipleship is knowledge and belief.	Discipleship is holistic faith and action.
Discipleship is education.	Discipleship is spiritual formation.
Being a disciple and evangelism are two distinct things we do.	Being a disciple is being on an evangelistic mission.
Spiritual formation primarily occurs through presentation and teaching.	Spiritual formation primarily occurs through experience and participation.
Discipleship is something that happens after people attend the worship service.	Discipleship is the center of the mission of the church.

bled to set up systems and programs for discipleship. In the emerging post-seeker-sensitive church, making disciples needs to be the lifeblood of the church from the beginning. This is critical so we don't make some of the mistakes we have seen in the past.

Our definition of discipleship must be clear and known by everyone in our church. Each church should have a written definition, known by everyone, which serves as a reference point for every decision, program, and strategy. In my church setting, we spend time each year going over our definition plus the disciplines and marks of a disciple. Sometimes we'll have worship gatherings focused on what it means to be a disciple, and we often include a sheet in our bulletin with a full "portrait of a disciple" even if we aren't teaching on it that day. We title this sheet, "Vintage Christianity: Being a Mission-Minded Disciple of Jesus." We have planned worship services in which we set up prayer stations with props that indicate various marks of a disciple, listing some of the things Jesus told us as his disciples to do. People can go to each table, read Scriptures, and ask God to produce these marks in them. It is beautiful to see people from emerging generations on their knees at these prayer stations. Prayer is an extremely critical key in all of this because it shows us that discipleship is not something we do but a relationship or an apprenticeship we are in.

✢ Relying on the Spirit, not the disciplines, to transform us

It is critical for the emerging church that we not teach that discipleship is simply a set of things to do. Otherwise discipleship becomes works-oriented and leads to legalism. If we are striving to be disciples of Jesus, then we must be in relationship with him. Practicing his presence through prayer is vital as we ask for the Spirit's help. While memorizing verses or going through study booklets is good and necessary, we can miss the whole point. We need to remember that the disciplines of an apprentice are only a means. The Holy Spirit is the one who changes, grows, and sanctifies us (Rom. 6–8).

We need to set systems in place that won't be obstacles for emerging generations. Churches need a strategy for drawing people toward discipleship. Dallas Willard states that there is "a strong absence of effectual programs of training that enable His people to do what Jesus said in a regular and efficient manner."[3] But keep in mind a few things that will shape your strategy.

The emerging church must not settle for attending events and programs. Rather, we must be disciples of Jesus who are dependent on the Holy Spirit to transform us into people who love God with all our being and who love people so much that we cannot help but be mission-minded.

First, an effective way many modern churches steer people through the initial steps of spiritual formation is through a numbered class system—101, 201, 301, and so on. Although this system has worked wonders in churches across the country, I can't tell you the number of awkward conversations I have had, with younger people in particular, trying to explain this program and approach. For one thing, emerging generations tend to suspect or resent any form of organized religion. Any approach that smacks of turning sacred spirituality into a formal, corporate, and rigid pursuit, even with the best of intentions, can easily backfire. Of course, the purpose behind 101, 201, etc., classes needs to be fulfilled, but we need to rethink how we approach them.

Second, emerging generations are responsive to much more fluid forms of learning. A numbered, step-by-step prescription for spiritual progress many times can prohibit organic growth. I've struggled to explain to new believers why they had to go through three classes before learning to share the faith. It was the first thing they wanted to learn, because they have so many non-Christian friends! Obviously we need to be well-rounded in our understanding of our faith, our spiritual habits, and our giftedness. But I believe we will continue to find emerging generations resistant to structures which box up something as mysterious and holistic as spiritual growth into a prescribed system.

So how can we create systems for discipleship that do not smack of modern business or academic structures and don't feel programmed but rather embrace the mystery, awe, and wonder of God's transforming work? One thing we can do is simply rename the classes to emphasize the spiritual aspect and to reflect values of the emerging culture. Mosaic church in Los Angeles uses names like River to describe a spiritual formation retreat that "is an immersion of your senses, emotions, body and intellect as we quest to explore our connection to God." They have another retreat called Snow, which is a "quest for forgiveness." Cedar Ridge Community Church in Maryland has spiritual formation classes named Soul Findings, Journey, and Kindle.

Titles which sound more spiritual as well as classes which encompass depth with an organic approach fit much better in the fluidity of the emerging culture. But titles are only the packaging; we need to think through how to encourage spiritual formation through a holistic approach of mind, heart, senses, and bodies. We can't just change the name and then just keep dispersing information. We need to change how we approach spiritual formation.

The focus of our strategy must be to produce mission-minded disciples. We need to evaluate everything we do in our churches by how each activity is producing mission-minded disciples. How is this class steering people toward becoming mission-minded disciples? In what ways do we

> This makes incredible sense. How can you build on what you don't have?
>
> —HOWARD HENDRICKS

hope to see God use this event to build mission-minded disciples? How does this sermon move people toward being a mission-minded disciple? Everything should be thought of in this way. Everything.

✟ The emerging church must see generations connecting

Remember your leaders, who spoke the word of God to you. Consider the outcome of their way of life and imitate their faith. —HEBREWS 13:7

> Connecting generations is the most frequently overlooked aspect of spiritual formation.
>
> —HOWARD HENDRICKS

I met Stuart Allen when I was in my early twenties, living in London and playing drums for a rockabilly-punk band. Stuart was pastor of a tiny church in London, a church in which the average age of his parishioners must have been seventy. We met when I wandered into this church one afternoon during a small lunch-hour Bible study. Stuart took me under his wing. Picture this unlikely combination: an eighty-three-year-old man, and me, dressed all in black with a very tall pompadour, spiked wrist bands, a metal belt, a skull bolo tie, and thick-soled Creeper shoes. Stuart never seemed to see any of that. He looked right past my exterior and showed me Jesus. And it didn't matter to me whether Stuart dressed in the latest fashion or whether he knew all the bands I was interested in. What mattered to me was that he loved God and that he unconditionally cared about and loved me.

Some weekends Stuart and his wife would invite me to stay at their house in the countryside. I saw how he would wake up before dawn and pray in a chair in his living room. I saw how he treated his wife with respect and love. I saw how he loved the Scriptures and memorized them.

And I was embraced by the tiny group in Stuart's church. On Sundays after the service, all fifteen of us would descend into a rather cold and dank basement for lunch and tea. I enjoyed being the young one and the center of attention; they would all bring sandwiches and cookies and argue with each other over the privilege of feeding me. Every Sunday afternoon in that little smelly basement, I experienced community with a group of elderly English people. As Stuart mentored me that year, I enjoyed an incredible intergenerational experience, which God used to change my life. A man in his eighties passed down the faith and wisdom to someone almost sixty years younger.

After that God placed Dr. John Mitchell in my life. I had the privilege of meeting with him almost weekly while I was a student at Multnomah

Biblical Seminary in Portland, Oregon. Quite honestly, I didn't think his teaching was riveting, but I found that sitting in his office listening to him pray was a life-changing experience. The advice and wisdom of Dr. Mitchell, who was over ninety when I met him, left an indelible impression. Seeing his love for the Scriptures inspired me far beyond any sermon ever could and instilled in me a love for God's Word that remains to this day. His intimate walk with Jesus was something I can only explain as being truly supernatural.

A third major influence in my life has been Rod Clendenen, who is over eighty years old. Rod continues to show me that worship is something you do not just at a service on Sunday but all day long. He teaches, by his life, how important it is not to depend on the church for your Bible intake but to learn to feed yourself from God's Word. These lessons could never have been taught with the same impact they had in sermons or classes. They can be taught only through mentoring, as generations interact with one another outside of a church setting.

Each of these men, who were in their sixties, eighties, and nineties when I met them, have made a huge impact on my life. Their photographs hang on the wall in my office and frequently remind me of the lessons these men have taught and that it's possible to make it through to old age as a disciple.

+ Looking for a Gandalf

Howard G. Hendricks from Dallas Theological Seminary was the guest speaker for one of our staff retreats. When he sat down across from me at breakfast, we had a conversation during which the topic of intergenerational relationships came up. Dr. Hendricks took out a napkin and drew two long arrows. Here's what his drawing looked like:

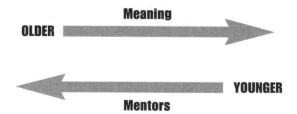

"That's what we have in our churches," he said. "Our churches are full of older people looking for meaning. They have walked with God, they have learned great lessons in life, and now they find themselves retired, with time on their hands, often lacking a sense of purpose and meaning.

"And then we have the younger generations," he said, "who are craving someone to mentor them, someone who will invest in their lives and show them the ways of the Lord. Our churches, meanwhile, are doing everything possible to keep these generations apart. The future of our churches hinges on the passing of faith from one generation to another through mentoring and intergenerational relationships."

I couldn't agree more.

Despite what some may believe, people in emerging generations deeply desire older spiritual mentors who will guide them in their spiritual formation. You can read in 2 Timothy 1:3–5 how Timothy's grandmother shared her faith down the generations. Titus 2:3–4, Psalm 71:18, and Joel 1:2–3 show how older generations were to impart the faith to younger generations.

Think about the changes that have affected the American family in the past fifty years. Not too long ago it was common for older people to share a home with their children and even grandchildren, or at least to live only a short distance away. People in different generations would regularly relate with each other. But clearly things have changed. Most families move several times due to career demands, or they split and relocate following divorce. Many children see their grandparents only rarely because they live in entirely different parts of the country.

Perhaps as a result of this void, younger generations are obsessed with the styles, tastes, and experiences of those who have gone before them. Think of the popularity of "Seventies Night" theme parties and the revival of the swing music of the 1930s and 1940s. Music legends like Johnny Cash, Frank Sinatra, and Tony Bennett are enjoying a resurgence of popularity. Despite obvious cultural differences, emerging generations have a deep longing for connection with and guidance from those who have wisdom and experience beyond their own.

To borrow another example from Tolkien's *The Lord of the Rings,* we see Frodo's reliance on his wise and elderly mentor, Gandalf. We all need Gandalfs in our lives, and I believe that emerging generations are searching for Gandalfs today.

We must do whatever we can to encourage these mentoring relationships. We spend so much energy trying to get generations to worship together, but I really don't believe it makes any meaningful difference if they do. As you've no doubt discovered, it's impossible to please everyone with one style of worship service, due to our differences in values, heart, mindset, and styles of worship.

But how does true community happen, anyway? Probably not as a result of sitting in a room together. We must think of ways to connect generations outside of the worship service.

A mentoring program in which smaller groups or individuals can be matched with those who are older is a fantastic way to accomplish this. Whenever we put out a call for leaders for Home Groups, which study books of the Bible during the week, we try to bring in mostly older people to lead these groups, to open their homes and share their wisdom.

If your church is mainly young people, consider establishing a relationship with another church of mainly older people. This could benefit both church bodies. Whatever it takes, the emerging church must work to establish mentoring relationships between older and younger generations. This intergenerational mentoring and passing on of wisdom must become a value in the emerging church.

✛ When it comes to spiritual growth, one size no longer fits all

Despite the best of intentions, and without realizing it, many of our modern churches have come to embrace a sort of one-size-fits-all approach to spiritual formation. We have systemized our faith so neatly that we've organized mystery and diversity right out of the picture. We've taught that if we fill in these blanks, memorize these verses, go through this booklet, we'll be disciples.

Of course, not all structured systems are bad. Some people grow and thrive in them. But because of the values differences we've discussed, more often than not, the emphasis on uniformity and logic in such a system is detrimental to the spiritual formation of emerging generations.

Gary Thomas, in his book *Sacred Pathways,* explains this diversity so well: "Expecting all Christians to have a certain type of quiet time can wreak havoc in a church. . . . We sometimes assume that if others do not experience the same thing, something must be wrong with them. . . . God wants your worship, according to the way He made you. That may differ somewhat from the worship of the person who brought you to Christ or the person who leads your Bible study or church."[4]

This gets complex, of course, but it makes sense that different people will relate to God in different ways, just as our personality temperaments affect how we relate with other people.

Thomas identifies nine spiritual temperaments, although there certainly might be more. Some people, for instance, tend to be more sensory.

> This strategy of developing mentoring relationships between generations is full of possibilities.
>
> —HOWARD HENDRICKS

They're drawn to the liturgical, the visual, the majestic. Trying to force people with this temperament to become disciples primarily through cognitive, rational training will only frustrate them. Conversely, if someone's spiritual temperament is more intellectual, they will grow naturally through a study of facts and logic.

This is a simple concept, but it has huge ramifications for the emerging church. We must think in terms of fluidity and diversity as we approach our goal of making disciples.

✠ Developing spiritual self-feeders instead of spiritual consumers

I am a Bible junkie. I don't worship the Bible, nor do I think of the Bible as the only way God communicates. But within its pages are life and direction and the grand love story of man and God. I love reading and thinking about the story. I love when the Bible convicts and encourages (Heb. 4:12). The Bible is a precious gift from God, and we need to saturate our minds and hearts with it (Psalm 119:9–16).

My father-in-law, Rod, who is over eighty years old, says he's noticed an unhealthy development in the contemporary church. He feels that we have created what he calls a gas-station mentality. As the modern church has gotten bigger and more proficient in preaching, we have subtly taught people that they come to church to get their weekly fill-up. And so in our eagerness to see disciples made, we create consumers.

> In fact, though by this time you ought to be teachers, you need someone to teach you the elementary truths of God's word all over again. You need milk, not solid food! Anyone who lives on milk, being still an infant, is not acquainted with the teaching about righteousness. But solid food is for the mature, who by constant use have trained themselves to distinguish good from evil.
>
> —Hebrews 5:12–14

Obviously, an adult who can drink only milk is sadly stunted and immature. Verse 14 tells us adults themselves, not any other person or institution, are responsible for their spiritual growth. "But solid food is for the mature, who by constant use have trained themselves." If someone who should be, or appears to be, a mature believer in Jesus tells you he "comes to church to be fed," he may not be as well grounded as he seems. Of course we should serve "healthy meals" at our worship services, but this shouldn't be the only meal people have throughout the week. Have we subtly trained people to come to the worship service for a weekly "feeding?" It's no wonder we are finding that many Christians who even attend weekly worship services are fairly illiterate biblically.

Dallas Willard, in *Renovation of the Heart,* states, "We must flatly say that one of the greatest contemporary barriers of meaningful spiritual formation in Christlikeness is overconfidence in the spiritual efficacy of 'regular church services,' of whatever kind they may be. Though they are vital, they are not enough. It is that simple."[5] I know for a fact that God moves in mighty ways in worship services. But if we look at the overall outcome of the evangelical Bible teaching and preaching, we are seeing some sad results. As a church designs its ministry, it must emphasize spiritual formation outside of the worship services. In the emerging church, we need to spend more time and effort teaching people how to feed themselves than we do on getting them to attend and enjoy our large weekend services.

+ Restoring the ancient disciplines to create vintage Christians

In the cases of wine and clothing, vintage refers to the high quality or value of something old. I think the same goes for the disciplines of our faith. The modern church has made being a disciple a rather limited thing, focusing on the disciplines of prayer, Bible reading, giving, and serving but virtually stopping there. We have neglected so many of the disciplines of the historical church, including weekly fasting, practicing silence, and *lectio divina*.

Emerging generations, in their search for proven, ancient, authentic forms of connection with God, are very much attracted to these ancient disciplines and historical spiritual rituals. Their willingness to participate is much stronger than many of us may have realized. Some of the things we might do include creating ancient midrash groups for discussion, or Greek forum–like discussions that teach how to interpret film theologically. I even heard of a junior high group taking prayer walks through the stations of the cross set up at a camp. At each station, they stopped, meditated on Scripture, and silently prayed. Last summer one of our midweek groups had a two-day fast, which was met with incredible excitement. I soon began to wonder why we weren't doing this all the time. I believe that emerging generations are simply waiting for their leaders to lead them into a new level of discipleship by practicing the ancient disciplines of the faith. Don't underestimate them.

✠ Social action in spiritual formation

Beyond the inward process of spiritual formation, our faith also includes kingdom living, part of which is the responsibility to fight locally and globally for social justice on behalf of the poor and needy. Our example is Jesus, who spent time among the lepers, the poor, and the needy. The New Testament instructs that "to look after orphans and widows" is a sign of pure religion (James 1:27). However, we've managed to hand these responsibilities over to others. We give money, but someone else goes into the slums, the homeless shelters, and the nursing homes. We have created such wonderful buildings and programs for our people that we can get them extremely busy running programs for themselves. With emerging generations, I believe that social action must be locked into our core values and incorporated into how we view our mission as a church, both locally and globally.

✠ A holistic approach to spiritual formation

We need to move to a holistic approach to discipleship instead of a compartmental one. We need to look beyond Bible studies and memory verses and look at our whole church. How do our worship gatherings fit in the holistic plan for discipleship? How does dialogue instead of lecture? How do the arts and creative expression fit in discipleship? (Yes, they do!) How does care of our bodies and health fit? Health and our bodies are rarely ever included in the discussion on discipleship, but they are a major part of being responsible for our "temples" (1 Cor. 6:19–20). How do the spiritual disciplines become part of the normal Christian life?

Emerging church leaders need to rethink the whole concept of discipleship, because quite frankly, if we're honest, the modern church hasn't done that good of a job. If making disciples is our primary goal, we'd better not be afraid to reconsider how we go about it.

In the post-seeker-sensitive emerging church, we all need to be practicing the presence of Jesus and arranging our lives in such a way as to live as he would live if he were us. This is not a shockingly new idea but is simply going back to the basics. It's simply vintage Christianity—the Christianity emerging generations are starving to see and experience.

EMERGING THOUGHTS

1. In your church, how would you say most people would define a disciple? What percentage of your church would you guess could give a reasonable definition of a disciple?

2. What systems are currently in place in your church for someone to grow in his or her spiritual formation? What would you think may be a first step to take if you have nothing in place now?

3. What is currently happening in your church to encourage intergenerational relationships and mentoring? Can you think of ways you could improve in this area in your church?

4. If you want older mentors for the younger, you need to have ways of caring for and nourishing the older ones. What are ways you do that in the emerging church?

Leadership for the Emerging Church

> **As he approached Jerusalem and saw the city, he wept over it and said, "If you, even you, had only known on this day what would bring you peace."**
>
> —Luke 19:41–42

Jesus walked down the Mount of Olives knowing what was ahead of him—arrest, trial, mockings, and merciless beatings. He would soon experience the horrible agony of the cross.

From a human perspective, Jesus might have been angry at Jerusalem for rejecting him. Or he might have been frustrated and fed up that after all of the teachings and miracles he had performed, they still weren't "getting it."

But instead of dismissing them for their stubbornness and disbelief, Jesus stopped, looked down upon the city, and wept for those who didn't know him. Jesus' heart was absolutely broken for the very people who rejected him.

✝ Compassionate leadership needed in the emerging culture

Compassion must be at the core of leadership in the emerging church. We see it demonstrated again in Matthew 9:36 when Jesus saw the crowds and had compassion on them because they were "like sheep without a shepherd." The word compassion is the strongest word for pity in the Greek language, formed from the word *splagchna,* which means "the bowels." It

describes compassion which moves a person to the deepest depths of his being.[1] Writers in the New Testament era used body parts to describe emotions. The bowels and stomach were associated with the deepest physical pain. In other words, Jesus ached for them with an incredibly deep pain because he saw that they were lost and helpless, the same status of many growing up in the emerging culture today. Our hearts need to break and ache for emerging generations who are lost and helpless, "like sheep without a shepherd."

It is not easy leading in the emerging church. We face many issues which didn't exist in prior generations. If we are motivated by the desire to build a big church or to create a safe subculture for Christians, or if we tend to believe that "these emerging generations just don't get it and probably never will," then we're in big trouble. We will become incredibly frustrated. We truly need to be motivated, like Jesus, by a broken heart.

✠ Leaders have lost a voice in the emerging culture

Leaders have a different place in this post-Christian culture than in the modern Christian era. Not too many years ago, Christian leaders had a voice and were generally well respected. Sure, we still see older leaders in government who respect Christian leaders. We still have Christians who respect other Christians. But if you move outside of those circles, it gets a little frightening. We barely have any voice with most of those who are influencing the worldview and opinions of younger generations in the media and entertainment cultures.

Christian leaders no longer automatically have a right to be heard and respected. In fact, we'll probably increasingly see the opposite. Most of those raised outside of the church view Christian leaders as power-seeking, finger-pointing, female-oppressing figures from an organized religion. In our culture today, there are many voices with various opinions, visions, and followers all competing for attention. As Christian leaders, we face the tremendous challenge of earning our right to be heard and respected and trusted.

+ The heart of church leadership must change for the emerging culture

Leaders absolutely still need to lead, but to engage the emerging culture, we need to shift our approach to leadership. The table illustrates some of the contrasts between modern and emerging-church approaches to leadership. Please keep in mind that these are generalizations.

Shifting Values in Approach to Leadership

Modern Leader	Emerging Church Leader
Captain Kirk: "Look to me; I have the plan."	Captain Picard: "I'll lead as we solve this together."
CEO/Manager	Spiritual guide/Fellow journeyer
Power is concentrated	Power is diffused
Hierarchical	Interconnected
Goals driven	Relationship driven
Values uniformity	Values diversity
Position and role give right to lead	Trust and relationship give right to lead
Leads by talking	Leads by listening

✢ The Captain Kirk CEO approach versus the Captain Picard relational approach

Stanley Grenz, in *A Primer on Postmodernism,* uses the TV shows *Star Trek* and *Star Trek: the Next Generation* as examples of modern and postmodern values. I'd like to take this idea one step further by contrasting the leadership values of Captain James T. Kirk with those of Captain Jean-Luc Picard. (*Star Trek* fanatics: please forgive my oversimplification of the characters. I realize that they are much more complex.)

Captain Kirk is the ultimate modern leader. He is staunchly individualistic, values power and knowledge, and desires to conquer and control. Whatever the crisis may be, Captain Kirk is always at the helm making the decisions. Most of the episodes clearly revolve around him. Everyone knows that he is in charge, ever the strong, directive leader: "Spock, take a landing party and explore the planet's surface." The show's female characters are generally far below Kirk on the leadership ladder, and he rarely asks for their advice. This is a male-dominated world led by Captain Kirk, who, for the most part, has it all together.

Captain Picard, on the other hand, is very much a leader, but his approach is quite different and fits much better with the emerging culture. When facing a decision, he asks others for input and gives them the

> This table is a grabber in terms of getting some perspective of the changing values in leadership.
>
> —HOWARD HENDRICKS

responsibility to make choices. He places females in key authority roles and frequently seeks their advice. Rather than solving problems as a conqueror, he talks frequently about putting yourself in another's shoes in order to see things from their perspective.

Another key to Picard's leadership style is diversity, an important value leaders in the emerging church will need to embrace. With diversity in leadership comes a diversity of styles and approaches. This means less standardization of a church's structure and more fluidity in the way its leadership team functions. Leadership teams will have to be much more intentional about being relational with one another, regardless of who earns more, knows more, or has more responsibility. Though lessening the grip of control goes very much against the grain of modern leadership, diversity also means less control with power diffused among many. In the emerging church, we need to move to a team approach. This will take more time, more relationship building, and the willingness to give up being the one person who makes all the decisions.

Note also that Captain Picard is conscious of what is happening around him, not only at the level of the dynamics between various governments but also at the level of galaxies and the universe. He is concerned with social justice among various peoples and life forms. Likewise, we also need to broaden our understanding of our roles to be more globally aware and concerned. We need to think more intently about matters of social justice. Haven't Christian leaders generally been more focused on inward Christian kingdoms than on the broken world outside?

Like Picard, who regularly is in contact with other leaders, we also need to go beyond denominations to seek friendships with one another. We are in this together. Gone are the days of superhero pastors who pioneer the way. The emerging church is about the friendship of leaders who are all on this journey together.

✠ CEO pastor versus spiritual guide and fellow journeyer

In his book *Dining with the Devil,* Os Guinness writes of an alarming observation made by a Japanese businessman: "Whenever I meet a Buddhist leader, I meet a holy man. Whenever I meet a Christian leader, I meet a manager."[2]

What a fascinating and perhaps uncomfortably true observation. I have attended many leadership conferences taught by modern leaders and pastors, and I have found that the terms and analogies most often used

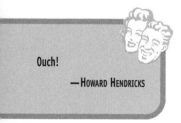

Ouch!

—HOWARD HENDRICKS

to define pastoral and staffing roles are drawn from the world of corporate executives, the senior pastor usually being the CEO.

Church leaders are taught to draw up organizational charts that reflect a top-down leadership style. Even the attire of those who lead the conferences says "corporate professional." It is common for church staffs to include an executive pastor, executive director of student ministry, senior associate pastor, and other similar positions.

As CEO pastors, we are taught to lead the church as we would a corporation. We sit behind desks in our offices writing out vision and mission statements and lists of our church's top ten values. We form management teams and executive steering teams. We run our churches efficiently like we would run a company, with cell phones on our belts and Palm Pilots in hand, walking with a purposeful CEO gait.

Granted, I am exaggerating to make a point, and I don't mean to undercut the effectiveness of this approach in so many contemporary modern churches. People who are in the corporate world relate to the use of executive titles and business terminology in ministry. Even Jesus used metaphors familiar to his disciples to help them understand that they would be "fishers" of men. But we are faced with different values in the emerging generations. To continue with the modern leadership approach in a post-Christian world will do more harm than good.

Let me explain. One of the often repeated criticisms of the church today is that it is an "organized religion," a "big business," a "modern man-made religion." So what are we communicating when we use terms such as executive pastor and management team to describe our church's "corporate structure?" Are we reinforcing negative stereotypes? Don't underestimate the power of words. I was serving on a "management team" at church and mentioned to someone, who was not a believer, that I was at our management team meeting earlier in the day. I remember the puzzled look I got. "Management team? I thought you worked at a church." I found it very awkward to explain that a church was using the terminology of the corporate world.

I know that in modern culture these terms may resonate with those who are used to hearing them in the business world, so hearing them in a church context may be refreshing and make sense. But for generations who are skeptical of the idea of the church as a business, we need to rethink this. Think of titles like senior pastor. Did Jesus have a senior disciple? A senior fisher of men? What signals do titles like these send to people in emerging generations?

What we need to grasp is that emerging generations are hungering for a spiritual experience, for spiritual leaders to point them toward God. Think of what a clash of values it is to offer them an executive director of finances, a senior pastor, or an executive associate pastor when they are looking for a prophet, a rabbi, a spiritual mystic, a philosopher, a shaman.

Deepak Chopra has tremendous influence both in Hollywood and at a national level in terms of spiritual direction. He has been described as a poet-prophet and a blender of physics and philosophy. This is what people in the emerging culture are looking for. In reality, we in Christian leadership, as messengers of the kingdom, should be the poet-prophets, the rabbis, the philosophers who translate Scripture for this culture.

✛ A pastor is a shepherd, not a CEO

I don't think it's by chance that pastor is the title the Spirit of God gave church leaders. There certainly were businesses during biblical times, so God could just as easily have used business terminology and titles. Even Jesus was familiar with the word manager (Luke 12:42; 16:1–9). But instead the Spirit chose to use the word pastor to describe those who would be caring for God's people. It's the Greek word *poimen,* which means "a shepherd, one who tends herds or flocks" (not one who merely feeds them). So it's used metaphorically of Christian pastors who guide as well as feed the flock (Acts 20:28). This involves tender care and vigilant superintendence.[3]

Won't people in the emerging culture be drawn to this type of leader? A pastor who tenderly cares for and loves them? A pastor is a shepherd who knows his sheep (John 10:4–13). Anything less makes him a hireling. Pastors don't just "do the job" or get people to come to their events. They are called to be shepherds who will go out and find the one lost sheep, leaving the ninety-nine to do so (Matt. 18:12–13).

I fully understand that in larger churches, leaders need to train and lead other "shepherds," that the people have to become the pastors in order to be able to care for everyone (Exod. 18:1–27). Yet we should never become so deceived by our cell phones, laptops, and pace of life that we lose the heart of a pastor. Emerging generations are looking for shepherds, not CEOs or executives.

✛ Would people in your church describe you as a manager or a holy man?

I know many pastors who, to eliminate the corporate sound, are changing their titles from senior pastor to lead pastor. Some pastors are

We also cannot forget the importance of being visionaries.

—HOWARD HENDRICKS

creative in how they use new titles. Some are even removing hierarchical titles entirely; they don't even use titles other than pastor at all. Don't underestimate how words shape people's viewpoints. How do you think the Japanese businessman Os Guinness mentioned would describe you and the pastors and leaders at your church? Managers? Or Holy Men?

+ The Nouwen-Maxwell leadership sandwich

In the emerging church, especially in churches larger than one hundred people, leaders will struggle with a great tension: How do we lead well yet keep our hearts soft? We need to approach leadership with author Henri Nouwen's heart of being like Jesus, compassionately caring for people, desperately dependent on the Spirit. At the same time, if your church grows, you need to develop the leadership skills of casting vision, developing multileveled teams, and recruiting and training leaders like author John Maxwell is well known for.

If you read these authors, you know that they approach leadership differently. But using one approach without the other will not be as effective in a larger emerging church. Josh Fox and I often joke that your reading diet should be a leadership sandwich of Nouwen and Maxwell. Both are needed to lead larger groups of people.

✢ What emerging generations are looking for in their leaders

I took part in a discussion with a group of church leaders—primarily church planters at a Leadership Network event in San Francisco. Some of these leaders had brought along one or two people from their churches. One such guest was a girl in her early twenties who was part of a church in southern California composed mostly of artists. Their church space functions as an art gallery as well as their meeting place. Most of this church community were recent converts to the faith and did not have a church upbringing. This girl also had recently become a Christian and was very articulate about her new beliefs and her love for Jesus.

As our discussion group focused on leadership, the pastors voiced various opinions, including many typical views about what a leader should look like. But I could sense a restlessness in this girl as she sat and listened. I finally asked her what she would look for in her pastor or leader at church. What she said was worth the two days I spent in San Francisco, because it resonated with what I believe is at the heart of the emerging church. Scribbling as fast as I could, I wrote down her words just as she spoke them. I know that we as church leaders are not to simply become whatever people want. If we do, we are in big trouble catering to the whims and wishes of those in the church. But as you read her statements, think about how they might affect the way you go about leading. Compare her words with what we usually hear that leaders are supposed to be.

✝ "I want the same kind of community with my leader that I used to get when I would smoke a bowl with my friends."

This was the first thought that came to her mind. For her, and for many others, smoking pot together represented a form of true (not shallow or rushed) community. When she used to do this, she enjoyed a sense of bonding and equality. What she missed wasn't the high from the pot but the sense of true community and companionship. She wanted this same experience with those in leadership. I thought this was a beautiful and an unusual way to describe her ideal experience (without the pot) of leadership and community.

What might this look like in the church? I know it might be much more difficult to accomplish in a larger church, but you might personally teach the membership class, if you have one, or you might open your house once a month to new people. People highly value the personal touch. If you want people to embrace you as their leader, you have to be willing to pay the price. But giving people even one chance to come into your home and get to know you a little, even just to see where you live, goes a long way. John 10:3–13 speaks of the strong bond a shepherd has with his sheep. It isn't just a job. It is a true caring relationship. You can't rush or fake community. You can't pretend to care.

If you don't already, I would encourage you to stay after the worship service and hang out until the last person leaves, no matter what size church you have. I make a commitment to do this so that I can be among people I pastor. I also linger in the hallways and in the coffee house between services. I am trying my best to communicate, in any way possible, that I am part of all this with them. I am not separate or distant.

We need to shift from a goals-driven leadership style to a relationship-driven style. We need to love people, not our goals and results. I try to schedule a meeting once a week with someone I don't know very well, someone who is just entering the community of our church or maybe someone on the fringes, someone who has been part of the church but

I agree with Dan that emerging church leaders must get outside of their church offices and buildings and be among the people in their world. Jesus didn't sit in the temple all day but got his feet and hands dirty meeting people where they were.

—Sally Morgenthaler

has never entered into serving or any form of leadership. I didn't always do this; I used to follow the "meet only with leaders" rule.

Because it isn't feasible or wise stewardship of our time to spend our entire week meeting with people, we need to be training many people in our churches to be shepherds as well. However, leaders are the ones up-front. We had better never see people simply as faceless numbers who fill our chairs.

Make it a habit to write at least one note a week to someone in your church community. One bit of encouragement written out, even an email just to check in, goes farther than you think. Do anything you possibly can to keep this value high, especially among emerging generations, with whom trust needs to be rebuilt and who put a higher premium on community than ever before.

Using personal vocabulary when addressing groups and when we preach is important, with warmth and care, feeling their pain.

—HOWARD HENDRICKS

✛ "I want a pastor who will help me to discover Jesus and the faith."

I absolutely love her choice of the word discover. She didn't say, "Tell me the facts about Jesus," or, "Preach to me about Jesus." She said she wanted a pastor who will help her discover Jesus. Of course we need to preach about Jesus, but does our teaching and preaching reflect a sense of the discovery she is asking for? Or have we grown accustomed to somewhat forcefully pushing the facts about Jesus onto someone as though we were trying to sell her a used car?

✛ "I want someone to listen to me and to hear me."

Do you notice she didn't say she wants a leader to tell her what to do in five easy steps? And it doesn't sound as if she wants to have conversations with a pastor who does 90 percent of the talking. She wants a leader who will listen to her. Emerging generations desire understanding, not quick analysis and solutions. Leadership in the emerging church is about a lot more listening than talking. Jesus talked and listened and asked a lot of questions. He didn't do all the talking.

✛ "I want my pastor and leaders to help me find out who I am, rather than telling me who I should be."

Again this requires listening. Evangelicals have really gotten good at telling people what a Christian should look like and how a Christian should act. Many times we even want them to look and be like us, instead of looking and being like who God made them to be under the leading of his

Spirit. It seems we are very eager to grab the microphone and tell people what they ought to do. But they aren't listening to us anymore, so we need to listen to them again.

Listening involves finding out first who the person is. Jesus was a questioner and a listener. We should follow his example, listening to find out where people are in their journey. Where are they coming from, and where have they been? How do they think? We may be surprised at what we learn.

✝ "I want someone to help me to see what my gifts are and then to use them for God."

Without realizing it, she nailed the biblical description of the Body found in 1 Corinthians 12. She desired to serve God with her gifts, but I don't think she was thinking of spiritual gifts the way we tend to, analyzing people with inventory tests and then plugging them in wherever we need them in our ministries.

Allow people to function in ministry the way God made them, so they will stretch and grow and be used by him in ways they have never imagined. We need to make the effort to encourage them, to give them confidence and support.

✝ "I want a leader who will encourage the artist in me, rather than squash or ignore it."

This young woman was a dancer who longed to see her pastor recognize this talent and then enable her to somehow use it for God. She represents an upwelling of those in emerging generations who have talents such as dance, art, and poetry and who need to be redeemed and lifted high in the church. I have heard far too many stories of how churches neglect certain gifts because they don't fit in the programs they offer. Think of the beautiful palette of color and creativity that might be revealed within our communities if we would only allow people with all sorts of gifts a forum in which to express them for God's glory.

✝ "I want parents."

This last comment was the most surprising to me, but the more I thought about it, the more it made sense. She was new in the faith, crying out for loving guidance and direction. She was saying that she wants leaders who will caringly protect her, parentally, even shepherd and guide her. She didn't expect all of her leaders to be youthful and culturally savvy.

Her leaders didn't have to dress hip and know all the latest bands. She simply wanted leaders who would unconditionally love, support, and encourage her the way parents should. In the emerging church, we need to break down generational barriers and see the older mentor the younger.

This young twenty-something's comments didn't include, "I want a courageous leader," or, "I want a leader who will be able to preach great sermons," or, "I want a leader who will cast a great vision." These things are absolutely needed, but her first thoughts were simple, community oriented, and beautiful. If you ran into a young person like this in your church, how would she describe you? Are these values part of your leadership ethos in your church?

✠ Leadership and the "empty chair"

Another major issue emerging church leaders need to focus on is what tools and methods we use for getting the job done. The modern culture has taught us to have businesslike meetings, get to the agenda at hand, make efficient use of our time, since it is so limited. And it's true we need to do so. There is no time to waste in carrying out our mission. But in our desire to lead and get ministry accomplished, we might be forgetting something—or Someone.

I have both led and participated in many staff meetings and church leadership gatherings, and I have observed that most such gatherings follow a certain flow. They usually begin with a prayer, asking God to guide us and help us as we walk through our agenda. After the prayer, we begin the meeting. Because time is precious, we want to be well organized and efficient. We take minutes to record what we discussed and who was delegated responsibilities. We may talk about new classes being offered or try to figure out why attendance may have been down the week before. We talk about programming and get frustrated with the problems we had with the video projector over the weekend. We talk about the two teenagers from last Wednesday night's youth meeting who were caught making out in the janitor's closet. We plan, we discuss, we problem-solve, our laptops working hard, and then we end the meeting. All this is well and good, at least until you consider what doesn't usually happen at the typical staff meeting.

Something that began nagging at me was that once we opened with prayer, we rarely mentioned the name of Jesus or God again in our meetings. I actually counted (including meetings I was leading) how often we would bring up Jesus' name, and I was rather disturbed to realize that I had fallen into the trap of trying to run things so efficiently that it was almost as though Jesus need not attend. We would ask Jesus for help and then leave him out of the rest of the meeting. But think about it! Everything we are doing is for him and about him.

After I realized this, I discussed it with the Graceland staff, and we decided to go to the extreme to change this pattern. Jesus taught us that "apart from me you can do nothing" (John 15:5). We all know this verse, but I know I so easily end up being self-dependent and running ministry on my own. I wanted to make sure we did not forget this verse, so we tried something. At the beginning of every staff meeting, we placed an empty chair in the middle of the room. We called this extra chair the Jesus chair. As we began our meetings in prayer, we would acknowledge the presence of Jesus. From that point on, the chair would remind us that Jesus was the reason for our meeting, the point of every discussion. If we came across a problem, we were easily reminded to pray and to ask Jesus to show us what to do.

One time a friend of mine gave me a really tacky six-inch-tall statue of Jesus that his mother had given him as a gift. He didn't know what to do with it, so he gave it to me, and I kept it near my desk. One day during a Graceland staff meeting, just for fun, I put the statue of Jesus on the Jesus chair. We were in the middle of the meeting when our senior pastor came in to visit us. He saw the chair and moved to sit down in it. When we said that he'd better not sit there because that was where Jesus was sitting, he looked down and saw the little statue. I'm glad he didn't just come in and sit down quickly or it could have been a problem! I tried to explain the Jesus chair, but with the little statue sitting there it seemed all the more odd, so I just gave up. More than ever in the emerging church we need to remember that our leadership skills will take us only so far. As leaders, we need to keep Jesus in the center of everything we do. May we always remember the empty chair and who is sitting in it.

+ Emerging church leaders need to be "snakes and doves" leaders

Jesus said, "I am sending you out like sheep among wolves" (Matt. 10:16). While most of us don't know what it's like to be arrested for our faith, we *are* living in a post-Christian culture that is hostile toward the gospel of Christ. More than ever we need to follow Jesus' instruction to his disciples to be "as shrewd as snakes and as innocent as doves."

I agree with what Dan says here. The snakes and doves illustration is a powerful analogy Jesus used for those serving him that we must take heed of.

—HOWARD HENDRICKS

✛ Leadership as shrewd as snakes

At first it seems odd that Jesus would tell us to be like snakes, since we think of them as symbols of sneakiness and deception. When Jesus uses the word "snakes" in Matthew 10:16, he's using snakes as an example of shrewdness and wisdom. In first-century Middle Eastern culture, snakes metaphorically embodied intelligence, cunning, and caution. Likewise, those of us in leadership should be strategic, cunning, and deliberate. Snakes are patient, waiting for the right moment to strike, and when they do, they are swift and effective—even deadly. In order to be effective, we should study the latest trends, attend relevant seminars, and read widely. We want to be skillful and wise in all we do and in how we use our time.

✛ Leadership as innocent as doves

Jesus also says we need to be as innocent as doves. Doves were known as the gentlest and most harmless of all the birds. They represented purity and innocence. Shouldn't this be characteristic of our leadership in the emerging church?

Let me share with you a growing personal concern. I have attended lots of conferences and leadership gatherings that focus on being shrewd as snakes, and I have heard plenty about postmodern preaching, strategic church planting, and ministry methodology. But missing from the discussion, for the most part, is anything about the nurturing and care of our souls. I don't hear much about integrity or holiness anymore, either at conferences or in leadership ministry books. I don't hear much about being careful to avoid conforming to the world (Rom. 12:2) or being polluted by the world (James 1:27) as leaders. Shouldn't this be unsettling?

After the TV evangelist scandals of the late 1980s, there was definitely a heightened sense of our need for personal holiness, innocence, and integrity. But over time, it seems the concern has slipped away. I am by no means a legalist and would never propose anything that would jeopardize the gift of freedom that comes with God's grace. But I am concerned that we whose hearts are broken for people in emerging generations may be neglecting the care of our own souls, which can result in lapses in integrity and purity. We forget that our own vessel, which God may be using to reach the people we care so much about, is fragile and in desperate need of the Spirit's strength and care.

Listen to what Reggie McNeal says in his book *A Work of Heart:*

I'm forty-six, and I've been pastoring (in one form or another) for over twenty years, but sometimes I feel like I'm eighty-six and should retire soon, because this thing is hard, very hard. So many of my colleagues have quit or burned out, victims of the absurdly contrary and excessive demands of ministry in these changing times. True, there are plenty of instances of clergy abuse, in the sense of clergy abusing parishioners, but there are probably equal if not greater numbers of clergy who are walking wounded, abused by sick congregational systems with inhuman congregational demands. However this change in leadership style is negotiated, I'm quite certain that two considerations will be required:

1. Churches will need to take care of their leaders as a cherished and needed asset.
2. Pastors will need to take care of themselves and one another when churches fail to do so.

—BRIAN MCLAREN

Leadership development efforts aimed at spiritual leaders all too often have neglected these issues of the heart. With the now decades-long emphasis on ministry as mechanic (how to counsel parishioners, how to grow a church, how to prepare a sermon, how to raise money, and the how-to list goes on and on), attention to the core being of spiritual leaders has gotten squeezed out in favor of more glamorous pursuits, or at least pursuits that would make the minister and his ministry "successful." ... However, all the leadership insight and expertise on the planet cannot, in the end, overcome a case of spiritual heart disease or "heart failure." ... Functionalism has replaced spiritual formation. Program manipulation and methodological prowess often serve as mere stop gaps to substitute for genuine spiritual leadership.[4]

What a sobering reminder that we can be as shrewd as snakes, seeing God use us tremendously in this emerging culture, but that if we are not as innocent as doves, it all means nothing.

Leadership in the emerging church is no longer about focusing on strategies, core values, mission statements, or church-growth principles. It is about leaders first becoming disciples of Jesus with prayerful, missional hearts that are broken for the emerging culture. All the rest will flow from this, not the other way around.

✢ A personal plea

I beg all who desire to have an impact in the emerging church to be "shrewd as snakes," thinking strategically, studying the culture, and functioning as missiologists like never before. We need to be the poets, theologians, and philosophers once again. We need not be afraid to rethink everything we are doing. We need to set the pace for social justice in our communities and be thinking globally. We need to be fluid when we lead, instead of being rigid or controlling. We need to be relational leaders instead of super-goal-driven leaders. But please, please, please, above all, pay ruthless attention to the prayerful care of your souls as leaders. Live holy and pure lives as innocent as doves in a corrupt and polluted culture. Be constantly connected to the chief Shepherd of the emerging church for his leading and guidance. Nothing is more important than this. Nothing.

EMERGING THOUGHTS

1. Do you relate more to a Captain Kirk approach to leadership or to a Captain Picard approach? Why? If you are not the primary leader in your church, how would you categorize the leadership style in your church? Do the leaders relate most closely to the modern church or to the emerging church?

2. What titles do you currently use for your church's leaders? Are they titles that would be understood by people in the emerging culture? Why or why not?

3. How would people describe the primary leaders of your church? What words would they use? Are they managers, or are they holy men?

4. How is the presence of Jesus acknowledged in the leadership and meetings in your church?

Personal Epilogue
The Road Goes Ever On

> **The road goes ever on and on, down from the door**
> **where it began.**
> **Now far ahead the road has gone, and I must follow**
> **it if I can,**
> **Pursuing it with eager feet, until it joins a larger way**
> **Where many paths and errands meet.**
> **And whither then? I cannot say.**
>
> —Bilbo Baggins in *The Fellowship of the Ring*

The epigraph to this chapter is a song Bilbo Baggins sings in J. R. R. Tolkien's *Fellowship of the Ring* as he leaves home for a journey to an unknown destination. I've always appreciated the words in this song because they are optimistic and cheery amid uncertainty. Doesn't this reflect the state of the emerging church? We live in a day of both great possibility and great ambiguity. New generations are spiritually open, and the church of Jesus Christ is poised like never before to carry hope to generations seeking truth and something to believe in. Exactly what the emerging church is going to look like and how it's going to go about its mission, we don't know. But no matter how confusing things are or how post-anything we may be, his church will prevail.

✛ Nothing will stop the church of Jesus

While in Israel a few years ago, my wife, Becky, and I drove our rental car up into the Golan Heights. We were heading for Banyas National Park, which was called Caesarea Philippi in the New Testament, a center of

Greco-Roman culture known for its pagan worship. After parking the car and following a few signs, we found ourselves at the mouth of a large cave at the base of a sheer mountain. From within this cave flowed a stream, which tumbled from the heights into the valley below to become the Jordan River. At the time of Christ, this place was known as the Gates of Hell because pagans believed that one could enter the underworld through this cave. In the walls of the cliff are niches where Pan and other deities, carved from the mountain itself, would receive sacrifices.

We stood within one of the larger altar niches, now empty and scattered with dusty rocks and the remains of some long-dead birds, and opened our Bible to read the words of Jesus from Matthew 16:17–18. In this passage, Jesus and his disciples were standing before this very mountain having an important discussion. After answering Jesus' questions about what others believed about him, Peter acknowledged that Jesus was the Christ, the Son of God.

Jesus replied, "Blessed are you, Simon son of Jonah, for this was not revealed to you by man, but by my Father in heaven. And I tell you that you are Peter, and on this rock I will build my church, and the gates of Hades will not overcome it."

What an incredible and memorable word picture! People who worshiped false gods believed that, from this location, they could enter hell. At this place, they worshiped the gods Pan and Baal. From here, of all places, Jesus chose to declare that his church would prevail.

Becky and I prayed inside that carved altar for a long time, thanking God for the example Jesus gave us and for his promise that his church would always stand strong. We felt that the similarities between that first band of followers and ourselves were poignantly clear. In that pagan place before the Gates of Hell is exactly where all who choose to take Christ to emerging generations stand today. We are surrounded by false gods and by religious and nonreligious philosophies that either ignore or blatantly oppose the gospel of Christ. We are encircled by pagan influence and false teachings, and the result is a "harassed and helpless" generation.

But I can think of absolutely nowhere else I'd rather be! Since you've chosen to read this book, I assume you feel the same way. We have lots of great ministries for professing Christians and lots of wonderful contemporary seeker-sensitive churches which God is using to expose modern-thinking people to the gospel. North America has more than its share of Christian entertainment at rock festivals frequented by Christians. But I want to be smack in the middle of the pagan worshipers. I want to be right among the altars of Pan and Baal, just like Jesus was at Caesarea Philippi, having full assurance that his church will prevail. I want to be sitting among the sinners and tax collectors (Matt. 9:11) like Jesus was, dialoguing with them about the truth that is light and the peace that's found in Jesus. I want to be part of a church that truly is not a place where people go but rather is a people who are. I want to be among those who are praying about and thinking through what the emerging church of Jesus is going to be like in the post-Christian culture.

It's no easy road that stretches ahead of us. But as Bilbo sang, we must be "pursuing it with eager feet" for the sake of the emerging church of Jesus. We must follow the Spirit of God's leading until he shows us what "larger way" he has in store for us.

What brings me great joy and makes the journey seem not as hard is knowing that I am not alone. So many of us out there are beginning to think the same things. So many of us sense something is changing. We don't know exactly how to explain it, but we all know it is real. I can't thank God enough for the friendships I have made along the road and the conversations we have had in helping one another on this journey. There are no solo acts or lone rangers in the emerging church. May our paths on this journey meet, as we truly are all in this together. Where it takes us, we cannot say. But I am eager to find out. I hope this book has helped you in some way, for the sake of the emerging church.

By the way, I wanted to mention that I just spent some time with Sky yesterday, our anti-Christian, antichurch, post-seeker friend from the first chapter, who eventually became a believer. He still has his cool sideburns and still dresses like Sky! He was sharing how much fun it is for him to serve in children's ministry. He teaches a kindergarten age group. He also still faithfully attends his midweek home group, working through books of the Bible with Rod and Connie, who are generations older than he. Sky even leads and teaches in the home group on occasion, as he loves to study the Scriptures.

Sky is now married, and I had the privilege of performing a Christ-centered wedding. Sky's personally written vows to his beautiful wife, Melissa, had Jesus all throughout them. I remember watching Sky and Melissa kneel during the ceremony while they took communion together as their first act of marriage. Sky then led them in a private prayer. Sky wanted me to make sure I clearly explained their faith and love for Jesus in the ceremony, since so many of his nonbelieving friends would be present.

You know, I don't believe that Sky is an isolated case. Many Sky's live in your communities and might respond in the same way. If only they experienced a church—that is, people—that passionately cared about them and made the effort to build loving relationships with them. If only there were a church that didn't hide or hold back its spiritual worship in front of others, a church that talked intelligently about kingdom living and the gospel and invited them to be a part of it. If only there were a church that took its role of caring for the environment, the poor and the needy, and global justice so seriously that the Skys in its community would take notice. If only there were a church that had a big enough heart for new generations and wasn't afraid to rethink what it might take to reach them, even if it meant giving up control or neat systems and coming up with new (and ancient) ways of doing ministry. If only there were a church that focused more energy on making kingdom-minded disciples than on running programs and events. If only there were a church that went back to the simple and raw beginning and became vintage Christians again. If only.

Sample Layout of a Vintage Worship Gathering

Many emerging-church worship gatherings will not be large and won't need the level of planning shown in this layout. I believe, however, that when you have a gathering for several hundred people, your level of planning does change. We need to be responsible for what we do, and that requires prayerful planning. Although the following sample layout may look very linear, down-to-the-minute, and rigid, it truly isn't. The complexity means we need to at least approximate the timing. Laying out time boundaries actually allows for the worship service to flow even more smoothly. We allow the Spirit to change things as we go, and we sometimes pause at a spot where we weren't planning to or extend a prayer time.

Ninety-nine percent of the time, we do not hit the timing, but if we didn't think the service through in advance, we would probably run way late and mess up the children's ministry by detaining parents in the service. Having some structure allows all the more freedom.

Following the table are diagrams contrasting a modern contemporary approach to setting up a worship center and an emerging church approach.

Communion Night 8:00 P.M.	Projected Time*	Actual Time	Elements	Mic/Source	Lighting/Curtain
Preservice stained-glass logo on screen	7:30		Scripture on screens (slides)		
CD music—reflective	7:45		Personal preparation for worship		
Worship Set *We Want to See* *Solid Rock* *River* *Those Who Trust* *Holy, Holy, Holy*	8:00		Band on front stage	Band	Stage House—Dim 30%
Baptism/Testimony	8:20			Baptism mic	House—Dim 30%
Welcome/ Announcements *Christine*	8:25		Announcement slides	Wireless mic	House—75% Stage
Mexico Team sendoff and Prayer	8:28		Team on stage— Mexico slides	Wireless mic	House—75% Stage
Offering Prayer *Alisa Cizar*	8:31		Ushers/Band interlude	Wireless mic	House—75% Stage
Song and Testimony *Dan Ryan*	8:33		Scriptures on screen	Band	House–45%
Communion Message *Dan K.*	8:38		Scriptures/Images	Wireless lapel	House—80%
Art/Scripture during message			Scripture readings— Christa M.	Wireless mic	Stage
Silent Reflection and Prayer	9:11		Scriptures/Images		House–Dim 20%
Worship Set/Rear Stage *Only You* *Hungry* *Sing Alleluia* *Run to You*	9:14		Communion taken from tables up front—people come given time to pray for rest of night **Band plays from rear stage	Band	House—Dim 25% Stage light low on back
Hymn Time *My Jesus I Love Thee*	9:30		Story chair—side stage	Wireless mic	Light on drama area
Corporate Scriptural Reading *Joe*	9:35		Scripture on screen	Wireless mic	Stage only
Worship Dance *Kendra Karnes*	9:36		Image on screen	CD	Stage only
Worship Set *Amazing Grace* *Forever I'm Yours*	9:39			Band	House–45% Stage
Closing Prayer *Dan K.*	9:45		Prayer Team up front	Wireless mic	House—45% Stage
Outro Music *mellow*				CD	House—30%

*NOTE: Times are given only as estimates. Allow the Spirit to change the actual gathering as it is in progress.

248

A modern, contemporary approach to the set-up of a worship center

Band plays from stage well removed from people

Curtain closes when band is finished

Pastor speaks from stage raised several feet higher than the people

People are situated in rows all facing the stage and the focus of attention is clear

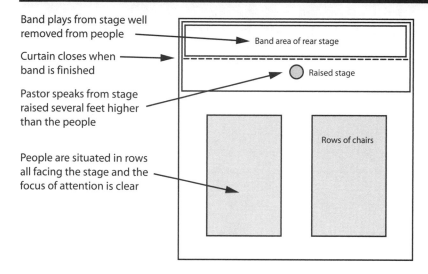

Band area of rear stage

Raised stage

Rows of chairs

A vintage-Christianity approach to the set-up of a worship gathering

same room, different set-up because of different values

Band moved to lower stage much closer to the people

Pastor speaks from lower stage among the people

Rows of chairs angled along with tables to create more of a sense of community

Experiential prayer, journaling, and art stations placed around the room for people to go to during worship

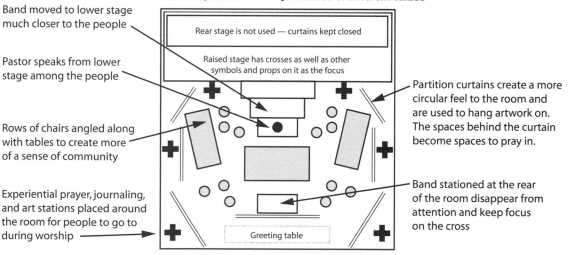

Rear stage is not used — curtains kept closed

Raised stage has crosses as well as other symbols and props on it as the focus

Partition curtains create a more circular feel to the room and are used to hang artwork on. The spaces behind the curtain become spaces to pray in.

Band stationed at the rear of the room disappear from attention and keep focus on the cross

Greeting table

This set-up is NOT intended as a model. It is intended to stimulate creativity as you consider changing the set up of a meeting place to incorporate the values of the emerging church in worship gatherings.

249

Sample Teaching Topics

Here are some of the "theotopical" messages we have used, categorized by the series titles and the theological intent behind them. The goal of each series is to tell the story in order to shape a theological worldview, not to just talk about the issues themselves. Our dream is that our church is the embodiment of our theology, that our theology is not just knowledge we learn. Usually a series runs from three to six weeks. Although I categorized several in the area of sanctification, we really address the Spirit's role in sanctification in almost every series as the application. Every message also ties into what it means for kingdom living as a mission-minded disciple.

"Mission Santa Cruz"; the book of Jonah. The very first series we did, going through the entire book with the initial college group in casting a vision for the start of our vintage-faith service. The theme was "If God could change Ninevah, then surely he can change Santa Cruz." (Missiology, ecclessiology, our role in God's story)

"Created for Community"; 1 John. The second series we did, with a focus on building community among those attending. (Ecclesiology, how we are each part of one another's story)

"The Invisible World"; various passages. This is a thrilling story to tell, especially what we know happens to evil in the end. (Angelology, angels, demons, Satan, prayer)

"Vintage Christianity"; the Sermon on the Mount, Matthew 5–7. We took several months to walk through these three chapters. This was the first series in which we encouraged people to bring others to hear the true heart of the Christian faith to break stereotypes they may have. (Sanctification)

"Knowing God"; various passages. A four-week series on the Trinity. (Doctrine of God, the way we are in relationship with the triune God)

"Romeo and Juliet"; various passages. A series on dating, relationships, and human sexuality. (Doctrine of man, sanctification, how our sexuality and relationships are part of kingdom living)

"Origins"; Genesis 1–4. An eight-week series on the story of creation, man, sin, Sabbath, Satan, marriage, divorce, and sex. (Doctrine of God, man, sin)

"Original Blues"; Psalms 73, 22, 51, 86, 63. A five-week series covering five emotional psalms. (Sanctification)

"On the Road." A four-week series on knowing God's will. (Sovereignty of God, how to live in the story)

"Welcome to the Jungle"; highlights from Daniel 1–6. A six-week series on the story of Daniel, who was immersed in pagan culture but still lived as a child of God. (Prayer, temptation, holiness, decision-making, engaging the culture)

"Life after Death?" A four-week series on heaven and hell, reincarnation, various passages about the big and future story. (Doctrine of future things)

"Swing Lessons." A five-week series on the spiritual disciplines, emphasizing that the results of the disciplines are the important thing, not the disciplines themselves. (Spiritual life, sanctification)

"Cool Cats." A four-week series looking at biblical characters from the story in both the Old and New Testaments—Esther, Rahab, Barnabus, Daniel, etc. (Character of God, sanctification)

"Decisions, Decisions." A series on making biblically based decisions as ambassadors of Jesus living in the kingdom. (Sovereignty of God, holiness, the Spirit-led life)

"The Bible: Food for the Soul." A four-week series on the doctrine of the Bible, based on various passages. (Doctrine of the Bible)

"Ways of Wisdom"; Proverbs. Six weeks of highlights from Proverbs on practical living before God. (Sanctification)

"End of Days." A five-week overview of the end times story and biblical prophecy, giving several views of the end times. (Eschatology)

"Contact: Communicating with an Invisible God." A four-week prayer series. (Sanctification, holiness, the Spirit-filled life)

"Reasonable Doubt." A five-week series based on surveys of the non-church-attending peers of those who attend. Typical apologetics, but fitting them in the story. (Origin of the Bible, problem of evil, hell, salvation)

"The Last Days of Jesus." A three-week walk through the narratives of Passion Week leading up to the resurrection. (Christology, soteriology)

"Freedom: Understanding Who We Are as Christians"; Romans 6–8. A six-week series on the spiritual life. (Sanctification, the work of the Holy Spirit)

"Lessons Learned." A look at the meaning and purpose of life and our existence. Highlights from the book of Ecclesiastes from the angle of hearing what lessons the wisest man on earth at the time learned. (Sanctification, life perspective)

"God with Us." A three-week look at the Trinity and the role each person played in the Christmas story. (Christology, doctrine of God)

"Reconstructing Jesus." A five-week look at the outrageous claims Jesus made. (Christology)

"Soul Mates: A Biblical Look at Marriage and Relationships"; Ephesians 5. A four-week series on redefining the covenant of marriage and what it means to be one flesh. (Sanctification, the doctrine of man, human sexuality, how marriage fits in the story and kingdom living)

"Sacred Family: A Fresh Look at Family the Way God Designed It to Be"; Ephesians 6:1–4, Deuteronomy 6:4–9. A four-week look into the biblical portrayal of family, introducing what it is to those who have never experienced one. (Sanctification, kingdom living)

In our ministry, we also try to relate what we teach or do to these themes of our mission.

With Jesus as the center and head of the church, we then desire in our mission to:

Explore truth: to dialogue, learn, teach, and live the biblical story of God and what it means to be a follower of Jesus (Acts 17:11; Acts 17:20; John 14:6).

Express faith: to passionately and creatively live out our mission locally and globally through the arts, social justice, and inviting others into kingdom living (Gal. 5:6; Col. 4:3–6; 1 Peter 3:15).

Experience God: to deeply connect to and love God with our heart, mind, strength, and soul as we live worshipful lives in all that we are and all that we do (Eph. 3:14–21; Matt. 22:37; Heb. 12:28–29).

Enter community: to participate in sharing life together as a church that is equipped to serve God and one another in love and in relationships through our unique diversity, dreams, and giftedness (Acts 2:42–47; John 34–35; 1 Cor. 12:27).

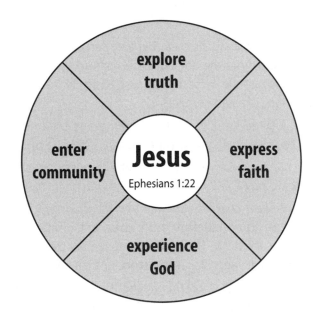

Resources for the Emerging Church

+ Websites

Websites come and go, so I have limited the list to a few that probably will be around for a while. These sites provide links to hundreds of others.

www.vintagefaith.com. This website provides updates on the topics discussed in this book, along with more examples and photographs, plus additional ministry samples and ideas. The website is an ongoing interactive supplement to this book. It provides links to various emerging churches, webzines, art sources, and other useful websites to explore.

www.emergentvillage.org. The Emergent website posts articles and information about conferences, and brings together voices for the emerging church.

www.next-wave.org. Next-Wave is a webzine that contains many articles about the emerging church from a wide range of perspectives.

www.Sacramentis.com. Sally Morgenthaler's website provides links to art on the web, as well as articles and helpful resources.

www.theooze.com. The Ooze is a great resource for provocative articles about the emerging church, and it also is a great source for links to emerging churches in America and globally.

www.youthspecialties.com. Youth Specialties always is a great source for emerging ministry. Even if we work with adults, we should be following youth ministry trends to track where the emerging church of the future will be.

☩ Books

Culture and Postmodernism

Grenz, Stanley. *A Primer on Postmodernism*. Grand Rapids, Mich.: Eerdmans, 1996. Some view this as the classic book that treats postmodernism in a readable manner, dealing with its origins and impact.

Grenz, Stanley J., and John R. Franke. *Beyond Foundationalism: Shaping Theology in a Postmodern Context*. Louisville: Westminster John Knox, 2000. Although I do not go into theology and the emerging church in my book, this book grapples with issues that emerging church leaders must think through.

Jones, Tony. *Postmodern Youth Ministry*. Grand Rapids, Mich.: Zondervan, 2001. Although this is a youth ministry book, it teaches more details about postmodernism than I have addressed in my book.

McLaren, Brian. *Church on the Other Side*. Grand Rapids, Mich.: Zondervan, 1998, 2000. I couldn't put this book down after I started reading it.

———. *A New Kind of Christian*. San Francisco: Jossey-Bass, 2001. Written as a story, this controversial book gets you thinking. I read it in two sittings because it touches on many of the issues we in leadership are facing. I highly recommend it to people who are new to the whole emerging church conversation.

McLaren, Brian, and Tony Campolo. *Adventures in Missing the Point*. Forthcoming from: emergentYS.

Rabey, Steve. *In Search of Authentic Faith: How Emerging Generations Are Transforming the Church*. Colorado Springs: Waterbrook, 2000. A book that examines specific churches that are reaching the emerging generations and what they are doing.

Sweet, Leonard, ed. *Four Views of the Church in Postmodern Culture*. Forthcoming from: emergentYS. An important book to help you sift through where you stand in response to postmodernism and to learn how others are responding.

Wilson, Jim. *Future Church: Ministry in a Post-Seeker Age*. Littleton, Colo.: Serendipity, 2002. A book which looks at the common links among several emerging churches.

Yaconelli, Michael, ed. *Stories of Emergence*. Forthcoming from: emergentYS. A great book of emerging leaders' stories of their struggles with modernity and the church. You may find yourself identifying with many of them.

The Church and Mission

Beckham, William A. *The Second Reformation: Reshaping the Church for the Twenty-first Century*. Houston: Touch Publications, 1995. This is a fairly balanced but opinionated book that looks at how far we have drifted from the early church model. Instead of simply stating that we need to go back to house churches, Beckham proposes a balance of both large gatherings and home churches.

Bercot, David. *Let Me Die in Ireland: The True Story of St. Patrick*. Tyler, Tex.: Scroll, 1999. A book to encourage us when we think we have it hard in ministry, as well as to inspire us about not giving up on reaching the people we feel God has called us to reach.

Gruder, Darrell, ed. *The Missional Church: A Vision for the Sending of the Church in North America*. Grand Rapids, Mich.: Eerdmans, 1998. This book is worth purchasing for chapters 4 and 5 alone.

McManus, Erwin. *An Unstoppable Force: Daring to Become the Church God Had in Mind*. Loveland, Colo.: Group, 2001. Erwin leads Mosaic, a missional and very creative church in Los Angeles. His insights are worth paying attention to.

Newbigin, Lesslie. *The Gospel in a Pluralistic Society*. Grand Rapids, Mich.: Eerdmans, 1989. When Newbigin returned to England from his work as a missionary to India, he faced a post-Christian culture, which he described as harder to reach than the culture in India.

Leadership

Nouwen, Henri. *In the Name of Jesus: Reflections on Christian Leadership*. New York: Crossroad, 1993. There are plenty of great books on leadership, but this book goes against the grain of most evangelical and business leadership books, and it's one I believe we in the emerging church need to read for sure. Nouwen raises issues of the heart for those in leadership.

Mallory, Sue. *The Equipping Church*. Grand Rapids, Mich.: Zondervan, 2001. In the emerging church, ministry needs to be in the hands of the people more than ever, as the Bible describes it should be in Ephesians 4:11–12. The emerging church must be an equipping church.

Maxwell, John. *Developing the Leaders around You*. Nashville: Thomas Nelson, 1995. While we need to embrace the issues Nouwen raises, we also need to develop some practical leadership skills, especially if your church is hoping to develop layers of leadership, extending its mission by growing larger or by planting new churches. The books which I have found the most practical for use in the church are this one and the following one by John Maxwell. I have to admit that I personally do not resonate with so many of the "principles," "laws of leadership," and other modern approaches that he uses. But we still need to lead and build teams, and these two books provide principles that I believe emerging church leaders need.

————. *Developing the Leader within You*. Nashville: Thomas Nelson, 2000.

Spiritual Formation

Case, Steve. *Book of Uncommon Prayer: Contemplative and Celebratory Prayers and Worship Services for Youth Ministry*. Grand Rapids, Mich.: Zondervan, Youth Specialties, 2002. If you are looking for examples of how to put into practice some of the ancient disciplines in a worship gathering, this is a good resource. It is geared for youth, but it can be used with adults as well.

Talbot, John Michael, and Steve Rabey. *The Lessons of St. Francis: How to Bring Simplicity and Spirituality into Your Daily Life*. New York: Dutton, 1997. Explores some ancient lifestyle disciplines that resonate with the emerging church.

Willard, Dallas. *The Divine Conspiracy: Rediscovering Our Hidden Life in God*. New York: Harper Collins, 1998. Without a doubt, the books that have had the most influence on my thinking on discipleship and spiritual formation for the emerging church are this one and the following one by Dallas Willard.

————. *Renovation of the Heart: Putting on the Character of Christ*. Colorado Springs: NavPress, 2002.

Yaconelli, Mike. *Messy Spirituality*. Grand Rapids, Mich.: Zondervan, 2002. More than ever, we need to admit that Christianity is not just a neat set of principles or steps to follow. This book beautifully admits the fact that the Christian faith is neither predictable nor a nice clean package. This is a message emerging generations need to hear so that they are not overburdened by guilt, defeat, and disappointment.

Evangelism

Hunter, George. *The Celtic Way of Evangelism*. Nashville: Abingdon, 2000. Probably my favorite book on evangelism that relates to our current culture.

Kallenberg, Brad. *Live to Tell: Evangelism for a Postmodern Age*. Grand Rapids, Mich.: Brazos, 2002.

McLaren, Brian. *More Ready Than You Realize*. Grand Rapids, Mich.: Zondervan, 2002. Based on a true story of how McLaren interacted primarily through email with a postmodern seeker.

Richardson, Rick. *Evangelism outside the Box*. Downers Grove, Ill.: InterVarsity, 2000. A practical book of ideas to implement regarding evangelism in our culture today.

The Early Church and Jewish Culture

I believe it's critical for emerging church leaders to study and learn about New Testament Jewish culture and the world in which the early church was birthed. All the criticism about the Christian faith being a modern organized religion can be diffused by sharing our historical and ancient roots. And it's even critical that we take a fresh look at Jesus and his message to help us identify how our modern biases have slipped into our view of him and his teachings.

We also must revisit where we came from and not assume that the modern presuppositions about what church is were the ones practiced in and taught by the Scriptures. The following books do not have "Five Steps to Leading an Emerging Church Small Group" in them, but they will broaden our perspective of what vintage Christianity was really about. You may be surprised at how far we have drifted in our modern culture from what was considered a high value in the early church.

Edersheim, Alfred. *The Life and Times of Jesus the Messiah*. Rev. ed. Peabody, Mass.: Hendrickson, 1997.

———. *Sketches of Jewish Social Life*. Rev. ed. Peabody, Mass.: Hendrickson, 1997.

Zondervan Illustrated Bible Backgrounds Commentary. Grand Rapids, Mich.: Zondervan, 2002.

Howard, Kevin, and Marvin Rosenthal. *The Feasts of Our Lord*. Nashville: Thomas Nelson, 1997. This book walks through the Jewish holidays and their messianic meaning. My wife and I practice many of the Jewish holidays through what is taught in this book and try to teach these in our church.

Martin, Ralph P. *Worship in the Early Church*. Grand Rapids, Mich.: Eerdmans, 1975.

Patzia, Arthur G. *The Emergence of the Church: Context, Growth, Leadership and Worship*. Downers Grove, Ill.: InterVarsity, 2001.

Stevenson, Kenneth. *The First Rites: Worship in the Early Church*. Collegeville, Minn.: Liturgical Press, 1990.

Vander Laan, Ray. *Faith Lessons: That the World May Know*. Grand Rapids, Mich.: Zondervan, 1998. Video series.

Wright, Norman T. *The Challenge of Jesus*: *Rediscovering Who Jesus Was and Is*. Downers Grove, Ill.: InterVarsity, 1999. I highly recommend this book for a refreshing look through a New Testament lens at who Jesus is.

Yancey, Phillip. *The Jesus I Never Knew*. Grand Rapids, Mich.: Zondervan, 1995.

The Arts

De Borchgrave, Helen. *A Journey into Christian Art*. Minneapolis: Fortress, 1999. A great resource for reading the history of the development of Christian art, as well as a source of images to use for worship gatherings.

Doré, Gustave. *The Doré Bible Illustrations*. New York: Dover, 1974. For biblical artwork, my favorite by far is Doré. His art is not tacky, and it powerfully communicates many biblical scenes from both Old and New Testaments.

Dyrness, William A. *Visual Faith: Art, Theology, and Worship in Dialogue*. Grand Rapids, Mich.: Baker, 2001. This book takes a theological look at why art is an important part of how God communicated and how we can also incorporate art in worship.

Notes

Introduction

[1]*The American Heritage Dictionary of the English Language,* 4th ed. (Boston: Houghton Mifflin, 2000) and *The New Lexicon Webster's Dictionary* (New York: Lexicon, 1987).

[2]Tom Clegg and Warren Bird, *Lost in America* (Loveland, Colo.: Group, 2001), 25.

Chapter One

[1]I use the term seeker in reference to a person who is investigating spiritual things, only because it has become so well known and widely used. I agree with many others that the labeling of someone as a seeker actually is a limited way to describe someone on their spiritual journey. In a way, when people become Christians, they remain seekers as they seek God in all they do.

[2]*Oxford American Dictionary* (New York: Oxford University Press, 1980).

Chapter Three

[1]George Barna, "How Americans See Themselves," *Barna Research Online* (28 May 1998). See www.barna.org/cgi-bin/PagePressRelease.asp?PressReleaseID=13&Reference=D. (Accessed January 4, 2002.)

[2]Ibid.

[3]George Barna, "Adults Who Attended Church As Children Show Lifelong Effects," *Barna Research Online* (5 November 2001). See www.barna.org/cgi-bin/PagePressRelease.asp?PressReleaseID=101&Reference=D. (Accessed January 4, 2002.)

[4]George Barna, "The Year's Most Intriguing Findings, from Barna Research Studies," *Barna Research Online* (17 December 2001). See www.barna.org/cgi-bin/PagePressRelease.asp?PressReleaseID=77&Reference=D. (Accessed January 4, 2002.)

[5]Ibid.

Chapter Four

[1]Stanley J. Grenz, *A Primer on Postmodernism* (Grand Rapids, Mich.: Eerdmans, 1996), 12.

[2]See www.emergentvillage.com/defpostmodern.html (accessed November 13, 2002).

[3]Terry Mattingly, "Mixed Messages: Spears' Naughty Image Belies Her Christian Belief," *San Jose Mercury News* (2 September 2000), 3E.

[4]John Leland, "Searching for a Holy Spirit," *Newsweek* (8 May 2000), 61.

[5]Dave Tomlinson, *The Post-Evangelical* (London: Triangle, 1995), 75. (A new edition of this book has been published by EmergentYS in 2003.)

[6]Ibid., 75–76.

Chapter Five

[1]Peter Drucker, *Post-Capitalist Society* (New York: Harper Collins, 1993), 1.

Chapter Six

[1]Lesslie Newbigin, *Unfinished Agenda* (London: SPCK, 1985), 249.

[2]Tom Clegg and Warren Bird, *Lost in America* (Loveland, Colo.: Group, 2001), 25.

[3]Newbigin, *Unfinished Agenda,* 249.

[4]Diana Eck, *A New Religious America: How a "Christian Country" Has Become the World's Most Religiously Diverse Nation* (New York: Harper Collins, 2001), inside cover flap and back cover.

[5]Ibid.

[6]Jeffrey L. Sheler, "Faith in America," *U.S. News and World Report* (6 May 2002), 42.

[7]John Leland, "Searching for a Holy Spirit," *Newsweek* (8 May 2000), 61.

[8]Ibid., 62.

[9]Susan Hogan Albach, "Teaching Values without Religion," *San Jose Mercury News* (23 December 2000), 1E.

Chapter Seven

[1]Rick Levin, "Christapalooza: 20,000 Christians Convene at the Gorge: God Doesn't Show," *The Stranger* (Seattle): 8 no. 48 (19–25 August 1999). See www.thestranger.com /1999-08-19/feature.html (accessed February 9, 2002).

[2]Stern on his detractors' efforts to influence advertisers against sponsoring his radio program.

[3]Blink-182's top-selling albums have the "explicit lyrics" stickers on them. One album cover and video featured a porn star, and the title of one of their albums is a sexual joke: "Take Off Your Pants and Jacket."

Chapter Eight

[1]Millard Erickson, *Introducing Christian Doctrine* (Grand Rapids, Mich.: Baker, 1992, 2001), 347.

[2]Darrell Guder, ed., *The Missional Church: A Vision for the Sending of the Church in North America* (Grand Rapids, Mich.: Eerdmans, 1998), 79–80.

[3]Ibid., 83–84.

[4]Erwin Raphael McManus, *An Unstoppable Force: Daring to Become the Church God Had in Mind* (Loveland, Colo.: Group, 2001), 29–30.

Chapter Ten

[1]Charles Ryrie, *Basic Theology* (Colorado Springs, Colo.: 1986), 428.

[2]Ralph P. Martin, *Worship in the Early Church* (Grand Rapids, Mich.: Eerdmans, 1964), 11.

[3]Sally Morgenthaler, *Worship Evangelism* (Grand Rapids, Mich.: Zondervan, 1995), 81.

Chapter Eleven

[1]Rick Warren, *The Purpose Driven Church* (Grand Rapids, Mich.: Zondervan, 1995), 165.

[2]Jim Cymbala, *Fresh Faith* (Grand Rapids, Mich.: Zondervan, 1999), 78.

Chapter Twelve

[1]I am greatly indebted to Paul Engle (executive editor and associate publisher, Zondervan) for much of what was written in this chapter. Paul's D. Min. teaching notes on "Aesthetics in Worship: Does Beauty Matter?" were the source for the chart within this chapter as well as many of the key points made.

Chapter Thirteen

[1]*Oxford American Dictionary* (New York: Oxford Univ. Press, 1980), 595.

[2]Rick Warren, *The Purpose-Driven Church* (Grand Rapids, Mich.: Zondervan, 1995), 266–67.

Chapter Fifteen

[1]Joseph Pine II and James H. Gilmore, *The Experience Economy* (Boston: Harvard Business School Press, 1999). Quote is from the dust jacket.

[2]Kalle Lasn, *Culture Jam*, (New York: Harper Collins, 1999), 19, 14–15.

Chapter Sixteen

[1]Excerpt taken from "Eucharist," a liturgy composed for the 1999 Greenbelt Festival in England.

[2]Philip Yancey, *The Jesus I Never Knew* (Grand Rapids, Mich.: Zondervan, 1995), 50.

Chapter Seventeen

[1]Leadership Network, *Explorer* no. 57 (11 March 2002).

[2]Ibid.

[3]Leith Anderson, *A Church for the Twenty-First Century* (Minneapolis: Bethany, 1992), 46.

[4]E. M. Bounds, *Preacher and Prayer* (Grand Rapids, Mich.: Zondervan, 1946), 26.

Chapter Eighteen

[1]Dallas Willard, *The Divine Conspiracy* (San Francisco: Harper Collins, 1998), 37.

[2]Darrell Gruder, ed., *The Missional Church* (Grand Rapids, Mich.: Eerdmans, 1998), 97.

[3]George G. Hunter III, *The Celtic Way of Evangelism* (Nashville: Abingdon, 2000), 53.

[4]George Barna quoted in an interview "Seven Questions with George Barna": www.ginkworld.net/current_7q/archives_7q_2002/7_questions_04012002.htm.

Chapter Nineteen

[1]*A Greek-English Lexicon of the New Testament and Other Early Christian Literature,* compiled by Walter Bauer, trans. and adapted by William F. Arndt and F. Wilbur Gingrich, 2d ed. rev. and augmented by F. Wilbur Gingrich and Frederick W. Danker (Chicago: University of Chicago Press, 1979), s.v. "mathetes," 486–87.

[2]Dallas Willard, *Renovation of the Heart* (Colorado Springs: Nav Press, 2002), 241.

[3]Ibid., 313.

[4]Gary Thomas, *Sacred Pathways* (Grand Rapids, Mich.: Zondervan, 2000), 16.

[5]Willard, *Renovation of the Heart,* 250.

Chapter Twenty

[1]William Barclay, *The Gospel of Matthew,* vol. 1 (Louisville: Westminster John Knox, 1956), 354.

[2]Os Guinness, *Dining with the Devil* (Grand Rapids, Mich.: Baker, 1993), 49.

[3]*Vine's Expository Dictionary of Biblical Words* (Nashville: Thomas Nelson, 1985).

[4]Reggie McNeal, *A Work of Heart: Understanding How God Shapes Spiritual Leaders* (San Francisco: Jossey-Bass, 2000), ix.

Contributors

I wanted to reflect in this book that the emerging church consists of many voices and opinions. So scattered throughout the text are comments from church leaders whom I have developed friendships with and whom I respect and through whom I have seen God significantly working to impact their culture for Jesus. They span several generations in age and have different approaches in their ministries, both modern and postmodern, in the contemporary and emerging church. However, by no means do these commentators represent the wide array of denominations, ages, races, countries, cultures, and philosophies of emerging churches and emerging church leaders.

Howard Hendricks. Dr. Hendricks is chairman of the Center for Christian Leadership and distinguished professor at Dallas Theological Seminary (www.dts.edu). For over fifty years he has touched the lives of thousands of students. He has written or cowritten numerous books, including *As Iron Sharpens Iron, Living by the Book,* and *Coloring Outside the Lines,* a book on creativity. He and his wife Jeanne have been married for over fifty years, have raised four children, and are the proud grandparents of six granddaughters.

Chip Ingram. Chip is president of Walk Thru the Bible and is the teaching pastor for the national radio broadcast *Living on the Edge,* (www.lote.org). Chip was the senior pastor of Santa Cruz Bible Church (www.santacruzbible.org), a large nondenominational church located in Santa Cruz, California, where he and Dan Kimball served on staff together for over twelve years. Chip is the author of *Holy Ambition: What It Takes to Make a Difference for God* and *I am with You Always: Experiencing God in Times of Need.*

Brian McLaren. Brian McLaren is founding pastor of Cedar Ridge Community Church (www.crcc.org) in Spencerville, Maryland. He is the author of several books, including *A New Kind of Christian, Finding Faith, More Ready Than You Realize,* and *The Church on the Other Side*. He is a senior fellow in Emergent (www.emergentvillage.org).

Sally Morgenthaler. Sally is president of Sacramentis.com and the author of *Worship Evangelism: Inviting Unbelievers into the Presence of God*. Her book has become a touchstone for postmodern, worship-driven ministry and a work whose popularity spans denominational boundaries. Her newest book, *The Uncharted Now,* focuses on worship in a postmodern culture. Samples of Sally's writing and photography along with more information about her ministry can be found on her website (www.sacramentis.com).

Mark Oestreicher. After having served about twenty years in youth ministry, Mark Oestreicher is now the president and publisher of Youth Specialties (www.youthspecialties.com). He's written a couple of dozen books for youth ministry. Marko is giving leadership to Emergent-YS, a partnership with Emergent (www.emergentvillage.com), to provide resources and training for emerging church leaders. He and his wife, Jeannie, live in San Diego with their nippers, Liesl and Max.

Rick Warren. Rick is the senior pastor of Saddleback Church in Lake Forest, California (www.saddleback.com), which has grown to over 16,000 in weekly attendance and has started over thirty daughter churches. Rick is the author of several best-selling books, including *The Purpose-Driven Life* and the Gold Medallion Award–winning book *The Purpose-Driven Church,* which has been translated into sixteen languages in over 116 countries. Along with his wife, Kay, Rick's heart is to provide proven resources, tested at Saddleback, to encourage pastors, ministers, and church leaders with tools and resources for growing healthy churches through their website: www.pastors.com.

the EMERGING church

Continuing the Discussion . . .

For information on continuing the conversation of this book, for more examples of ministry spoken of in this book, for more photographs of various emerging church worship experiences, and for links to other websites and ministries engaged in the emerging church conversation, go to www.vintagefaith.com.

If you have stories or examples of ministry you'd like to share, or input about this book, I'd love to hear from you, as we are all in this together. You can contact me through the website.

—Dan Kimball

We want to hear from you. Please send your comments about this book to us in care of the address below. Thank you.

GRAND RAPIDS, MICHIGAN 49530 USA

WWW.ZONDERVAN.COM